The Art of Diplomacy
The American Experience

THOMAS A. BAILEY
Byrne Professor of American History
Stanford University

New York
APPLETON–CENTURY–CROFTS
Division of Meredith Corporation

PRINTED IN THE UNITED STATES OF AMERICA
E 04990

Preface

My hope—no doubt a vain one—is that this book will fall into the hands of the President of the United States, the Secretary of State, and other denizens of Foggy Bottom who fashion American foreign policy. I also have in mind the small army of foreign service officers who implement that policy abroad and the host of intelligent citizens, including students, who help shape it at home.

I have set forth 267 basic guidelines or maxims and then have illustrated them briefly from our experience, mostly recent (a Chronological Overview rearranges the material by era). The emphasis is on principles rather than particulars. Fuller coverage may be found in the basic histories of American diplomacy, including my own, for which this may serve as a companion volume.

Like other maxims, those presented here are not invariably true for all times and climes. Occasionally one may seem to contradict another, but that may be the exception that "proves the rule." Some are undeniably obvious, but the obvious is often so undistinguished as to escape us.

For critical and helpful readings I am indebted to Professor Raymond G. O'Connor, of Temple University, and to three experienced and perceptive foreign service officers: John K. Emmerson, George F. Jones, Jr., and John C. Pool. Useful counsel was provided by Professors Claude A. Buss and James T. Watkins, IV, both of Stanford University. Mr. George D. Bullock and Mrs. Elaine D. Atkins served most capably as research assistants.

Thomas A. Bailey

Contents

Preface   v

Chronological Overview   ix

Part I. Personnel Problems   1

I	The Role of the President	3
II	The Department of State	21
III	Picking the Right Ambassador	35
IV	Utilizing the Ambassador	52
V	Advice for the Diplomat	62

Part II. Policy Formulation   79

VI	The Supremacy of National Interest	81
VII	The Shaping of Policy	89
VIII	The Power of Economic Interests	102
IX	The Domestic Front	113
X	The Pressure of Public Opinion	122

Part III. Diplomatic Techniques   135

XI	Top-Level Diplomacy	137
XII	Ethics and Morality	156
XIII	Allies and Alliances	173

Part IV.   The Fragmented Globe   183

XIV   The Role of the Foreigner   185
XV   Foreign Aid Programs   194
XVI   The Communist World   205
XVII   The Non-Communist World   215

Part V.   War and Diplomacy   227

XVIII The Politics of Power   229
XIX   The Mission of the Military   240
XX   The Iron Dice of War   249

Part VI.   Problems of Peace   259

XXI   The Perils of Peacemaking   261
XXII   Neutrality and Neutralism   271
XXIII The Mirage of Disarmament   279

Epilogue   287

Bibliography and Notes   289

Index   299

Chronological Overview

Where an item receives a fuller treatment than most, pages are boldfaced.

A. **Diplomacy of the Revolution and Confederation**
French Alliance, 166–167, **174–176**, 189–190. Netherlands loan, 42. Treaty of 1783, 53, **146**, 159, 161. French trade, 103.

B. **Presidents Washington and Adams, 1789–1801**
French relations, 69, 166, 200. Jay's Treaty, 146, **154**. Washington's Farewell Address, 74, 173, 190. XYZ Affair, 8, 125.

C. **The Jefferson and Madison Administrations, 1801–1817**
Tripoli War, 111, 114. Louisiana Purchase, 58, 92. British relations, 72, 147. Embargo, 107. Florida designs, 170–171. War of 1812 (causes and course), 7, 40, 130, 142, 230, 233, 241, 246, 254, **266**. Peace of Ghent, **265**.

D. **From Monroe to Tyler, 1817–1845**
Monroe Doctrine (origins), 68; (history), 176, 191–192. Texas question, 114–115.

E. **From Polk Through Buchanan, 1845–1861**
Oregon boundary, **68**, 230, 253. Mexican War (California), 145; 146n., 159, 253. Cuba, 77, 115.

F. **The Lincoln–Johnson Years, 1861–1869**
British relations, 67, 72, 115, **249–250**. Emancipation Proclamation, 132. French relations (Mexico), 115, **142–143**, 246. Spanish relations (Santo Domingo), 93, 115. Russian fleets, 192. Alaska Purchase, 12–13.

G. **From Grant Through Cleveland, 1869–1897**
Motley Affair, 67. *Alabama* Claims, 115, **155**. Blaine's Pan Americanism, 28. Relations with Austria–Hungary, 50. Sackville–West

ix

Incident, **75**, 78. Italian relations, 54. McKinley Tariff and Hawaii, 105, 114. *Baltimore* Incident, 231. Wilson–Gorman Tariff and Cuba, 105. Cuban crisis, 125.

H. **The McKinley Years, 1897–1901**
    Cuba, 118. De Lôme Letter, 78. Spanish–American War, 123, 125. Philippines, 67, 93, 148, **160**. Open Door, 93, 149n. Boxer Rebellion, 157.

I. **The Roosevelt–Taft Era, 1901–1913**
    Panama problem, 155n., 158, 162, 168–169, 175, 231. Monroe Doctrine corollary (1904), 130. Japanese problem, 147, 153, 213. Russo–Japanese War, 17–18, 86. Dollar Diplomacy, 111. Manchurian neutralization, 142, 153.

J. **The Wilson Administration, 1913–1921**
    State Department relations, 4, 9, 11, 22, 23, 27, 52. China policy, 9. Latin American policy, 9, 81, 86; (Mexico), 86, **96**, 167, 218, 220. Japanese relations, 40. Russian relations, 58–59. European alliances (pre-1917), 164, 170, 178–179, 241, 251. Prewar America (1914–1917), 7, 130, 242, 275; (German friction), 7, 9, 15, 27, 59, 83, 158, 159, 165–166, 242. British relations, 12, 53, 66–67. War vote, 8. Fourteen Points, 81, 87n., 129, 169, 268. War propaganda, 87, 117, 129. Peace Commission, 13, 119. Peace Conference, 138, 139, 160–161, 261; (world opinion), 17, 193. League of Nations, 170, 268n.; (fight for), 4, 13, 74, 95, **119–120**, 125. Treaty of Versailles, 74, 161, 164, 189, 267, 268–269, 270. Security Treaty of 1919, 85. Postwar policy, 95, 236.

K. **Harding, Coolidge, and Hoover, 1921–1933**
    League of Nations, 72. Isolationism, 94. Colombian Treaty, 158. Washington Conference, 18, 146, 171–172, 175, **284–285**. War debts, 107. Japanese relations, 97, 114. Kellogg–Briand Pact, 254. Hawley–Smoot Tariff, 106. Sino–Japanese War, **108**, 118, 222–223, 238, 254. Hoover–Stimson Doctrine, 238. Good Neighbor Policy, 96–97. Hoover–Roosevelt relations, 19–20.

L. **Franklin D. Roosevelt, 1939–1941**
    State Department relations, 10–11, 23, 60, 66. Chinese relations, 114. Good Neighbor Policy, 91, 219. Recognition of Russia, 103, **167–168**. Reciprocal Trade Agreements, 10, 106. Italy embargo, 108–109. Spanish Civil War, 127. Invasion of Poland, 241, **246, 251**,

253, 273. Prewar statements, 15, 55, 123, 125. Japanese relations, 63, 72n., 91–92, 104, 108, 127, 187, 216, 244; (negotiations), 45, 59–60, 91–92; (Pearl Harbor), 55, 98, 144, 172, 244, 252. German relations, 50, 151; (Munich), 98, **145**, 241, 247. Russian relations, 59n., 159, 174–175, 252–253. British relations, 125, 126, **131**, 191. Vichy, 17, **69**. Neutrality, 125, 126, 131, 274, 275, 276. Declaration of War (1941), 8.

M. **Franklin D. Roosevelt and World War II, 1942–1945**
American attitude, 129. Relations with France, 69, 76. Spain, 46–47, 278. Lebanon, 32. Italy, 179. Britain, 60, 95. Russia, 15–16, 84, 88, 95, 171, 177–178. Japan, 83. Conferences, 16, 66, 138, 144n.; (Yalta), 64, 127n., 139, 147, 152, 180. Unconditional Surrender, 10, 146, **262–263**, 269. United Nations, 120–121. Postwar policy, 10, 33, 86–87, 95, 180, 236.

N. **The Trials of Harry Truman, 1945–1953**
State Department relations, 5, 6–7, 9, 22, 29. Potsdam Conference, 43, 138, 144n. Atomic bomb decision, **132**, 252, 262–263. Unconditional Surrender policy (Japan), **146–147**, 262. Postwar European policy, 124, 216, 236–237, 243, 263, 269–270. Japanese Treaty, 267. British loan request, 197–198. Rio Pact, 220. Argentine policy, 74. Truman Doctrine, 180, 195, **212–213**, 237. Marshall Plan, 23, **82**, 111, 131–132, 149, 201, 203, 212. Italy, 199. NATO, 132, 175, 180, 241. China policy (Chiang Kai-shek), 49, 94, 127; (Red China), 99, 109, 148, **168**, **210**. The Cold War (Russian relations), 84, **113**, 124, 148, 161, 206, 243, 250; (India), 159, **277–278**; (Yugoslavia), **195–196**, 206; (Austria), 277. Creation of Israel, 11. Korean War (American commitment), 13, 26, 121, 148n., 212, 221, 254, 255; (strategy), **71**, 176–177, **235**, 251–252, 256, **263–264**, **266**; (negotiations), 43, **265**. MacArthur dismissal, 256.

O. **The Eisenhower Years, 1953–1961**
State Department relations, 4, 6, 22, 23. Travels, 4, 18, 19, 138. Latin American policy, 163–164. Guatemala, 28, 33. Indo–China, Laos, 34, 98–99. German relations, 57, 170, 246. Italian relations, 68. Vietnam policy, 123, 257. Food for Peace, 202–203. Mutual Security program, 195. China policy, 13, 14, 25, 64, 144. Austria policy, 43, 277. Geneva Summit, 138, 139. Open Skies proposal, 143. Suez Canal seizure, 31, 87, **162–163**, 178, 186, 191, **250**. Hungarian Revolt, 120, 134, 179. Egyptian Dam, 144, 151. Eisenhower Middle East Doctrine, 14, 208. Little Rock incident, 115.

Sputnik, 212. Antarctica Treaty, 145n., 209. Cuban relations, 163, 169, 220. Bolivia, 219n. U-2 incident, 18–19, 41, 128, 138, **171.** South African relations, 28, 93. Paris Summit, 138. Negotiations on Berlin, 138. Cuban relations severed, 20. Military spending, 244–245, 248.

P. **Kennedy and the New Frontier Diplomacy, 1961–1963**
Peace Corps, 201. Alliance for Progress, 111, 201. Bay of Pigs invasion, **6**, 11, 33, **100**, 128, 149, 162. Vienna Conference, 16. Vietnam commitment, 257. Cuban Embargo, 109. "Old Miss" riots, 116. Cuban missile crisis, 76, 76n., 121, 282; (U.S. policy), **25–26, 123**, 144, 162, 187, 220, **232**, 235, 247; (Khrushchev confrontation), 15, 16, 149–150, 211, 221, 243; (world attitude), 158, 178, 187; (Turkish missiles), 101, **145**. Nuclear testing, 133. Indonesian relations, 181. West German visit, 18. Grain to Russia, 118–119. Birmingham riots, 116. Italy policy, 32. Proposed Soviet pact, 152. Nuclear Test-Ban Treaty, 57, **142**, 209–210, 284.

Q. **Lyndon B. Johnson and Foreign Relations, 1963–**

Panama Canal crisis, 54, 151–152. Cyprus situation, 180. Egyptian relations, 196. Congo crisis, 224. Dominican intervention, 14, 91n., 93, **97–98, 162**, 220–221. Vietnam War, 14, 70, 84n., 129, 130, 134, 165, 177, 212, **221–222**, 233–234, **253–254**, 257; (U.S. policy), 153, **160**, 207; (peace overtures), 97, 150, 150n., 251, **264–265**. Russian relations, 77, 127. French relations, 174, 178, 186, 196.

PART I

Personnel Problems

CHAPTER I

The Role of the President

"I make American foreign policy."

PRESIDENT HARRY S TRUMAN, 1948

PROLOGUE

The Constitution of the United States, partly by inference, makes the President commander-in-chief of foreign relations. His powers were formidable before the Atomic Age; now they are enormous, largely because the global stage on which he strides has become infinitely bigger. He now has a world constituency, although only about one percent of its people vote for him. We might almost say that a whisper on the Potomac is a shout in Peking; or that if the President catches a cold, mankind runs a temperature.

Global worries are of growing concern to the American public. The electorate, in choosing presidential standard-bearers, should give high place to the capacity of the candidate to handle foreign affairs, especially if he is up for reelection, and to his probable capacity if he is an untried candidate. During the campaign of 1960 Vice President Nixon, who had considerable background in global diplomacy, ran against Senator John F. Kennedy, who had little. "Experience Counts" was a potent pro-Nixon slogan.

The following principles are directed to the Chief Executive. But they can be useful to the workaday citizen in enabling him to decide whether or not the expectant President or the reigning President can measure up to the overwhelming responsibilities of his high office in the dangerous arena of foreign affairs.

THE PRESIDENT SHOULD PROVIDE LEADERSHIP

If the President does not lead, then Congress will try to, as was painfully true after Woodrow Wilson's physical collapse in 1919. But a legislative body that is unwieldy, windy, partisan, and seniority-strangled cannot lead effectively, any more than a committee can govern effectively.

One of the chief criticisms the Democrats leveled at the Republican President Eisenhower was that, despite undeniable magnetic gifts, he failed to provide the dynamic leadership that the Nuclear Age demanded. He was further criticized for jetting off on exhausting good-will safaris, ranging from Latin America to Europe to Asia. Although he elicited amazing outpourings of esteem, many Americans (chiefly Democrats) charged that his "dynamic drifting" was not providing the aggressive and constructive leadership that the Cold War required. His critics further claimed that personality was no substitute for policy and that showmanship was no substitute for statesmanship.

LEADERSHIP IS IMPOSSIBLE WITHOUT FOLLOWERSHIP

President Franklin Roosevelt once remarked that nothing is quite so disheartening for a leader as to look back and see that no one is following him. On the other hand, if he lags so far behind as to merge with the crowd, he is a timeserver rather than a leader.

A President who proposes to lead his people into greener pastures should educate them in advance to their new responsibilities, that is, if he wishes to be sure of popular support. President Wilson in 1919–1920 tried to persuade the nation to forsake its centuries-old isolationism and step into the chill waters of internationalism. He launched a campaign of education, but it was too little and too late. The people wearied rapidly of well doing and eventually cold-shouldered the League of Nations. One world war and millions of casualties later, they enthusiastically embraced the

United Nations. By this time the harsh tutelage of events had educated them to their new responsibilities in a rapidly shriveling world.

THE PRESIDENT CANNOT SHIRK HIS RESPONSIBILITIES

The President must stay on top of events or events will soon be on top of him. On his White House desk President Truman kept a plaque with the arresting motto: "The buck stops here." The "buck" can be passed up from the lower echelons but not beyond the White House, except occasionally to the United Nations.[1]

Truman lived up to his motto. He had on tap numerous advisers, with whom he repeatedly huddled. But his dozen or so earth-shaking decisions had to be made in the White House—"the loneliest place in the world." He reached these decisions—ranging from dropping the atomic bomb on Japan to dumping MacArthur in Korea—in the light of the facts available. He then refrained from tying himself up in mental knots by second-guessing about what he should have done. Uneaten by remorse, he lived to a ripe, if somewhat irascible, old age.

The price that the President pays for being a leader is to be damned if he does and damned if he does not. High-level executive decisions are seldom revocable; second chances seldom occur. A rare exception came in 1945 when the United Nations provided a brand new substitute for the defunct League of Nations.

THE POWER AND PRESTIGE OF THE PRESIDENCY
SHOULD BE PRESERVED

The Chief Executive has an obligation to pass on to his successor the powers of his office undiminished. He may not care to exercise all the authority within his grasp, but his successor might.

In the atomically-fused world of today, the President needs more power rather than less. The so-called Bricker amendment,

[1] Early in 1966 the Johnson administration attempted to pass the Vietnam problem on up to the United Nations. See *Department of State Bulletin,* LIV (Feb. 14, 1966), pp. 229–239.

pushed to a showdown by Senator Bricker of Ohio in 1954, was designed to restrict the right of the President to make Executive Agreements (which do not need senatorial approval) as substitutes for treaties (which need senatorial approval). This proposed addition to the Constitution was finally sidetracked in the Senate by the narrowest of margins. President Eisenhower opposed it, but his efforts were not so vigorous as his critics desired or demanded.

Similarly, the prestige of the presidency should not be lightly hazarded. The office is a priceless trust that the Chief Executive must at all times safeguard.

The Bay of Pigs blunder in 1961 is a dramatic case in point. President Kennedy, new on the job and partially committed by his predecessor, reluctantly supported the abortive invasion of Cuba by a band of some 1400 American-trained and American-armed Cuban exiles. In his determination not to become directly implicated, Kennedy became deeply involved in a tangled web of furtiveness, deceptiveness, and indecisiveness. The humiliating failure blackened not only the good name of the nation but the prestige of the presidency as well.

PRESIDENTIAL POWERS SHOULD NOT BE MOTHBALLED

Presidential power should be used in the national interest, not hoarded. In the 1950's Senator Joseph R. McCarthy of Wisconsin besmirched the national image by instigating book-burning in American embassies and by leading a hysterical witchhunt against alleged Communists in government. Few other antics could have done more to play into the hands of Communist propagandists abroad. President Eisenhower, the decent old General, refused "to get into the gutter with that guy," even when McCarthy assailed the President's own Defense Department.

Despite the dirtiness involved, Eisenhower had the power to chastise McCarthy. He could have withheld federal patronage, limited federal funds for Wisconsin, and wielded various other potent weapons in his arsenal. But the aging General, a professional fighter but a rookie in politics, was unduly concerned about avoiding a fight. The worst he would do was to cut the Senator off the White House social list.

By contrast, the peppery Harry Truman denounced McCarthy,

but he did so more frequently and more strongly after he had left the White House for his safer house in Independence, Missouri.[2]

NEVER LEAD A DIVIDED PEOPLE INTO WAR

President Madison, smarting from near-intolerable grievances, led a disunited nation into a conflict with Great Britain in 1812. Federalist New England bitterly opposed "Mr. Madison's War," with the result that in a sense the United States fought both Old England and New England simultaneously. Madison was unhappily aware of this opposition, but he threw forward the flag in the hope that the Federalists, their patriotism touched, would pick it up. They were content to let it lie in the mud. To expect war to unite a disunited people is about as risky as to expect marriage to reform a drunkard.

President Wilson, early in his administration, remarked that he and Madison were the only two Princetonians ever to occupy the White House and that he was not going to repeat his predecessor's blunder and lead a disunited nation into the global conflict then raging. In the face of repeated German outrages, Wilson held back until April, 1917, waiting for public opinion to ripen, perhaps over-ripen. One result was that America's war effort was not hampered by internal opposition, which invariably plays into the hands of the enemy.

Complete unity in a democracy is seldom possible, but a strong minority of dissentients invariably spells trouble.

NEVER PRESS BIG DECISIONS ON SMALL MAJORITIES

In 1812 the Congress, reflecting the popular mood, was badly split, yet President Madison urged it to declare war on Britain. The vote in the House was 79 to 49; in the Senate, 19 to 13. A change of four votes would have defeated the resolution in the Senate. This reversal almost certainly would have occurred had there been a transatlantic cable, because two days before the fateful roll call the British government had announced its decision to suspend the

---

[2] "The son of a bitch ought to be impeached," McCarthy had told a press conference after President Truman's sacking of General MacArthur. Richard H. Rovere, *Senator Joe McCarthy* (1959), p. 12.

odious Orders in Council, which had partially shackled American shipping. The closeness of the congressional vote in 1812 was an unmistakable augury of the appalling disunity with which the war was going to be fought.

When President Wilson asked Congress for war in 1917, the Senate responded 82 to 6 and the House, 373 to 50. The conflict was fought with unusual unity, despite some stifled opposition from pro-German elements.

When President Franklin Roosevelt called for a declaration of war in 1941, after Japan's attack on Pearl Harbor, only one negative vote was cast in either house of Congress.[3] The declarations of war on Germany and Italy were passed unanimously, and the ensuing conflict was fought with extraordinary unity. Roosevelt, perhaps profiting from Wilson's experience, had held back until the Japanese bombs at Pearl Harbor had sunk the large and vociferous isolationist element in the United States.

THE PRESIDENT SHOULD ALWAYS PUT COUNTRY ABOVE PARTY

The Chief Executive must repeatedly remind himself that he is President of all the people, not just Democrats or Republicans. In 1798 President John Adams, after rashly leading the Republic to the brink of war with France over the XYZ insult, belatedly recovered his balance. Full-blown hostilities would have been popular with much of the public, though by no means all of it, and might possibly have improved his chances for reelection. (Americans are disinclined in wartime to swap presidential horses midstream.) In any event, President Adams resolutely adopted what he regarded as the right course (it may even have been the cleverest one politically) and patched up the quarrel with France.[4] He was defeated for reelection in 1800, albeit by a narrow margin.

Whether or not Adams would have fared better at the polls by unsheathing the sword cannot be proved. But he finally did what he thought was best for the country, and for this he is generously praised by posterity.

---

[3] By Miss Jeannette Rankin, Representative from Montana, who had also voted against war with Germany in 1917.

[4] See Page Smith, *John Adams* (1962), II, 1001–1002.

A President should also remember that a sound foreign policy is not governed by the whirligig of politics. Yet on a number of occasions the incoming Executive has sharply changed or even reversed the course set by his predecessor, especially one of the opposition party. After the Democratic Woodrow Wilson had been in office only two weeks, he jerked the rug from under the Latin American and China policies of his Republican predecessor, William H. Taft. He acted peremptorily and without consulting the Department of State, one of whose officials resigned in a scorching letter of protest.

The national interest does not revolve in four-year cycles, with Democratic policies alternating with Republican. If a fundamental policy is a sound one, its life expectancy is usually more than four years.

THE PRESIDENT IS NOT THE SECRETARY OF STATE

The Chief Executive should have a hand, whether large or small, in making or shaping foreign policy. At the very least he should approve all important decisions that are reached by the Department of State.

The stronger Presidents, like Woodrow Wilson and Franklin Roosevelt, had a dominant voice in the formulation of major policy decisions, and they normally shoved their Secretaries of State onto back seats. The weaker Presidents, like Harding with his masterful Secretary, Charles Evans Hughes, have generally been content to serve more or less as rubber stamps.

The job of Secretary of State is now so onerous that not even the Secretary himself can handle it alone, much less his overburdened Chief. The President would do well to be his own President rather than his own Secretary of State. But the Secretary should be an active partner, even though at times a junior partner, in all vital decisions, as was notably true of the Truman–Acheson relationship.

If a President feels that he must be his own Secretary, he should concentrate on the major issues and leave the State Department to manage the secondary or minor ones. This is essentially what Woodrow Wilson did. He drafted critical notes to Germany on his own typewriter (they were signed by Secretary of State

Bryan) and left Bryan, in whom he had scant confidence, to negotiate some thirty "cooling off" peace treaties. President Franklin
Roosevelt, while habitually keeping Secretary Cordell Hull in the
dark during the war years, gave him a relatively free hand to
negotiate a packet of path-breaking tariff reciprocity treaties with
the Latin American republics and other nations.

SHORT-CIRCUITING THE STATE DEPARTMENT IS DANGEROUS

It is one thing for the President to go over the head of the
State Department in crucial decisions, while notifying the Department of what he has done or proposes to do. It is another to go
behind the back of the State Department and keep it in the dark.
Such a practice, if repeated, results in confusion, cross-purposes,
fouled lines of communication, bruised feelings, and shattered
morale.

Secretary Cordell Hull was too important a political figure to be
dismissed, so President Roosevelt kept him on and repeatedly by-
passed him. Roosevelt gave more heed to the disastrous advice of
Secretary of the Treasury Morgenthau about punishing postwar
Germany, at least at one crucial stage. He took Hull to none of the
summit conferences abroad; he did not consult with him before an-
nouncing the fateful policy of "unconditional surrender" at Casablanca in 1943. Ambassador Winant in London had authority to use
the United States naval code in communicating with the White
House; Ambassador Bullitt in Paris used the transatlantic telephone
in reporting directly to Roosevelt. When Ambassador Robert Murphy left for his hazardous North African mission, Roosevelt remarked casually, "If you learn anything in Africa of special interest,
send it to me. Don't bother going through State Department channels." [5] Many commitments were thus made without even being put
on the official record, all of which compounded the confusion.

There are doubtless times when the red tape ensnarling the
State Department has to be snipped and business expedited. But
Roosevelt evidently regarded the Department as a "sieve," which
at times it proved to be. He also distrusted it because he believed
that some of the permanent officials were fossilized bureaucrats, and

[5] Robert Murphy, *Diplomat Among Warriors* (1964), p. 70.

hence responsible for the mistaken policies of Hoover and his other Republican predecessors. If a President loses confidence in his Secretary of State, he should replace him, not ignore him. During the anxious months when Wilson was prostrated by a paralytic stroke, Secretary Lansing held more than a score of informal Cabinet meetings in an effort to keep the machinery moving. Wilson regarded these well-meaning efforts as gross insubordination. When he had sufficiently recovered, he abruptly dismissed Lansing in an ill-tempered and ill-advised letter. Secretary Colby, Lansing's successor, enjoyed the confidence of the President and did a creditable job.

THE PRESIDENT SHOULD GIVE EAR TO THE EXPERTS

The White House has on tap the advice of a formidable fact-gathering machine in the Department of State and other federal agencies. President Roosevelt was understandably annoyed in 1939 when Senator Borah, a member of the Senate Foreign Relations Committee, insisted that his own private sources of information had on occasion proved superior to those of the Secretary of State.

This does not mean that the recommendations of the State Department must necessarily be followed, but at the very least they should be listened to with respect. The "generalists" are often better advisers than the specialists, especially if the latter have devised the policy in question and have a vested interest in seeing it adopted. A green-on-the-job President Kennedy learned this lesson the sad way in 1961 when he was sold a bill of goods by overzealous officials who were promoting the invasion of Cuba by way of the Bay of Pigs.

President Truman, who was not a college graduate, had poorly concealed contempt for many of the "overeducated," "striped pants boys" in the State Department and overseas.[6] He was determined to press for the creation of the state of Israel, not unaware of the potency of the large Jewish vote in the New York area in the upcoming presidential election of 1948. But experts in the State Department opposed the creation and recognition of the new Jewish nation. They feared that such a course would fatally undermine our

---

[6] "Protocol and striped pants give me a pain in the neck," Truman once wrote to Charles W. Thayer. Thayer, *Diplomat* (1959), p. 224.

long-range policy of maintaining friendly relations with the embittered Arab nations, which controlled some of the greatest oil pools in the world. President Truman brushed aside such objections and extended recognition and aid to the infant state of Israel on a pell-mell basis.

Truman may have been right or he may have been wrong. But it was regrettable that political and emotional factors played a major role in a decision which critically involved the larger national interest.

SPECIAL EXECUTIVE AGENTS SHOULD BE USED DISCREETLY

In modern times the President has increasingly used special agents to supplement the work of the minister or ambassador abroad. Such appointments are easy to make because an executive agent, unlike an ambassador, does not require the approval of the Senate, or even the knowledge of the Secretary of State.

The use of executive agents can lead to cross-purposes, as when Colonel House, President Wilson's confidant, worked out a secret code for communicating with the British foreign secretary over the head of Ambassador Page in London. Many Presidents have been suspicious, often with good reason, of the slow-moving, hide-bound foreign service and have desired more immediate and more personalized contacts. Others have distrusted the objectivity of the ambassador, as Wilson did that of Walter H. Page. At times even the envoy's loyalty is suspect, especially when a Democratic holdover serves under a Republican President, or vice versa.

An especially disturbing result of the use of executive agents or special ambassadors is, as we shall later note, an undermining of the prestige and authority of the resident ambassador.

PRESIDENTS SHOULD LEARN TO LIVE WITH CONGRESS

As the Constitution specifies, Congress is a coordinate body in the making and executing of foreign policy. The House of Representatives has a direct hand in the passing or nonpassing of all money bills, including the purchase of foreign territory and appropriations for foreign aid. The House in 1868, for example, made a determined but unsuccessful attempt to sabotage the $7.2 million appropriation for the purchase of Alaska. In various other ways Congress can throw monkey wrenches into the diplomatic machinery.

The President, in shaping his foreign policy, must be keenly aware of what he can or cannot get through Congress, especially the Senate, which has a final whack at treaties. President Wilson, himself an unsuccessful attorney, had scant respect for the successful lawyers ("ambulance chasers") who dominated the Senate. His contemptuous attitude partially reflected itself in his decision not to include a single senator on his commission of five peace negotiators in Paris in 1918. Nor did he stoop to solicit the views of the Senate in advance. The senators later got their revenge when they tacked onto the resolution of ratification the fourteen reservations (later fifteen) that resulted in the fateful deadlock between Lodge and Wilson. The treaty was finally trampled to death, as far as America was concerned, beneath the feet of the antagonists in Washington.

Congress, for its part, should show maturity and responsibility. From time to time either the Senate or the House, notably the House, will shout through certain irrelevant or provocative resolutions, such as those that were repeatedly passed prior to 1921 favoring the independence of Ireland (and Irish–American voters). In the 1950's, at a time when the Eisenhower administration was trying to keep Chiang Kai-shek on Formosa and out of trouble, the Republican majority (later minority) leader, Senator William F. Knowland, was sounding off in favor of drastic measures to back Chiang. Many foreigners, unfamiliar with the quirks of the American system, assumed that the headline-making Knowland was speaking for the administration when, in fact, he was not.

BLANK CHECKS FROM CONGRESS CAN BE USEFUL

In 1950 President Truman was assailed for sending American troops into Korea without a declaration of war by Congress. The truth is that Congress never did pass a formal declaration, and as the blood-letting became increasingly unpopular, outcries mounted against "Mr. Truman's War."

President Eisenhower was able to guard against similar criticism by inducing Congress to give him two precedent-shattering blank checks. The first, in 1955, authorized him to use the armed forces to defend Chiang Kai-shek's Formosa against Communist China; the second, in 1957, authorized him to defend the Middle East against Communist intrusion. These two measures were insurance against the Korean-type condemnation, and they undoubtedly strengthened Eisenhower's hand. But the General was criticized for weakening the presidential office by seeking from Congress the power he already possessed under the Constitution as Commander-in-Chief of the armed forces. Actually, the United States has undertaken more than a hundred and fifty interventions on foreign soil involving American troops, all acting under presidential authority, without a declaration of war.[7]

President Lyndon Johnson requested and received from Congress a blank check to bomb North Vietnam in August, 1964.[8] The authorization followed an alleged attack by several North Vietnamese torpedo boats on two American warships in the international waters of the Gulf of Tonkin. The Vietnamese war gradually escalated into a large-scale affair, for which many Congressmen had not bargained when they had impulsively but patriotically voted for a limited operation on a small scale. Many members wanted to recall the blanket authorization, but with American boys dying in the steaming jungles, such a negative move was certain to bring an angry outcry from the voters.

These three blank-check precedents inspired the fear that Presidents thereafter would not dare to employ troops, though empowered to do so by the Constitution, without first seeking permission from Congress. President Lyndon B. Johnson partially quieted any such misgivings (while raising others) when he sent a large contingent of American troops into Santo Domingo in 1965 without first asking for the approval of Congress. Time was too pressing, he felt, for a protracted congressional debate.

The President is clearly in a stronger position politically, at least temporarily, if he has a go-ahead from Congress in advance of a possible declaration of war, whatever the adverse long-range effects on his office may be. At the very least, he should alert the

---

[7] See *House Reports,* 82nd Cong., 1st Sess., No. 127.

[8] The vote on August 7, 1964, was 416 to 0 in the House and 88 to 2 in the Senate.

leaders of Congress to an imminent crisis, as President Kennedy did on the eve of his confrontation with Soviet Premier Khrushchev over the Cuban missiles in 1962.

NEVER GIVE ONE'S ADVERSARY A BLANK CHECK

The Chief Executive should ordinarily try to retain the initiative at all times. He is guilty of ineptitude, not to say folly, if he deliberately surrenders it to his opponent.

In 1916, following the attack by a German submarine on an unarmed French passenger liner, *Sussex*, an outraged President Wilson in effect sent a blank-check ultimatum to Berlin. He declared that if the German government ever resumed this inhumane kind of undersea warfare, he would have no alternative but to sever diplomatic relations. (In those days a rupture of relations between great powers was almost inevitably a prelude to a declaration of war.)

Early in 1917 the Berlin government filled in the blank check when it announced a resumption (and expansion) of its brutal submarine warfare. Wilson was honor-bound to sever relations, and Congress declared war a few weeks later. If he had not so rashly gone out on the end of a limb, he might have resorted to other alternatives. As it was, national honor restricted him to a rigid course, and the decision to fight was made in Berlin, not in America.

Closely related to issuing a blank check is a hand-tying political pledge. Franklin Roosevelt erred in the presidential campaign of 1940 when he assured a cheering Boston audience, "Your boys are not going to be sent into any foreign wars." They were ultimately sent overseas, to the probable embarrassment of the President. Unequivocal statements like these tend to foreclose options, and a flexible policy requires that as many options as possible be kept open.

STUDY YOUR OPPONENT'S STRENGTHS AND WEAKNESSES

President Franklin Roosevelt, not renowned as a bookish man, had evidently never read much of Karl Marx or of latter-day Communist dialectic. Supremely confident of his ability to charm dictator Joseph Stalin out of his nasty Communist ways, he eagerly sought a face-to-face confrontation with the hardened conspirator of the Kremlin. "I can handle that old buzzard," was his reputed boast before the summit meetings at Teheran and Yalta. The record does not reveal that the steely "old buzzard" was melted by the Roosevelt charm, including the use of the breezy nickname, "Uncle Joe."

Just as baseball players have a "book" on one another's weaknesses and strengths, the President should study his adversary for his weaknesses and strengths. Wisely, President Kennedy went to great pains to find out what he could about Premier Khrushchev of the Soviet Union before their first (and only) face-to-face meeting, early in 1961 in Vienna.

KEEP ALL CHANNELS OF COMMUNICATION OPEN

The chilling conference in Vienna between Kennedy (aged 44) and Khrushchev (aged 67) was a grim experience for the younger man. The bullying Bolshevik gave no ground on Berlin and certain other hot spots. But one unexpected boon grew out of the meeting: the Soviet leader initiated a lengthy and protracted private correspondence with his youthful opponent.[9] The familiarity thus cultivated probably made easier a meeting of minds when the dangerous Cuban missile crisis boiled up in October, 1962.

Amicable relations are usually easier to achieve between acquaintances than between strangers. This basic truism was evidently lost on the American public, the President, and the State Department when we continued our strait-jacket policy of having no dealings with Red China during the 1950's and well into the 1960's. Responding to strong anti-Communist pressure at home, the State Department forbade American journalists and travelers to go behind the Bamboo Curtain to see for themselves what was churning up.

Decisions based upon full information may be unwise, whether reached by officialdom or by the public. But they have practically no chance of being wise if based on blind prejudice rather than basic facts. The more understanding, the less likelihood of misunderstanding.

[9] Theodore C. Sorensen, *Kennedy* (1965), p. 552.

AVOID APPEALS OVER THE HEADS OF GOVERNMENTS

President Wilson, thwarted at the Peace Conference at Paris in 1919, went over the heads of the Italian delegates to appeal to the Italian people on the issue of self-determination in Fiume. (He wanted the Yugoslavs to obtain this Adriatic port.) His plea backfired badly. In pursuit of their own selfish interests, foreign peoples normally stand behind their own officials, rather than idealistic foreign statesmen.

President Franklin Roosevelt, after the fall of France in 1940, appealed directly by radio to the French people. He urged them not to support the puppet government at Vichy, which Hitler had propped up under the semi-senile Marshal Petain. The results were of questionable value, but this was a critical wartime dilemma which called for desperate measures.[10]

Public appeals also tend to become confused with unofficial or semi-official appeals. Radio Free Europe, supported by private American funds, urged the peoples of Central Europe in the 1950's to throw off the Communist yoke. The Hungarians, many of whom wishfully interpreted this message as a promise of armed aid by the United States, arose in revolt, only to be crushed under Soviet tanks.

THE HONEST BROKER RUNS GRAVE RISKS

In 1905, during the Russo–Japanese War, President Theodore Roosevelt consented to mediate between the two partially exhausted combatants at a meeting place near Portsmouth, New Hampshire. Although invited by both sides, he knew that he would risk his popularity. But he acted in the conviction that the preservation of the balance of power between these two belligerents in the Far East was to our advantage.

Neither Russia nor Japan, both traditional friends of the United States, came away from the peace table with such favorable terms as desired. Roosevelt, the honest broker, was bitterly blamed. Anti-American demonstrations erupted in once friendly Japan, and in

---

[10] An American official in Paris remarked to the present writer in 1947 that Roosevelt's spoken French was "so terrible as to be moving."

Russia the press (anti-Semitic) falsely and irrelevantly charged that the Roosevelt family was descended from the Jewish Rosenfelts.

We must not conclude that the President should never mediate when the national interest is involved, but he should realize that the mediator is more likely to make at least one enemy than two friends. If the settlement is lopsided, one enemy is almost certain; if it is a fair one, two parties will be about equally displeased.

PRESIDENTIAL PRESS CONFERENCES MUST BE USED WITH CAUTION

The ordinary press conference, conducted off-the-cuff, involves definite dangers. But the hazards are greatest in a televised conference, presented "live" and witnessed by tens of millions of people. First, there is the drawback of decreasing effectiveness through "overexposure." Second, there is always the fear of a disastrous slip of the tongue, even though the President may have subjected himself to a preliminary dry-run briefing in an effort to anticipate questions posed by inquisitive newsmen. On a number of occasions White House spokesmen have had to issue hasty "coverups" to explain to the world that the President did not really mean what he said.

Perhaps the worst blunder of all came in a news conference that President Harding held in 1921, at the time of the so-called Washington Disarmament Conference. He told the correspondents that the recently drafted Four Power Treaty did not apply to the homeland of Japan, whereas the exact opposite was the case. When the truth came out, the people were left with the impression that a confused President Harding did not know what he was doing, which unfortunately was true.

PEOPLE-TO-PEOPLE DIPLOMACY INVOLVES HAZARDS

When Chief Executives have gone abroad on visits of state, they have almost invariably expected and received red-carpet treatment. The receptions accorded Wilson in Italy, Eisenhower in India, and Kennedy in West Germany were incredible popular outpourings.

Before America's U-2 spy plane (and reputation) was shot down over Russia in 1960, President Eisenhower had accepted invitations to visit both the Soviet Union and Japan. After the U-2 episode, Moscow cancelled its invitation and anti-American fanatics in Japan ran wild. They condemned not only the basing of U-2 planes in Japan but also the Japanese–American security treaty then pending. A courageous President Eisenhower persisted in his determination to visit Japan, despite the grave risk to which he was exposing the presidency, not to mention his person. The riots finally became so frenzied that the Tokyo government was forced to "postpone" the invitation indefinitely. America lost face, but this was better than losing the President's life. Certainly less face would have been lost if Eisenhower and his advisers had been willing to propose a postponement earlier in the game.[11]

Similarly, the Vice President should not demean his high office and risk involving his country in disaster by going to places where he is subjected to stones, spit, and other forms of contempt. Vice President Nixon's South American trip in 1958 resulted in such a debacle. With proper soundings in advance, it would never have been scheduled. With a realistic appraisal of the rising tide of resentment, it should have been cancelled long before the dangerous climax forced a face-losing backdown.[12]

LAME DUCKS SHOULD COOPERATE WITH THEIR SUCCESSORS

A lame-duck President, the quip goes, is one whose goose has recently been cooked at the polls, or one whose successor has been chosen in the recent election. The incumbent since 1933 has somewhat more than two months to serve (early November to January 20). During this interval he should avoid committing the nation to new courses, especially those that may prove distasteful or disastrous to his successor. Ideally, he should establish a close liaison with the incoming President, whether of the same party or not. And for his part, the President-elect should treat his predecessor in a like manner.

In 1932–1933 Herbert Hoover, a Republican, was the outgoing President-reject. He did not hit it off well in several conferences

[11] For Eisenhower's own version see his *Waging Peace* (1965), pp. 560–563.
[12] For Richard M. Nixon's story see *Six Crises* (1962), Sec. 4.

with Franklin Roosevelt, a Democrat, the President-elect. This was partly because the dying king was desperately trying to commit the uncrowned king to conservative courses which, as Hoover wrote privately at the time, would mean "the abandonment of 90% of the so-called 'New Deal.'"[13] In American politics the victor, not the vanquished, ordinarily scoops up the spoils. Roosevelt naturally avoided commitments on the Allied war debts and other pressing issues, while Hoover and his supporters continued to berate Roosevelt for noncooperation.

President Eisenhower, in the last few weeks of his lame-duck period, broke diplomatic relations with Castro's Cuba, thereby presenting President-elect Kennedy with an accomplished fact. But this drastic step was reportedly taken only after consultation with spokesmen for the incoming administration.

Blessed are the Presidents who can cooperate with both their predecessors and their successors.

[13] Hoover to Senator David A. Reed, Feb. 20, 1933, in W. S. Myers and W. H. Newton, eds., *The Hoover Administration* (1936), p. 341.

CHAPTER II

The Department of State

"A President may, and will, listen to whom he wishes. But his relationship with the Secretary of State will not prosper if the latter is not accepted as his principal adviser and executive agent in foreign affairs, and the trusted confidant of all his thoughts and plans relating to them."

FORMER SECRETARY DEAN ACHESON, 1960

PROLOGUE

The President has a back-breaking job, but let us reserve a little sympathy for the Secretary of State. Secretary John Foster Dulles once listed his sixteen major tasks, the last of which was "making long-range policies." This in itself is more than a full-time chore.

In some respects the Secretary has a tougher job than his chief. Perched on the peak of a globally-based pyramid, he is responsible to the President, and not to the electorate, which is more easily misled. Like most diplomats, he is always on duty, for world-shaking events are no respecters of weekends. He is at the beck and call of Congress, whose various committees think nothing of wasting hours of his precious time as he patiently and respectfully repeats information that he has already imparted to other committees. He dare not offend the legislative branch, lest he bite the hand that doles out the appropriations. He has no power to coerce Congress, as the President has with various weapons at his command. If the Secretary's policies (actually the President's) turn out badly, he is often the whipping boy. Of course, he has to defend those policies or bow out in favor of someone else who will.

For all this he is paid $35,000, or less than some college presidents and football coaches.

THE SECRETARY SHOULD ENJOY THE PRESIDENT'S CONFIDENCE

The Secretary of State has always been the premier officer in the Cabinet, and his appointment is probably the most important single one that the President can make.

Ideally, there should be reciprocal confidence, respect, and loyal support. Some Secretaries have not thought too highly of their Chief, as was evident in Secretary Webster's patronizing attitude toward President ("Old Tippecanoe") Harrison. Some Presidents have not had too high a regard for their Secretaries, especially those forced upon them by the exigencies of politics. This was painfully true of Woodrow Wilson's feelings toward Secretary Bryan, and their shotgun marriage not surprisingly ended in a disorderly divorce.

Happier and more fruitful relationships can readily be cited. President Truman worked hand in glove with the brilliant but somewhat condescending Secretary Dean Acheson; the two men evidently respected each other and gave each other loyal support. President Eisenhower reposed great confidence, perhaps too much, in Secretary Dulles, who for protracted periods was given virtually a free hand. Andrew H. Berding, then a State Department official, quotes Dulles as saying, "I've never found myself in any disagreement whatsoever with the President."[1] This statement is more alarming than reassuring, for it suggests that one of the two, probably Eisenhower, was not doing much profound thinking about foreign policy.

THE SECRETARY OF STATE SHOULD SPEAK FOR THE PRESIDENT

The President, as we have seen, may speak for himself in handling foreign policy, without the approval or even the prior

[1] *Dulles on Diplomacy* (1965), p. 15. Berding states that he recorded Dulles' lengthy remarks at the time in shorthand.

knowledge of the Secretary. But the Secretary cannot or should not enunciate policy unless he has advance clearance from his Chief. Secretary Dulles, as befitted the subordinate of a former active General (Eisenhower), referred to himself as the "President's chief of staff in foreign affairs."

The Secretary often serves as a "front" for the President. Secretary Marshall, in his famous speech at the Harvard commencement in 1947, unveiled what proved to be the basis of the Marshall Plan. But he was actually the mouthpiece of President Truman, who had carefully worked out this epochal scheme after close consultation with a small army of advisers, including Secretary Marshall and Under Secretary of State Dean Acheson. Marshall's speech was no routine commencement address.

A STRONG SECRETARY OFTEN INDICATES A WEAK PRESIDENT

As already noted, the power of the Secretary of State as a rule is inversely proportional to the strength of the President. Strong Presidents often have colorless Secretaries, and strong Secretaries often serve relatively colorless Presidents, in teeter-totter fashion.

Secretary Dulles, under Eisenhower, was a strong Secretary who, in the words of the British journalist Richard Goold-Adams, "held more power in his own hands than any modern American except Franklin Roosevelt." [2] Even making allowance for exaggeration, we may doubt the wisdom of clothing nonelected officials in a democratic government with this much authority. The teeter-totter theory that a strong Secretary indicates a weak President does Eisenhower's reputation no good.

On the other hand, a strong President like Woodrow Wilson looked upon his Secretaries as glorified clerks or "administrative assistants." They were supposed to take orders with a minimum of back talk. Secretary Bryan was squeezed out and Secretary Lansing was thrown out when they refused to toe the line. After more than eleven years, President Roosevelt finally got rid of the ailing but assertive Secretary Hull and replaced him with a nonassertive nonentity, Secretary Stettinius—a handsome, tooth-flashing figure of a man. Cynics remarked that there was less there than met the eye.

[2] Richard Goold-Adams, *John Foster Dulles: A Reappraisal* (1962), p. 300.

THERE CAN BE ONLY ONE SECRETARY OF STATE
AT A TIME

Other Cabinet members must be careful not to poach on the preserves of the State Department.

In 1946 Secretary of State Byrnes delivered a get-tough-with-Russia speech in Germany. A week later Secretary of Commerce Wallace made a go-soft-on-Russia speech in New York. Foreigners and Americans alike were confused as to the policy, if any, of the Truman administration. Wallace claimed that the President had read and approved an advance copy of the speech, but Truman finally explained that he had only approved the speaker's right to express his views. The left-leaning Wallace was soon dropped.

There is ordinarily enough confusion about our foreign policies without free-wheeling members of the Cabinet issuing conflicting views. As the Republican Senator Arthur H. Vandenberg acidly observed regarding Wallace, "We can only cooperate with one Secretary of State at a time."

The problem has been complicated in recent years by the Ambassador of the United States at the United Nations in New York. Ambassador Lodge, serving under President Eisenhower, remarked to Robert Murphy, "I am not bound by instructions from the State Department. I am a member of the President's cabinet and accept instructions only from him." [3] The perpetuation of this two-headed foreign office was continued under President Kennedy, when Adlai Stevenson, the two-time loser as a presidential candidate of the party, exercised unusual influence in New York as Ambassador at the United Nations.

BRINKMANSHIP IS A DANGEROUS SHIP

On January 16, 1956, *Life* magazine published an explosive article about Secretary of State Dulles, obviously based on an interview or interviews. He was reported as practicing "brinkmanship," although he did not use this precise term. He said in effect that a powerful nation like the United States, must, if need be, show a willingness to back its policies by going "to the brink" of war and

[3] Robert Murphy, *Diplomat Among Warriors* (1964), p. 367.

forcing its adversary to back down. In short, avert war by a willingness to go to war.

This, of course, is elementary. If a nation with enormous strength repeatedly "chickens out" in a crisis, its expensively maintained armaments become largely useless. The classic instance of "brinkmanship" occurred during the Cuban missile crisis in 1962, when the Soviets pulled in their horns after President Kennedy and Premier Khrushchev had gone to the brink.

Even though "brinkmanship" is a standard practice of the great powers, the American Secretary of State should not boast about it in public. To do so is to create fears and excite alarms that may eventually push the nation over the brink. Speaking of Dulles, Winston Churchill remarked in 1954, "He is the only case of a bull I know who carries his china closet with him." [4]

NEVER GLOAT OVER DIPLOMATIC VICTORIES

Secretary Dulles, something of a "headline hog," talked too much to the "brinkmanship" interviewer about how he had forced his adversaries to back down over Quemoy and Matsu (the Chinese offshore islands) and other danger spots. He forgot (if he ever fully learned) one of the ABC's of diplomacy: the best diplomatic work is done without fanfare. To boast is to rub salt into wounds, put one's adversary on his guard, and make future accommodations with him more difficult. In some instances he may not realize that he has suffered a sharp defeat until he hears the Secretary bragging about it. If anything, the Secretary or the ambassador should quietly congratulate the other side on having scored some good points. [5] "Grandstanding" or "showboating" has no more place in diplomacy than it does in the espionage operations of the Central Intelligence Agency.

Nor should the President himself resort to boasting. Kennedy won an impressive, though incomplete, diplomatic victory in the Cuban missile crisis of 1962, but he was wise enough not to crow over it. He helped the Soviets to save face and to beat a reasonably graceful retreat. In fact, they insisted they had won a diplomatic

[4] Kay Halle, ed., *Irrepressible Churchill* (1966), p. 325.
[5] After the Cuban missile crisis, Secretary Rusk, taking his cue from President Kennedy, urged the reporters not to write of a Soviet "capitulation." Elie Abel, *The Missile Crisis* (1966), p. 207.

victory by forcing the United States to agree not to invade Cuba, which (they alleged) had been their only objective in the first place.

If Washington can win diplomatic victories in substance, it should not be too unwilling to permit its opponents to claim victories on paper. Diplomatic failures, all too often, make the headlines, while triumphs are filed away in the archives, or should be.

AVOID THE OPEN-MOUTH POLICY

The Secretary should make few speeches, and when he does make them he would be well advised, as a rule, to confine himself to platitudes. There is always the danger of a slip of the tongue. For the same reason he should be more than cautious in press conferences and carefully limit their number.

Secretary Dulles was unfortunately afflicted with a bad case of foot-in-mouth disease. Such catchwords as "unleashing Chiang," "massive retaliation," "agonizing reappraisal," "liberation" of captive peoples, and "brinkmanship" will long be associated with his name. He stirred up a tremendous uproar in 1955 when he offended the people of India by referring to the tiny Portuguese enclave of Goa, dating back to 1510, as a "province" of Portugal. "Peace-loving" India eventually ended the debate by forcibly reclaiming Goa in 1961.

Far more unfortunate, seemingly, was Secretary Acheson's famous National Press Club speech of January 12, 1950. On this occasion he excluded South Korea from the American defense perimeter. But he did acknowledge that South Korea was a responsibility of the United Nations, of which the United States was a member. The assumption is that Acheson's indiscretion encouraged the North Koreans, backed by the Soviet Union, to launch their fateful invasion of South Korea later that year.

THE SECRETARY SHOULD RISE ABOVE POLITICS

Traditionally, the Secretary of State has been an important political figure. Sometimes he was the uncrowned king of the party, who, as the result of various mischances, never quite attained the presidency. Such were Henry Clay, Daniel Webster, W. H. Seward, James G. Blaine, and William J. Bryan. Secretary Cordell Hull (under Franklin Roosevelt) and Secretary James F. Byrnes (under Truman) were the last Secretaries who could boast considerable political stature. Those of more recent vintage—Marshall, Acheson, Dulles, Herter, and Rusk—were all without substantial political influence in their own right. A politically potent Secretary can be useful in such ways as lobbying important legislation through Congress, as Bryan did in 1913. But he usually cannot be dismissed, when his usefulness has ended, without an unseemly row, such as accompanied the resignation of the pacifist Bryan in 1915 over the submarine crisis with Berlin.

Whether a political figure or not, the Secretary, like the President, should put the welfare of the country above that of the party. Bryan brought the foreign service into disrepute when he undertook to find places in it for "deserving Democrats," many of whom had voted for him in three presidential elections. Caustic criticism poured forth from "resolute Republicans," who had for years been doing much the same thing. In truth, Bryan was not so much of a spoilsman as certain other fellow Democrats, but the only really rotten egg whom he nominated for the legation in Santo Domingo, James M. Sullivan, was not soon forgotten.[6]

This is not to suggest that a reasonable number of able and aggressive nonprofessionals should not be brought into the Department from time to time. Fossilized professionals are to be as much deplored as bungling amateurs. But stuffing the service with political hacks is a practice to be shunned.

SELF-RIGHTEOUSNESS DOES NOT BECOME A SECRETARY OF STATE

There are always two sides, sometimes many sides, to any complex international controversy. The Secretary of State inevitably arouses annoyance and opposition if he speaks as though God were an American citizen and as though we invariably have a monopoly on being right.

Secretary Dulles, himself a prominent lay churchman, was

[6] Sullivan was a New York lawyer under heavy obligation to unsavory elements who had large financial interests in the Dominican Republic. See Paolo E. Coletta, "Secretary of State William Jennings Bryan and 'Deserving Democrats,' " *Mid-America,* XLVIII (1966), pp. 75–98.

prone to preach at other nations in terms of moral righteousness, sometimes moralistic legalism. Critics complained that he was ponderous, platitudinous, and pious, and that he acted as though he were the Almighty's foreign minister. His under-the-table dealings, which involved the overthrow of the Communist-tainted government of Guatemala in 1954, seemed to belie his pretensions.

Moral righteousness can easily shade into Phariseeism. In the 1890's the Department of State complained to Spain about the mistreatment of Cubans, all the while ignoring our shameful mistreatment of the Indians and the wholesale lynching of Negroes. Other examples could easily be cited, including the protest by a spokesman for the State Department in 1960 against mistreatment of Negroes in the Union of South Africa. At this very time Negro sit-in demonstrations were sweeping the South, and the government of South Africa pointedly told us to mind our own business.

REVERSING POLICY CAPRICIOUSLY IS BAD POLICY

As noted in connection with the presidency, American foreign policies should not be valid for only a four-year stretch, or within a four-year stretch.

The flamboyant Secretary Blaine, appointed by his friend President Garfield, embarked upon a far-visioned policy of Pan-Americanism. Garfield died from an assassin's bullet after only six months in office, and President Arthur, who succeeded him, did not hit it off well with Blaine. The result was that Blaine resigned, as all Secretaries should who do not enjoy the confidence of their Chief.

The new Secretary was Frederick Frelinghuysen. Disapproving of Blaine's ambitious plans, he summarily recalled the invitations to the first Pan American Conference in Washington which had been issued and for which some acceptances had been received. This species of rudeness did not lessen the overbearing image given by Latin America to the Colossus of the North.

NEVER ANTAGONIZE CONGRESS UNNECESSARILY

The Department of State stands in an uneasy relationship to Congress, which votes the necessary appropriations, albeit on a cut-rate basis. Unlike farm leaders and labor leaders, the foreign service has no constituency that can bring pressure to bear on Capitol Hill. Living by sufferance, it is one of the smallest of the executive departments in both personnel and budget. The Senate confirms (or rejects) presidential appointments and approves (or disapproves) treaties. Painful though some of the knifings may be, the Senate is merely doing its constitutional duty, and its members are often able to detect flaws in the pacts presented. Secretary John Hay looked upon the Senate as his natural enemy, and petulantly wrote the famous lines about a treaty entering the Senate having the same chances as a bull entering a Spanish arena.

Secretary of State Dean Acheson did not get along conspicuously well with Congress, and he was subjected to much verbal abuse by its members, chiefly of the opposition Republican party. In appearing before its committees he was too bright, too clever, and too sophisticated, much in the manner of the supercilious "damned Englishman," whom he rather resembled in appearance. All this was unfortunate because, from the standpoint of intellectual equipment, Acheson was one of our ablest Secretaries of State.

Secretaries Hay and Acheson were never members of Congress. The record reveals that Secretaries of State who have served for long periods in that body, notably Cordell Hull, understand it better and generally get along more harmoniously with it. The President could well bear this fact of life in mind when he makes his choice.

THE SECRETARY OWES LOYALTY TO HIS STAFF

Secretary Acheson (a Democrat) and Secretary Dulles (a Republican) served during the years of the McCarthy madness in the 1950's. Senator McCarthy wildly accused the State Department of being wormy with scores of known Communists and homosexuals, and tried to purge it of such alleged undesirables. Secretary Acheson, backed by a peppery President Truman, loyally undertook to defend his subordinates against such "red herring" attacks by the opposition Republican party.

Secretary Dulles, keenly aware of Acheson's strained relations with Congress, was determined to get along with it, whatever the cost. He permitted McCarthy to install his own hatchet man, Robert W. S. McLeod, as chief security officer in the Department of State in 1953.[7] Heads rolled. The morale of the Department and of the foreign service, already scraping bottom, received a shattering blow. Its prestige drooped, both at home and abroad, and its program for recruiting able new personnel received a staggering setback. Perhaps worst of all, foreign service officers in the field were now under enormous pressure to report that Communism was losing out, even though such an interpretation may not have squared with the facts.

Loyalty begets loyalty. The Secretary of State can hardly expect loyal support from his subordinates unless he is prepared to support those who are unjustly accused.

THE SECRETARY SHOULD NOT BE A GADABOUT

Secretary Dulles enjoyed airplane travel, with its freedom from telephone calls and other jangling interruptions. He broke new paths in flying to various parts of the world to confer with important officials, including heads of state. All told, he logged about 560,000 miles, or the equivalent of more than twenty times around the globe. Cynics said, with obvious exaggeration, that he "carried the State Department in his hat."

Critics voiced various complaints about "airport diplomacy" and Dulles' capacity for taking "infinite planes." Such "perpetual motion" was so fatiguing that the Secretary obviously could not be at his best; the expectations of foreigners were aroused beyond reason; bypassed nations felt slighted; there was no time for careful study in advance or patient deliberation afterward; the American ambassador was downgraded by the vote of "no confidence" cast by the presence of the Secretary; world perspective was better in the United States than inside the crater of the volcano; and decision-making in Washington was lamed when the Secretary was not "tending store." A popular reversal of the old adage was applied to Dulles: "Don't just do something, stand there."

On the other hand, there are genuine advantages in face-to-face dealings, especially when the alternative is to inch through red-taped channels. In this Nuclear Age speed is of the essence. The

[7] In 1957, after Senator McCarthy's power had been broken, McLeod was sent as Ambassador to Ireland, where some of the Irish newspapers were critical of the obvious political maneuver. *New York Times,* April 15, 1957, 12:3.

jet airplane is here to stay, and no one can deny the Secretary's right, or even obligation, to use it. Dulles' immediate successors followed in his vapor trail and traveled even more miles on an annual basis. The Henry M. Jackson Senate Subcommittee, frowning somewhat on "commuter-trip" diplomacy, concluded in 1965 that jet travel will not necessarily "convert indecisiveness in Washington to decisiveness in the field."[8] The ancient Greek philosophers counseled moderation in all things, and this would include travel. A good rule would be: when in doubt stay at home and get a bird's-eye view, rather than a worm's eye view, of global perplexities. A commander-in-chief should never go on patrol duty.

SICK MEN CAN MAKE SICK POLICIES

When President Nasser of Egypt seized the Suez Canal in 1956, Secretary Dulles was operated on for cancer, and a portion of his large intestine was removed. Many diplomats have resigned because of "illness" when their policies have collapsed, as Dulles' had, and the ailing Secretary might properly have bowed out. But dedicated grimly to duty and needed by an unsure President Eisenhower, he persevered, finally winning worldwide respect for his courage and his "martyrdom." After having virtually ruptured the NATO Alliance, he managed to bring relations with our principal allies from the disastrous level to the endurable level. Finally forced by a recurrence of cancer to resign and enter a hospital in 1959, he was sworn in on a sickbed as a special consultant to the President on foreign affairs. He died a month later.

Few will deny Dulles' courage, but many will doubt his common sense. He was dealing with issues that involved the lives and deaths of hundreds of millions of people. Who among us, when indicted for murder, would employ an attorney, no matter how dedicated or gifted, who is dying of cancer? What is a good rule for the Secretary is also a good rule for his Chief; when suffering from a fatal illness, both have an obligation to turn over the reins to healthy men.

[8] *Administration of National Security* (1965), p. 60.

ELIMINATE BUREAUCRATIC STRANGULATION

When the President sends a request to the Secretary for advice, a common procedure is for the paper to pass over numerous desks, involving various layers of experts, on its way down and back. This process often takes about ten days and reveals bureaucracy at about its clumsiest.

During World War II, Admiral Leahy and President Roosevelt decided to send naval units to Beirut, Lebanon, despite objections from the Free French. When Ambassador Robert Murphy asked Leahy if the State Department had concurred, he was informed that it had not even been consulted. "We decided what to do in twenty-five minutes," he explained. "If we referred this to the Secretary of State, it would take twenty-five days." [9]

The slow-motion procedure can be further slowed by personal biases. At various desks in the State Department sit men of various persuasions: liberals and conservatives, Democrats and Republicans, Catholics and Protestants, Jews and Gentiles. Some of them do not approve of the policies that the President asks them to implement, and they are sometimes able to exercise quiet but effective sabotage.

President John F. Kennedy ordered the execution of a new policy regarding a more liberal regime in Italy. Despite repeated proddings, nearly two years elapsed before his instructions were reluctantly carried out in the teeth of opposition from conservative foot-draggers in the State Department. Arthur M. Schlesinger, Jr., who helped prepare what he called a "melancholy memorandum" for President Kennedy, added: "Lest you think you run the United States Government, the matter is still under debate." [10]

LEAVE FOREIGN POLICY TO THE FOREIGN POLICY AGENCIES

There is a disturbing tendency, as we have seen, for other Departments to thrust a hand into the affairs of the State Department and the foreign service. This trend has been especially conspicuous since World War II, when diplomatic problems, like the occupation of Germany and Japan, merged with military problems, and when

---

[9] Robert Murphy, *Diplomat Among Warriors* (1964), p. 447.
[10] A. M. Schlesinger, Jr., *A Thousand Days* (1965), p. 881.

men like Generals Clay and MacArthur were summoned to perform useful civilian service. Yet the necessity for having diplomatic instructions cleared by the Department of Defense or other agencies inevitably results in delays and contradictions.

Astronomical sums of money are involved in modern American diplomacy, and, not surprisingly, Secretary of the Treasury Morgenthau, a Dutchess County neighbor and longtime friend of President Roosevelt, often had more ready access to the President than did Secretary of State Hull. In 1944 Morgenthau, understandably embittered by the fate of his Jewish co-religionists, convinced Roosevelt of the wisdom of punishing Nazi Germany by destroying its industry and reducing it to an agricultural state—the so-called "potato patch" theory.

The Morgenthau Plan leaked out, played into the hands of Nazi propagandists, and otherwise did infinite harm. Secretary of State Hull had nothing to do with this policy and thoroughly disapproved of it, but such are the bitter fruits of officious interference. President Roosevelt had more judicious second thoughts and finally dropped the ill-conceived scheme.

THE CENTRAL INTELLIGENCE AGENCY SHOULD NOT MAKE POLICY

The CIA is designed to gather covert information on which the architects of foreign policy in Washington can base their decisions. This cloak-and-dagger outfit had a large hand in engineering the Guatemalan *coup* in 1954, which resulted in the overthrow of a Communist-oriented government. Thereafter afflicted with the "Guatemala disease," the CIA evidently concluded that the overthrow of Castro's Cuba could be similarly contrived. It had a large hand in planning and attempting to carry off the disastrous Bay of Pigs landing in 1961, as a result of which cynics dubbed the CIA "the Cuban Invasion Agency."

Allen W. Dulles, who in the Cuban aftermath lost his job as director of the CIA, claims in his book that the agency never carried out any action of a political nature without proper approval "at a high political level in our government *outside the CIA*." [11] This

[11] Allen W. Dulles, *The Craft of Intelligence* (1963), p. 189. Secret agents can also shape policy by withholding essential information.

may have been true of the CIA in Washington, but Dulles could not exercise complete control over his small army of secret operatives in the field. Being human (and prejudiced), they could influence high policy by reporting the facts (or the presumed facts) as they saw them through their colored spectacles. Having a large slush fund for bribery and other purposes, these agents were sometimes guilty of pushing causes or backing persons contrary to the policy established in Washington. Such sabotage was notorious in Laos in the 1950's and contributed richly to the dangerous debacle in this lotus land.

If we should have only one Secretary of State at a time, we should have only one agency at a time making and directing foreign policy. The State Department should not be backward about asserting its primacy over rival or competing agencies.

CHAPTER III

Picking the Right Ambassador

"When an Ambassador overseas negotiates, or speaks in private or in public, his audience needs to feel that he has the confidence and speaks with the authority of the President of the United States."

THE HENRY M. JACKSON SENATE
SUBCOMMITTEE, 1965

PROLOGUE

Diplomats have traditionally suffered from a bad public "image." They have often been portrayed as frock-coated bunglers whose chief occupation is to get us into wars, or at least to stir up more trouble than they settle. "Fortunately," some wit has said, "they have long noses, because they cannot see beyond the ends of them." In the United States they were long branded as "cooky pushers" and "tea gladiators," whose chief skill lay in balancing a teacup or hoisting a cocktail glass.

The truth is that a good ambassador should possess all the virtues, for he is the eyes, ears, nose, voice, and brain of his government at the foreign capital. The best diplomats, like the best musicians, are born, not made. They can learn some lessons from books and from experience, especially experience. But if they do not have the proper qualities of mind, character, temperament, and personality, they are almost certain to fall short of a completely satisfactory performance.

The eighteenth-century manuals declared that the ideal envoy should have "a quick mind but unlimited patience, know how to dissemble without being a liar, inspire trust without trusting others, be modest but assertive, charm others without succumbing to their charm, and possess plenty of money and a beautiful wife while remaining indifferent to all temptations of riches and women."[1]

Agitation has developed periodically in the United States to establish a West Point for diplomats, that is, a school where future foreign service officers are drilled to perfection. But we should note that the art of diplomacy cannot be adequately taught in schoolrooms. Basic principles may be imparted, but a graduate of a diplomatic charm school can give no guarantee that he will prove to be an able diplomatist. A broad education in the liberal arts is still regarded as the best background, and this can still be secured in existing colleges, which do not isolate the trainee from the mainstream of American life.

CHOOSE AMBASSADORS OF
INTELLIGENCE AND TALENTS

François de Callières, the veteran French diplomatist, wrote in 1716 that while a king may equip an able man with the necessary financial means, "it is not in his power to endow with intelligence one who does not possess it."[2] Some of the ablest American diplomats have been the brainiest. It was no accident that men like John Quincy Adams, Charles Francis Adams, John Hay, and Dwight W. Morrow were elected to Phi Beta Kappa while in college.

A superior intelligence is related to a deep interest in international affairs, a studious and inquiring mind, powers of analysis, a capacity to separate the essential from the nonessential, a balanced judgment, the ability to think clearly and logically in a crisis, and good political horse sense. Deputy Under Secretary of State Loy Henderson in the 1950's, when asked what he sought for most in

---

[1] Fred C. Iklé, *How Nations Negotiate* (1964), p. 253.
[2] François de Callières, *On the Manner of Negotiating with Princes* (1716; trans. from French by A. F. Whyte, 1919), p. 39. This is a classic work.

recruits, replied, "Political sensitivity—without it a Ph.D. is useless. With it, a high school student is invaluable."[3]

The ambassador should be ingenious and clever, but not so clever as to overreach himself. He should be shrewd in evaluating evidence, resourceful in expedients, firm in his grasp of realities, far-visioned in his imaginative foresight. Perceptiveness, especially in seeing trouble looming on the horizon, is highly important, for one good man on the ground is ordinarily worth two at the desk in Washington. The ideal diplomat also needs to be a first-rate psychologist. As Callières remarked, he should be able to read his adversary's thoughts (like a poker player) by noting the changes in his facial expression.

Finally, the model ambassador should be a gifted administrator and a competent businessman, as was Ambassador Chester Bowles in India in the 1950's. Many of the embassy staffs are huge and cumbersome affairs, and economic problems are among the most pressing in the world today.

SEND ABROAD MEN (AND WOMEN) [4] TO MATCH OUR MOUNTAINS

A diplomat is more likely to succeed if he has dignity and "presence"—that is if, without being a stuffed shirt, he looks like a diplomat. He must command respect if he expects to receive it. The wealthy career man Henry White, who served early in the century under Theodore Roosevelt, was tall, well-proportioned, well-rounded, gray-haired—every inch a diplomatist.

A strong physique and steel nerves should accompany an imposing presence. Only a vigorous body and iron self-discipline enabled Townsend Harris in Japan in the 1850's to stick it out for three lonely years in his outpost at Shimoda and finally emerge with an epochal treaty. A healthy body is likewise related to energy, enterprise, and industry, all of which the ideal envoy should possess

[3] Quoted in Charles W. Thayer, *Diplomat* (1959), p. 243.
[4] A few women have occupied ambassadorships, notably Mrs. Clare Boothe Luce, the politically appointed Ambassador to Italy. The Latin world is a man's world, and although she did some commendable work, she was not universally admired. See E. Wilder Spaulding, *Ambassadors Ordinary and Extraordinary* (1961), pp. 195–202.

in full measure. The foreign service has no place for the lazy man.

The diplomat must also be prepared to dine for his country. He must eat all kinds of strange concoctions (lest he insult his host), ranging all the way down to stewed cat and fried lizard. Little wonder the ex-Ambassador Robert Murphy could note that ulcers were "the occupational disease of professional diplomats," who have often regretted that they had but one stomach to give for their country.[5]

The importance of a good physique is underlined by the fact that many of the "hardship" posts are dangerous, what with vermin, disease, lack of sanitation, and extremes of heat and cold. In the "old days" before penicillin, La Paz (Bolivia) was especially feared; there the atmosphere is so rarified that to contract pneumonia was to flirt with death. The ultimate in folly occurred in 1830, when John Randolph of Roanoke, afflicted with tuberculosis, was sent as minister to damp and chilly St. Petersburg. After less than a month, he beat a hasty retreat to the less lethal climate of England.

SELECT ENVOYS OF EXEMPLARY CHARACTER

The ambassador is generally regarded in the host country as the personification of the virtues and vices of the nation that he represents. The highest character embraces a sense of self-sacrifice, dedication to the public service, unimpeachable integrity, and complete trustworthiness. We should above all avoid appointing boors, drunks, or crooks, all of whom at times have disgraced the service.

The practice was not uncommon in nineteenth-century America to get rid of troublemakers by awarding them diplomatic appointments. Especially useful for this purpose were Peking and St. Petersburg, both of which were far removed from Washington. In the case of St. Petersburg, the chances were fairly good that the appointee would die of pneumonia. But a change of climate seldom results in a change of character.

President Lincoln did the foreign service no good when he

[5] The American Ambassador to Britain, Charles G. Dawes, stated in 1930, "Diplomacy is not too hard on the brain, but it's hell on the feet." See Paul R. Leach, *That Man Dawes* (1930), p. 326. Dawes may have been thinking of standing at receptions. Ex-Ambassador to Italy, Henry P. Fletcher, commented, "It depends on which [end] you use."

named Secretary of War Cameron as Minister to Russia, primarily to get him out of the country and hush up scandals that were bubbling up in the War Department. This practice has led to the quip that some men are sent abroad for the good of the country and others for the good of the party.[6]

Courage—moral and physical—is an essential ingredient of a strong character, and foreign service officers need their share of it. Ambassador Joseph P. ("Jolly Joe") Kennedy, stationed in London during World War II, experienced more than two hundred German air raids, several of them almost fatal. A plaque hanging in the State Department building in Washington lists the names of the more than seventy foreign service officers who have lost their lives in the line of duty, sometimes at the hands of frenzied mobs. In 1924, for example, Major Robert W. Imbrie, American Vice Consul in Persia, was beaten to death by religious fanatics. Other men have suffered even more disagreeable fates.

TACTFULNESS IS THE ESSENCE OF DIPLOMACY

Tact is virtually synonymous with diplomacy. The envoy must ordinarily keep his dislikes under control, and not repay disagreeableness with disagreeableness. He must develop skill in saying sweet nothings on those occasions when it is best to say nothing. A soft answer not only "turneth away wrath" but invites soft answers. This is probably what one wit had in mind when he observed, "Diplomacy is to do and say the nastiest thing in the nicest way." Antagonizing one's hosts usually accomplishes nothing but frustration, as Minister Pierre Soulé discovered in Spain in the 1850's when he tried to strong-arm Spain out of Cuba.

The envoy must never say "no," or almost never. He may say "let's consider it," "maybe," "perhaps," "tomorrow," but seldom a flat negative. Some quipster has said, "When a diplomat says 'yes,' he means 'perhaps'; when he says 'perhaps,' he means 'no'; when he says 'no,' he is no diplomat." Other words seldom used by diplo-

[6] In 1943 President Roosevelt, seeking a reward for a powerful Bronx politician, Edward J. Flynn, appointed him Minister to Australia, then being threatened by a Japanese invasion and defended by Americans. The resulting public uproar forced a withdrawal of the nomination. For Flynn's version see *You're the Boss* (1947), pp. 172–177.

matists of the old school [7] were "war," "never," "this is final." As
Secretary Bryan told the Japanese ambassador in 1913, at the time
of the California alien land crisis, "Nothing is final between friends."

SELF-POSSESSION IS A PRIME VIRTUE

Ideally, the envoy should exude charm and suavity; the social
graces and an ability to get along with people are of the utmost importance. He must be courteous, gracious, tolerant, and possess simple good manners. He should not emulate John Randolph, who,
when presented to the Russian Tsar in 1830, allegedly blurted out,
"Howaya Emperor? And how's the madam?"

While to a degree self-effacing, the diplomat should be decisive
and display powers of leadership, as Anson Burlingame did in China
in the 1860's. He not only became leader of the diplomatic corps
but so commended himself to the Peking officials that they chose
him to represent China as the head of a diplomatic mission to Europe, even though he spoke no Chinese.

Anger is a luxury that a true diplomat can seldom afford. He
must be prudent, moderate, restrained, at all times keeping his emotions under control. He must not blurt out his reactions but think
twice before he speaks, even if his words say nothing. He must
never give way to outbursts of temper, and certainly not become involved in a public brawl, as did our Minister to Bulgaria, George
H. Earle, in 1941, when provoked by an insolent German business
man who threw a wine bottle at him.[8]

The envoy must never leave his outpost in frustration and dis-
gust, as did the able William Pinkney when he quit the London
legation in 1811, leaving behind a much less able man as *chargé*.
If Pinkney had remained, he might have glimpsed that Britain's
maritime restrictions, the basic cause of America's grievances, were
about to ease. His departure was like desertion in the face of the
enemy.

The foreign service officer should be willing to assume responsibility and exercise initiative—to stick out his neck if he finds he

---

[7] The Soviets, as relative newcomers, have long practiced "diplomacy by
tantrum" or calculated rudeness, which in certain circumstances has brought the
desired results, especially where the nation was weak enough to be bullied.

[8] *New York Times,* February 23, 1941, 1:3–4; February 28, 1941, 2:7.

must make a crucial decision in the national interest. A white-spatted warrior is as expendable as an armed warrior. But there is a tradition in the foreign service against "making waves"—that is, speaking out of turn or advancing ideas unpalatable to the Secretary of State. The gifted professional, George F. Kennan, clashed with Secretary of State Dulles, who did not encourage public dissent in underlings, and as a result Mr. Kennan was put on the shelf for about eight years.

DISCRETION IS THE HANDMAIDEN OF DIPLOMACY

The envoy must have a capacity to keep secrets; the foreign service is no place for blabbermouths. Looking wise while bored, holding one's peace, and bridling one's tongue are all virtues highly valued. Heavy drinkers are not desirable material for diplomacy: many a secret has been dropped after the third or fourth cocktail has loosened tongues. François de Callières advised that one "should drink in such a manner as not to lose control of his own faculties while endeavoring to loosen the self-control of others." [9]

In the police states of the nonfree world, informers are everywhere. The embassy may in fact be "bugged" with recording devices. This happened to the large wooden eagle which was taken from the American embassy in Moscow, and which was displayed by Ambassador Lodge at the United Nations in 1960 during the debate over the U-2 spy-plane affair.

Even so gifted a diplomatist as George F. Kennan was guilty of an indiscretion that brought about his recall as Ambassador to the Soviet Union in 1952. Arriving in Berlin after a sojourn in Moscow, he allegedly remarked to reporters that life for Western diplomats in Russia resembled that of his internment in Germany after the outbreak of World War II. [10] The Kremlin promptly declared him *persona non grata*, and he was brought home.

So important a public official as the ambassador can hardly give vent to private feelings in public. The warfare on the diplomatic front is too serious.

[9] François de Callières, *On the Manner of Negotiating with Princes*, p. 61. Zealous members of the Woman's Christian Temperance Union have contended that America's so-called diplomatic setbacks at Yalta were caused by Stalin's secret weapon—vodka.

[10] *New York Times*, September 20, 1952, 3:1.

ADAPTABILITY IS PREFERABLE TO UNCONVENTIONALITY

The polished envoy accepts conditions in a foreign country as he finds them, unless perchance he is posted to one of the so-called backward countries that are undergoing reform with American money. He avoids excessive moralism regarding local customs, and refrains from reminding his hosts how much better conditions are in his own country. He tries to visualize problems, not as they appear to him through his American spectacles, but rather as they appear to the people among whom he is residing. Benjamin Franklin, the inventor of bifocals and our envoy to France (1776–1785), showed unusual talent in viewing the scene through both French and American eyes.

The diplomat should try to conform to local usages, including official dress. In this regard the United States in the nineteenth century often tried to show its democratic contempt for monarchical courts by attiring its diplomats in simple black clothes, thereby causing them at times to be confused with the waiters. John Adams, a colleague of Franklin in France, advised submission to those conditions that could not be changed, including walking backward when leaving the presence of royalty.

Other diplomatists have been unwilling to conform and to recognize that while in Rome one should shoot Roman candles. During the Christmas season of 1959, the American ambassador in Lebanon insisted on dragging his beloved dog to social functions, despite the well-known Moslem distaste for canine uncleanliness.[11]

THE DIPLOMATIST MUST BE PATIENT

Patience and persistence are the very soul of diplomacy. The negotiator must not try to force the pace of events; the future comes only one day at a time. The capacity to outsit the other fellow—"bladder diplomacy" it has been called—has frequently reaped rich rewards. John Adams, though a hot-tempered Yankee, showed infinite patience in negotiating a treaty and a loan in the Netherlands during the American War of Independence, at a time when the American cause looked like a bad risk.

---

[11] Spaulding, *Ambassadors Ordinary and Extraordinary*, pp. 289–290.

But Americans are on the whole an impatient, go-for-broke people. They are handicapped in negotiating with the Communists, who take the long view of history and who are in no great hurry. President Harry Truman, in negotiating with Stalin at Potsdam, became so annoyed by all the repetitions, irrelevancies, and petty bickerings that, as he later wrote, "I felt like blowing the roof off the palace." [12] He did manage to keep from exploding, but his impatience led to brushing the Yugoslav question off the agenda.

A primary task of the diplomat, who should be an optimist, is to keep the discussions alive, even when they seem hopeless. He must continue to hope that his opponents will finally see the light of reason (as he sees it) or that changing conditions will change their minds for them. The negotiations ending the Korean War in 1953 required two years and 575 meetings (most of them seemingly hopeless). The treaty that neutralized Austria in 1955 required eight years and some 400 meetings. But in the end an armistice came to Korea and neutralization to Austria, largely because the negotiators had the patience to continue to go through motions and to tolerate insulting behavior and verbal abuse.[13]

CHAMPAGNE IS THE LUBRICANT OF DIPLOMACY

François de Callières noted in 1716 that "a good table will greatly assist in the discovery of all that is going on" and that "good cheer is a great conciliator. . . ." Secretary of State Lansing, under President Wilson, discovered that a man whom he had met on a social footing the night before was a far more approachable person when he came to the State Department the next morning.

Entertainment, when reciprocated, opens many doors. And a prime objective of the diplomat is to open as many doors as possible and secure information that may be useful to Washington. Ambassador Dodd, an ex-professor of modest means who served in Berlin in the 1930's, decided to live on his salary, and when he did not

[12] *Memoirs by Harry S. Truman: Year of Decisions* (1955), p. 369.

[13] Arthur H. Dean, the chief UN negotiator in Korea, reported that his Red Chinese opposite number "habitually called me a capitalistic crook, rapist, thief, robber of widows, stealer of pennies from the eyes of the dead, mongrel of uncertain origin. . . ." He later said that "I had blood on my hands and was a murderer lying in the gutter with filthy garbage, wallowing in the filth of a ram. . . ." *New York Times Magazine,* October 30, 1966, p. 54.

"pay back" his social obligations, he was often not reinvited. By that much his usefulness was curtailed.

On the other hand, entertaining can be overdone. The wealthy Mrs. Pearl Mesta, "the hostess with the mostest [money]," entertained lavishly in the American legation in Luxembourg, where she served as minister from 1949 to 1953. More dedicated to dining than dossiers, she was not exceptionally well informed about the complicated European chessboard. After the Belgian foreign minister had conversed with her on one occasion, he reported to Robert Murphy that "We had a thorough discussion about the weather and all such matters."

Napoleon Bonaparte, in sending an ambassador off to Moscow in 1812, advised, "Keep a good table and look after the ladies." [14] The so-called "Whiskey Fund" may conceivably prevent a war, and no matter how lavish, is bound to be cheaper.

FOREIGN LANGUAGE COMPETENCE SHOULD BE ENCOURAGED

Ideally, a diplomat should be fluent in the language of the host country. But since there are now more than one hundred sovereign nations, and even more languages, this is an ideal frequently unattained.[15] A natural aptitude for languages and a natural aptitude for diplomacy are often not conjoined, and if we must choose between an agile tongue and an agile brain, we must settle for the brain that makes use of interpreters. A fool who speaks Russian is still a fool.

Occasionally an envoy will be so fluent in a given language as to arouse suspicion that he is more than the official spy he is supposed to be—perhaps an ex-CIA agent. On the other hand, as Under Secretary of State Sumner Welles assured Dr. Carlton J. H. Hayes—

[14] Looking after the ladies must be done discreetly, as the aged but amorous widower Franklin did in Paris. General Daniel E. Sickles, who had lost a leg at Gettysburg, not only did his best to provoke a war as Minister to Spain in the 1870's, but created a scandal by becoming the paramour of the adulterous ex-Queen Isabella, then exiled in Paris. W. A. Swanberg, *Sickles the Incredible* (1956), pp. 320–321.

[15] The McCarthyites bitterly opposed the appointment of Charles E. Bohlen as Ambassador to Moscow in 1953, even though he was unusually well qualified and fluent in Russian. They finally managed to get him transferred to Manila in 1957, where his language competence was of little use. The Russians were probably glad to see so perceptive an envoy leave their country.

the prospective Ambassador to Spain who pleaded ignorance of Spanish—some people resent having their language butchered. Sometimes an envoy overestimates his knowledge of the language and not only deceives himself but his own foreign office. Admiral Nomura, the Japanese Ambassador in Washington on the eve of Pearl Harbor, did not fully comprehend the seriousness of Secretary Hull's warnings (in English). He incorrectly reported to Tokyo that Hull was willing to make certain concessions, and when they were not forthcoming, Washington seemed to be falling back to a "hard" position, which helped trigger the explosion at Pearl Harbor.[16]

Often the best arrangement is for the American diplomat to know enough of the language to understand what is being said, even though he may not speak it at all well. He then has additional time in which to formulate his reply while the translation is being made by the interpreter. And while collecting his thoughts he can check on the reliability of the interpreter.

English, rather than French, is now the universal language. It is often spoken by the educated classes abroad, and they frequently prefer to use it (thereby displaying their cultural attainments) rather than to speak their own tongue with a fumbling tyro. Yet even Americans and Englishmen, while using a common language, sometimes fail to arrive at a common meaning.

PROFESSIONALS ARE GENERALLY PREFERABLE TO AMATEURS

American political hacks, especially in the nineteenth century, regarded the foreign service as the only important career in which training, experience, and ability were not needed. Nothing could be further from the truth. "Even in those cases where success has attended the efforts of an amateur diplomatist," wrote François de Callières, "the example must be regarded as an exception, for it is a commonplace of human experience that skilled work requires a skilled workman." [17] Diplomacy is dynamite, especially in the Nuclear Age, and handlers of dynamite should be experienced technicians.

[16] R. J. C. Butow, "The Hull–Nomura Conversations: A Fundamental Misconception," *American Historical Review*, LXV (1960), pp. 822–836.
[17] *On the Manner of Negotiating with Princes*, pp. 64–65.

In the nineteenth century the oceans were still wide, and blunders that would be fatal today were simple mistakes. This explains in part why President Pierce in 1853 could appoint as minister to monarchical Spain the preposterous Pierre Soulé of Louisiana, an impulsive, hot-headed, combative revolutionary exile from France. Matador rather than ambassador, he picked a quarrel with the French envoy, and in the subsequent duel lamed him for life.

A Venetian ambassador, apologizing to the Duke of Tuscany because Venice had sent to Florence an inept diplomat, explained, "We have many fools in Venice." The reply was, "We also have fools in Florence, but we take care not to export them." [18]

Ungifted amateurs are usually a liability. But gifted amateurs who have come up by other ladders, such as the banker Dwight W. Morrow in Mexico City in the 1920's, can often make valuable contributions. Superlative talent is the thing. The nonprofessional, though not familiar with the ropes at first, has one distinctive advantage over the professional: he can assume more responsibility and hence take more risks.[19] If he guesses wrong, he has another occupation to fall back on. If the professional guesses wrong, his lifetime career may end in frustration and disgrace.

All embassies are now significant outposts, and diplomacy is much too important to be left solely to the diplomats. This is especially true of the overprofessionalized, overbureaucratized, overcautious, striped-pants variety. A judicious leavening by talented newcomers has its place, and our ambassadorial posts even today are staffed by about one-fourth noncareer officers.

Over the years a number of able amateurs have made their mark. In 1942 President Franklin Roosevelt drafted a Catholic history professor, Dr. Carlton J. H. Hayes of Columbia University, for the post of Ambassador in Madrid. His primary task was to keep the Catholic dictator Franco out of the Nazi–Fascist camp during World War II. Dr. Hayes was berated by "professional liberals" in America

[18] *Ibid.*, p. 59.

[19] John B. Martin, the politically appointed Ambassador to the Dominican Republic (1962–1964), later wrote: "He [the career officer] is more likely to stand aside, let events take their course, and seek instruction from Washington. I sometimes acted first and then told Washington what I'd done. If I succeeded, I would get little public credit, for when diplomacy succeeds, all is quiet; newspapers cover crises—policy failures—not successes. If I failed, I would go home." John B. Martin, *Overtaken by Events* (1966), p. 714.

for "appeasing" Franco. But Dr. E. Wilder Spaulding, a former foreign service officer, reports that "in the opinion of the Department's European desk" he came the nearest of all our distinguished historian-diplomats "to doing a really satisfactory job." [20]

If praise or blame is called for, we should in all fairness single out the right people. The ambassador, like the soldier in the rear ranks, is simply carrying out orders, or should be. If Roosevelt's policy of not forcing Franco into the enemy camp was wrong, the President should receive the primary blame, not the ambassador in Madrid.[21]

THE SPOILS SYSTEM AND DIPLOMACY DO NOT MIX

In the nineteenth century the foreign service was the happy hunting ground of political wheelhorses, so much so that Marine General Smedley D. Butler could later define a diplomat as "A ward politician with a frock coat." These gentry sought overseas posts as rewards for enriching the party's campaign coffers, for making speeches in support of the winning presidential candidate, or for otherwise causing the party to become indebted to them.

A famous case burst into the headlines in 1893, when President Cleveland (a Democrat) nominated James J. Van Alen (a Democrat) as Minister to Italy. The nominee was a gentleman of considerable attainments, and in addition had contributed $50,000 to the Democratic campaign chest. Civil service reformers (especially opposition Republicans) raised such an uproar over "buying" the office that Van Alen, though confirmed by the Senate, finally declined the appointment.

[20] *Ambassadors Ordinary and Extraordinary* (1961), p. 177. The galaxy of historians who served as ministers or ambassadors would include Washington Irving (Madrid), George Bancroft (London, Berlin), John L. Motley (Vienna, London), Andrew D. White (Berlin), John Hay (London), William E. Dodd (Berlin), and Claude G. Bowers (Madrid, Santiago). Additionally, Richard Hildreth served as consul at Trieste.

[21] When Mrs. Clare Boothe Luce, ex-Ambassador to Italy, was being considered for the embassy in Brazil in 1959, she was criticized for having tried to induce the Rome government to change its policy and permit private capital to exploit oil properties. She replied to Senator Morse: "I was the instrument of my country's policy. I had no private policy of my own. I pursued no private policies of my own. And I certainly had no oil policy of my own." *Hearings before the Committee on Foreign Relations, United States Senate*, 86th Cong., 1st sess. (Apr. 15, 1959), p. 16.

In more recent decades this practice of appointing "fat cats" has fallen into increasing disuse, but it still persists to some degree. In 1957 President Eisenhower nominated Maxwell H. Gluck, a wealthy campaign contributor who was a purveyor of women's apparel, for the ambassadorship in Ceylon. Gluck confessed before the Senate Foreign Relations Committee that he could not name the Prime Minister of Ceylon, and not surprisingly, because it was S. W. R. D. Bandaranaike.[22] Gluck was finally confirmed but lasted only a year. While he did no great harm, he managed to make the foreign service look slightly ridiculous.

PRESTIGIOUS MEN FOR PRESTIGIOUS POSTS

If we must use men without previous diplomatic experience, their stature is enhanced if they have attained a distinguished reputation in other fields of endeavor. Prestige also adds to the self-confidence that is essential for the successful envoy.

In the nineteenth century, before Guggenheim and Fulbright fellowships and similar subventions were available to scholars, leading literary figures were sent abroad to consular or diplomatic posts, sometimes to enable them to continue writing. (These were the "damn literary fellers" at whom the politician Simon Cameron sneered.)

In 1852 Nathaniel Hawthorne wrote a campaign biography of his college friend President-to-be Pierce, and was rewarded with the lucrative consulate at Liverpool. James Russell Lowell, an eminent man of letters who was appointed Minister to Spain and then to Britain, received a far more friendly reception in British society than would have been accorded an ordinary politician. Other literary luminaries were Washington Irving (Minister to Spain), General Lewis Wallace of *Ben Hur* acclaim (Minister to Turkey), William Dean Howells (who wrote a campaign biography of Lincoln and was rewarded with the consulate at Venice in 1861), and Bret Harte (who held consulates in Germany and Scotland). This, of course, is only a partial list.

Prestige won in fields other than literature often carries weight.

[22] Less defensible was Minister Charles Denby in China in the 1890's; he believed that Cossacks came from Corsica rather than Russia.

General George C. Marshall, a five-star desk hero of World War II, was sent to Nationalist China in 1945 as the United States ambassador. Charged with the impossible task of inducing the Nationalist lamb to lie down with the Communist dragon, he finally failed. But his hosts were doubtless flattered by the presence of so distinguished a figure, and as a consequence failure probably came less rapidly than otherwise.

WEALTHY MEN FOR EXPENSIVE POSTS

One of the many ironies of American democracy is that the higher echelons of the diplomatic service have long featured a plutocracy. Only rich men could afford to shoulder the financial burdens of legations or embassies. The gap between their salary and allowances, on the one hand, and their necessary expenses, on the other, had to be bridged by their own bank accounts. The first question that the President was forced to ask about a proposed nominee for one of these bankrupting honors was: Is he rich enough to take the inevitable loss? In the 1920's, the press reported that Ambassador John W. Davis in London, on a salary of $17,500, laid out an additional $50,000 or $60,000 each year on entertainment, while Ambassador Whitney, in the 1950's, annually spent more than $100,000 above his $6,000 "booze allowance."

This deficiency has been substantially remedied in recent years. Yet even today the man (or woman) holding an ambassadorship in an expensive capital should have a considerable bankroll as a backlog. Lavish entertainment by the wealthiest of nations is far more fitting than niggardly hospitality, but Congress has never been overgenerous with funds for the "tea gladiators."

The American people, who have brought salesmanship to a high art, should recognize the value of an expense account. The task of "selling" the United States abroad obviously requires an appropriate outlay. Ironically, some of the poorer "backward nations," recipients of financial support from the United States, have often put on more of a splurge in foreign capitals than the American envoy.

When we send a fleet around the world, we do not ask the admiral to pay for the oil out of his own bank account. Beverages, as we have noted, are the oil of diplomacy, and we should not expect the diplomat to pay for them himself. Many an able man would like to serve his country without being forced to serve sandwiches out of his own pocket.

SEND ENVOYS WHO ARE *PERSONA GRATA*

The host nation reserves the traditional right to veto the appointment of any ambassador whom it finds objectionable. All it has to do is to declare him *persona non grata*. This was the case, for example, with Anthony M. Keiley, whom President Cleveland appointed Minister to Austria–Hungary in 1885. He was branded *persona non grata* by the Vienna government because he was "wedded to a Jewess by civil marriage." The Secretary of State, while conceding the legality of this discrimination, remonstrated that it was contrary to the Constitution of the United States (which had no relevance in Vienna). When the Austro–Hungarian government persisted in its stand, President Cleveland announced that by way of reprisal he would appoint no minister but would use a *chargé d'affaires*. The vacancy continued for more than two years.

Professor William E. Dodd of the University of Chicago, an eminent American historian, was named ambassador to Hitler's Germany by President Roosevelt in 1933. He was not a first-choice appointee, and his well-known dislike for the Nazi regime might properly have brought a protest from Berlin. After arriving at his post, he was so outspoken in his hostility that many channels were closed to him that should have been kept open. A veteran foreign service officer wrote in 1967, "The Ambassador's *first* job is still to cultivate the officials of the government to which he is accredited." [23]

François de Callières observed in 1716 that a *persona grata* could "uproot even the deepest suspicions," whereas a *persona non grata* would not be in a position to know what was "going on" and hence could not properly inform his "home government."

[23] Letter to author, March 1, 1967. Defenders of Dodd have pointed out that he predicted more accurately the war-mad course of Hitler than did some of his professional colleagues in the service. Perhaps no ambassador in Berlin could have changed the course of Hitlerian history, but by most tests the tactless Dodd was not a successful ambassador. A brief and critical appraisal by Franklin L. Ford appears in Gordon A. Craig and Felix Gilbert, eds., *The Diplomats, 1919–1939* (1953), Ch. 14.

HONOR THE RELIGION OF THE HOST COUNTRY

If the ambassador can publicly worship in the established church of the host country, his usefulness is increased because he can make more intimate social and official contacts.

William O'Dwyer, the scandal-tainted ex-Mayor of New York City, was sent to Mexico City in 1950 as the American ambassador, partly, some newspapers guessed, to get him out of the country. In spite of his alleged connection with grafting (or perhaps as a result of it) he was unusually popular. He not only spoke Spanish but was a Roman Catholic who could attend mass in the company of the Mexican people. Mrs. Clare Boothe Luce was also a Roman Catholic, the dominant faith of Italy, and this asset took off some of the curse (in Latin eyes) of her being a lady ambassador.

What is true of religion is also true of the prevailing political ideology. The ultraconservative Jefferson Caffery was out of his element in the 1930's as the ambassador in Cuba, which was then seething with radical discontent. The ultraliberal Claude G. Bowers, Ambassador in Madrid, had to withdraw from Spain after the fascistic Franco finally triumphed in 1939.

Empathy, rather than antipathy, makes for promising diplomatic dialogue. But the envoy should always exercise restraint.

CHAPTER IV

Utilizing the Ambassador

"If the Department of State is to take primary responsibility for foreign policy in Washington, it follows that the Ambassador is expected to take charge overseas."

SECRETARY OF STATE RUSK, 1961

PROLOGUE

If the President must have confidence in his Secretary of State, the Secretary of State must have confidence in the ambassadors through whom he has to work.

The post of ambassador, like that of the Secretary himself, has become more onerous as the nation's foreign affairs have become more complex. In 1965, in London alone, we operated at least forty-four agencies that had a finger in the pie of American foreign relations.

Such complexities call for ambassadorial talents of the highest order, but superlative talents are in short supply. The other professions, often with higher monetary rewards and better living and working conditions, draw off much of the cream. Little wonder that the President has met with much frustration in securing top-drawer men for the key diplomatic posts, especially those embassies that are earmarked for noncareer officers. Not one of Woodrow Wilson's major diplomatic appointments in 1913 was better than a third choice.

The foreign service officer cannot count on financial rewards, enduring prestige, or proper appreciation by his government or his countrymen. But at least he can find solace in doing his duty for his country on the diplomatic firing line.

BRING THE AMBASSADOR HOME PERIODICALLY

If the envoy lives abroad too long, he is liable, chameleon-like, to absorb too completely the outlook of the host nation, while losing contact with the shifting currents of opinion back home. He becomes less vigorous in presenting the case of his own government, and he falls out of step with the implementation of policy elsewhere.

Benjamin Franklin remained in Paris for nearly nine years (1776–1785) as the astute representative of the United States, and he appears not to have suffered unduly from overexposure. But the newly arrived John Adams and John Jay, both of whom joined him as peace negotiators, were evidently more vigilant and suspicious in promoting the interests of their homeland.[1]

At the other extreme stood Ambassador Walter H. Page, who swallowed too completely the British line during his five years in London (1913–1918). President Wilson finally brought him home in 1916 for a much needed "bath" in American public opinion, but the immersion evidently did not wash away his pro-British attachments. Just as a lawyer should not lose contact for too long a period with his client in an important case, so should the envoy not lose contact with the country he represents. In 1965 a Senate subcommittee headed by Senator Henry M. Jackson recommended that ideally the ambassadors should return to Washington two or three times a year, for a week or ten days each time. Only in this way can they reimmerse themselves in American policy-making, and keep properly in line with the diplomatic procession at home and abroad. A sabbatical year, involving refreshing contacts with the people represented, would also have much value.

LEAVING THE AMBASSADORSHIP VACANT IS RISKY

The Secretary of State sometimes brings the ambassador home as a dramatic way of expressing displeasure with the host nation. A *chargé d'affaires* is usually left in command.

If we may assume that the ambassador is more able and better

[1] See Richard B. Morris, *The Peacemakers* (1965).

informed than his subordinate, such a withdrawal is unwise. It suggests having the captain of a ship take off in a rowboat, while leaving his inexperienced third mate to steer the ship over dangerous reefs. In time of trouble the best procedure is to keep the best man possible on the spot.

The practice of spiteful withdrawal has probably been more used against the United States than the reverse. In 1891, following the lynching of eleven Italians in New Orleans, the Rome government withdrew its minister in protest. Washington retaliated by ordering the American minister in Italy to come home on a leave of absence. Both legations were left in the hands of *chargés*.

A somewhat related risk occurs when the ambassador resigns or is recalled, and his successor is not promptly appointed. When bloody anti-Yankee riots broke out in Panama early in 1964, we had not had an ambassador on the ground for four months. Ambassador Joseph S. Farland had resigned in August over differences with the State Department. In any case, a public notice of resignation or recall should be delayed as long as possible, because the influence of the lame duck begins to wane just as soon as the announcement is made.

The refusal to appoint a new ambassador as a mark of protest, following his predecessor's dismissal, is likely to hurt the protesting nation more than the offending nation. It suggests the legendary folly of cutting off one's nose to spite one's face.

KEEP THE AMBASSADOR FULLY ADVISED

The envoy who is well informed is twice armed, and ideally all relevant data should be fed to him. No information or wrong information may lead to mistaken assumptions and blundering decisions.

Ex-Ambassador George F. Kennan, testifying before the Jackson Senate Subcommittee in 1963 on his experiences in Yugoslavia, stated that in the "absence of any sort of liaison with the internal security organs of our own country, we simply had to bat in the dark. . . ."[2]

---

[2] *Administration of National Security* (1965), p. 361. Bismarck cold-bloodedly left his chiefs of mission in the dark, and on occasion deliberately misled them. They could then compromise themselves without compromising him. See Gordon A. Craig, *War, Politics, and Diplomacy* (1966), Ch. 10.

An ambassador can hardly be expected to carry out the policy of his government with effectiveness if he does not know in detail what it is and the reasons for it. Secretary Dulles was unaccountably puzzled when his chiefs of mission resented being kept in ignorance about issues that concerned them directly and about which they would be asked questions. The Washington government should keep its adversary in the dark, not its own diplomatic representatives. This is especially advisable when it plans a reversal of established policy, as occurred when Franklin Roosevelt delivered his famous "quarantine the aggressors" speech in Chicago in 1937.

Complete information naturally increases the hazards of leakage. On the eve of Pearl Harbor, the Washington nerve center did not fully inform its diplomatic and military agents in the field as to an imminent Japanese assault somewhere. The fear prevailed that such top-secret information might leak out and warn the enemy that we had "cracked" Japan's most important secret code.[3] In this eventuality, Tokyo would certainly have changed to another which might not have been "crackable" or which could have been "cracked" only after a dangerous delay.

AVOID DIPLOMATIC MUSICAL CHAIRS

The ordinary tour of duty at an American embassy is three or four years, often much shorter. The effort to avoid routinization often results in overrotation.

Ambassador Ellis O. Briggs was stationed at seventeen posts in thirty-seven years, or about two years to a capital. His two years and ten months in Brazil proved unusually frustrating. After studying the Portuguese language and after beginning to get the feel of the country and its leading men, he was ordered off to Greece. There he had to begin his apprenticeship anew.

On-again-off-again assignments are obviously too short to permit the United States to reap maximum advantages. Ex-Ambassador Robert Murphy writes that some prominent persons in foreign capitals will not bother to cultivate the American envoy simply because

[3] See Roberta Wohlstetter, *Pearl Harbor: Warning and Decision* (1962), pp. 176 *ff.* In the light of hindsight we can see that Washington might well have risked passing this information on to the commanders in Hawaii.

he will be there so brief a time. Lincoln Gordon, then Ambassador to Brazil, stated in 1963 that a short tour of duty might be adequate for a tiny Central American republic, but an enormous country like Brazil might appropriately engage the talents of a foreign service officer, perhaps in different capacities, for eight years.

Shortness of tenure, often caused by four-year political overturns in Washington, has traditionally cursed the American foreign service. Ambassador Jules Jusserand of France, while serving his country with balance and brilliance in Washington for twenty-three consecutive years, soon became a "fixture." During that same period we had a parade of eight ambassadors in Paris.

Experience and stability are priceless assets that should not be lightly squandered. The ambassador, like a tree, needs time to take root.

OVERSTAFFING IS POOR STAFFING

The tendency is for the foreign service (and the State Department) to be overstaffed in certain areas. Ex-Ambassador Ellis O. Briggs concludes that during and after World War II the military men implanted the idea that when a "ten-man job is to be tackled, one hundred men must be mobilized to undertake it." [4]

Briggs cites the example of the American embassy in Prague, which he headed but which he believed to be badly overstaffed. His appeals to Washington for reduction were in vain. But after the Communists seized the country in 1948, they sought to cripple his operations by declaring five-sixths of his personnel *persona non grata*. Unknowingly they conferred a favor on him. The remainder, reduced from 78 to 13, were able to do a more efficient job for less money than the original bloated staff, whose members had been falling over one another.

A report of the Jackson Senate Subcommittee observed in 1965 that "understaffing can be the best staffing. If officers have more to do than they can possibly do, they are more likely to do what is important." [5]

[4] E. O. Briggs, *Farewell to Foggy Bottom* (1964), p. 176.
[5] *Administration of National Security* (1965), p. 67.

BEWARE OF UPSTAGING THE AMBASSADOR

The sending of special agents or special ambassadors to "hot spots" as trouble-shooters, though sometimes necessary, should be kept within bounds. As we have seen, the arrival in various foreign capitals of roving envoys—men like Woodrow Wilson's Colonel E. M. House or Franklin Roosevelt's Harry Hopkins—could hardly have caused unrestrained rejoicing in the American embassies thus "honored."

The appearance of the peripatetic plenipotentiary, often from the skies, almost invariably weakens the position of the resident ambassador. Suspicious newsmen and other wiseacres jump to the conclusion that the regularly accredited envoy cannot ferret out the facts, is incapable of reporting them correctly, and is unable to handle current difficulties, with or without instructions. The high-flying newcomers seldom have time to remain on the ground long enough to become properly oriented and to carry through the subsequent negotiations.

The affront to the resident ambassador often leaves lasting bitterness. In 1959 President Eisenhower (a Republican) twice sent John J. McCloy (a Republican) to convey "personal" messages to Chancellor Adenauer of West Germany. The subsequent loss of face is presumed to have hastened the resignation of able Ambassador David K. E. Bruce (a Democrat).

Occasionally a prickly diplomatic problem calls for special technical skills or someone who is close to the President. Ambassador-at-Large W. Averell Harriman, appointed in 1961, is a happy example. He no doubt has caused the permanent ambassador to lose some face, but the favorable results in several instances have heavily outweighed this loss. We remember particularly Harriman's stellar role in negotiating the Nuclear Test-Ban Treaty in Moscow in 1963.

GIVE THE EXPERIENCED DIPLOMAT SOME LEEWAY

In the pre-cable days American diplomats, when confronted with emergencies not covered by their instructions, were often forced to make career-risking decisions. They had to guess what the State Department would approve. If they guessed wrong, their heads might be forfeit. This was the dilemma facing Robert R. Livingston and James Monroe in Paris, in 1803, when they decided to seize the opportunity to buy all of the Louisiana territory, even though they were not authorized to do so. Happily for them and their country, the American people were eager to accept the breathtaking bargain. "Them was th' days," later remarked the droll Mr. Dooley, "when ye'd have a good time as an ambassadure."

Now that modern technology has made possible instantaneous communication, the ambassador is often written off as a puppet dangling on the end of a transoceanic telephone wire. But if technology has reduced independence of judgment, it has enlarged the need for such judgment by increasing the tempo with which events tumble over one another. There is still no substitute for an able and perceptive diplomat on the ground, especially one who has a delicate sense of timing and who can sniff and assess the current political atmosphere. Unlike the bureaucrat in the State Department at home, he can operate without the immediate pressures of partisanship and public opinion. As a famed British diplomat, Sir Harold Nicolson, has observed, no large corporation or newspaper would risk being represented in a foreign capital by a mere clerk at the end of a wire.

An able diplomat who enjoys the confidence of Washington can often take a more active and useful part in making and executing policy than his predecessors of the pre-cable era. Senator Jackson's subcommittee reported, after extended hearings in 1963: "All too often an experienced envoy in the field is second-guessed by a junior official in Washington who is less qualified to judge either the issue or the tactics. Within the limits of general guidance and instructions, an ambassador should have broad discretion as to the timing, form, and level of approach to the government to which he is accredited." [6]

The ambassador in the field should not be overruled too readily. If he is worth appointing, he is worth heeding.

WEED OUT THE INCOMPETENTS

David Rowland Francis, a prominent but elderly St. Louis grain merchant, was named by President Wilson as Ambassador

[6] *Administration of National Security,* p. 59.

to Russia in 1916. He was there the next year when the Bolsheviks seized power, and his reports home were singularly unperceptive. He was a man of some political stature who evidently accepted this difficult assignment out of a sense of duty, but he was a misfit whose appointment must be blamed on the Wilson administration. A summary removal would have involved political embarrassment, so he was kept on to continue his bungling.[7] François de Callières remarked in 1716, "It is a crime against the public safety not to uproot incapacity wherever it is discovered, or to allow an incompetent diplomatist to remain one moment longer than necessary in a place where competency is sorely needed."[8]

Removal, not transferral, is the ideal solution. To shift a mediocre or incompetent person to another position of responsibility may ease a difficult situation temporarily, but such a change can hardly fail ultimately to create new difficulties elsewhere.

OPERATE THROUGH REGULAR DIPLOMATIC CHANNELS

Foreign offices and embassies are the normal means by which governments speak to one another. Occasionally, when a foreign office is unresponsive, the impatient embassy will appeal directly to the public through the newspapers, as the Germans did in 1915 through an advertisement in the New York newspapers warning American passengers not to sail on the British liner *Lusitania*. Such a public notice, of course, was highly irregular.[9]

In crisis situations, the President may occasionally appeal directly to the head of another state. Franklin Roosevelt did so on

[7] An abler man was the lawyer and lush campaign contributor, Joseph E. Davies, who served as Ambassador to Russia, 1936–1938. Although an experienced lawyer, he was taken in by Stalin's notorious purge trials, and his book, *Mission to Moscow* (1941), proved to be an important propaganda document in facilitating the wartime alliance with the Soviet Union. The story was made into a movie of that name, in which Dictator Stalin appeared in a benevolent role.

[8] *On the Manner of Negotiating with Princes*, p. 94.

[9] Tales were widely circulated about the pre-marital doings of Eva Perón, wife of the Argentine dictator. The Argentine Embassy in Washington (presumably acting under instructions) ill-advisedly placed a large advertisement in *The New York Times* (Sept. 23, 1947) urging the fair-minded American people to pay no attention to these lurid tales. This notice was not only highly improper but obviously self-defeating.

the eve of Pearl Harbor, when he vainly cabled a peace plea directly to Emperor Hirohito in Japan.

President Franklin Roosevelt, seizing the helm in a desperate war crisis, conducted much diplomacy on a highly personal basis with Prime Minister Churchill. Although they often clashed on high strategy, they respected each other and on the whole evidently enjoyed being comrades-in-arms, especially during the early years. Altogether they met in ten conferences and exchanged some 1750 messages. "It is fun to be in the same decade with you," ran one of these communications in 1942 from the White House to Downing Street.[10]

All this may have been "fun," but it often left the regular agencies groping in the dark and resulted in much misunderstanding and working at cross-purposes. The by-passed Secretary of State Hull, as we have seen, was understandably much distressed.

POOR HOUSING DOES NOT BEFIT A RICH NATION

During the nineteenth century, when the Republic was relatively poor, we maintained few permanent legations or embassies. The envoy often had to spend his time in house-hunting, and since he usually did not have surplus funds for rent and enjoyed no guaranteed tenure, the renter regarded him as a poor prospect. The newcomer often had to locate in an undesirable part of the city, renovate the residence out of his own pinched pocket (Henry White in Paris spent $35,000), and suffer such annoyances as having the premises sold out from under him. The impermanence of such quarters handicapped his business, for his legation was not always easy to find. Diplomatist Henry White recalled that in Paris he once asked a cab driver to take him to the American legation, and he wound up in front of the chancellery of a tiny Latin American republic.

After World War I (when we emerged the world's creditor), and particularly after World War II (when we emerged the world's great superpower), permanent housing was vastly improved. But many habits of penny-pinching days persisted, and the expanding agencies dealing with foreign affairs tended to cramp even the most spacious quarters.

[10] January 30, 1942. *Churchill: Taken from the Diaries of Lord Moran* (1966), p. 27.

In some conspicuous cases, we have now swung to the other extreme. We have splurged to such an extent that the buildings have not always blended with local architecture, and some are monuments of bad taste. Conspicuous in this category is the embassy in London, with its thirty-five foot golden eagle, bordering historic Grosvenor Square.

Expensive and exposed plate glass windows have attracted bricks in the hands of demonstrating Communists and other rioters. American architects would do well to subordinate originality and aesthetic values and to bear in mind that those who live in glass houses invite stones. The Russians, after long experience with anti-Tsarist anarchists and other bomb throwers, have on the whole been more realistic, for many of their embassies are sheltered within walled compounds. Americans could learn some lessons from the Soviets.

CHAPTER V

Advice for the Diplomat

"You are in a sense soldiers in the front-line trenches of our foreign policy. Nowadays anything of any importance that happens
anywhere in the world is of importance to the United States."

SECRETARY OF STATE DULLES, from customary speech to
foreign service officers while on his trips.

PROLOGUE

An American envoy to a foreign country stands in much the
same relationship to the Department of State as the foreign correspondent does to his newspaper. The journalist digs up the facts
upon which the editors at home in part base their editorial policy;
the ambassador digs up the facts upon which the officials in Washington in part base their foreign policy.

It would be difficult to name a single qualification that an ideal
foreign correspondent should possess that an ideal ambassador
should not also possess. Both men should have training, experience,
tact, the social graces, and the ability to report discriminatingly and
objectively in precise and concise English. Both should have an intimate knowledge of the host country—its language, history, economy, social structure, and aspirations. Both should be men of vigorous
and attractive personalities who circulate in all strata of society,
who genuinely like the people (within limits), and who in turn are
liked by them (within limits).

Such men are not easy to find or to persuade to enter upon this kind of demanding public service, whether in the fields of diplomacy or journalism.

THE AMBASSADOR SHOULD BRIEF HIMSELF ADEQUATELY

If the American envoy is to be the interpreter of the host country to the Secretary of State, he must discover all he reasonably can about it. He should steep himself in its traditions and history, primarily because such knowledge will help him to comprehend and interpret current trends. More than that, his hosts will be flattered by evidences of such interest and understanding, and the success of his mission will be furthered.

Several special sources are usually available. The ambassador should keep closely in touch with the abler foreign correspondents in the capital, for they are often better informed than the foreign service officers themselves. He should cultivate friendly relations with his colleagues of the diplomatic corps; Ambassador Grew in Japan in the 1930's at times got better information from the British envoy than he did from Washington.[1] Finally, the ambassador should study the back files of instructions and dispatches in the embassy, so as to discover the thrust of policy prior to his coming.

George F. Kennan, stationed in Moscow during the 1930's as a subordinate, spent considerable time reading the dispatches written by American ministers in the nineteenth century. He was to some extent comforted to find that there was little basically new about the Bolsheviks. Minister Neill S. Brown in the 1850's had been complaining about Russian secretiveness, dilatoriness, evasiveness, suspicion, and other traits—the selfsame traits that Americans were still complaining about in the 1930's.

The American ambassador should also be well informed about American history, for he is, in addition to other duties, an interpreter of his country to the host nation. He can hardly interpret it faithfully unless he knows it well, and this is one of the reasons why American history should form a substantial part of the liberal arts background expected of every candidate for the foreign service.

---

[1] Grew had to formulate his own policy at first, so scanty were his instructions from Secretary Hull. Joseph C. Grew, *Turbulent Era* (1952), II, 931.

EMPLOY RELIABLE INTERPRETERS

If the American envoy is unable to speak directly to foreign officials in their own tongue, he should make every effort to secure the ablest and most trustworthy interpreters. Communicating ideas is difficult enough even when all parties to a negotiation are thoroughly familiar with the same language. At the Yalta Conference, Roosevelt and Churchill had to speak to Stalin through an interpreter, and Roosevelt made use of the able and reliable Charles E. Bohlen, subsequently American Ambassador to the Soviet Union. Even so, some of the misunderstanding about what was supposedly agreed on at Yalta probably arose in part from faulty communication.

When Secretary Dulles flew to Formosa to confer with Generalissimo Chiang Kai-shek, the Madame insisted on being present and serving as interpreter. "The trouble was," Andrew H. Berding reported, "that the lovely Oriental was not content to be merely an interpreter; she was constantly injecting her own opinions, and one could never be sure that she was transmitting the Generalissimo's thought to the Secretary, or the Secretary's to the Generalissimo, without adding her own coloration and embroidery." [2]

The same caution about securing trustworthy interpreters applies also to translators. In the 1830's the quarrel with France over some unpaid damages worsened when the State Department was irked because the French used the word *prétendu* in connection with the American claims. The French foreign minister was forced to write a formal note solemnly explaining that the offensive word did not mean "pretended" but rather "so-called."

PRECISE AND OBJECTIVE REPORTING IS ESSENTIAL

A primary duty of the ambassador is to send home to Washington detailed descriptions and analyses of what is going on in the host country in reports (dispatches) that are prompt, clear, candid, succinct, interesting, comprehensive, and accurate. In theory, he is not supposed to make policy but to provide the facts upon which the officials in Washington, looking at the world spectrum, can formulate policy. But he can interpret the facts and make recom-

[2] *Dulles on Diplomacy* (1965), p. 65. The visits were in 1954 and 1955.

mendations based on those facts. Indeed, he is generally encouraged to do so. He can also help orient policy by handpicking facts which he regards as important, or misrepresenting the facts in such a way as to mislead the policy-makers in Washington. The ambassador is in such a critical position that he should be in the highest degree objective and truthful. If his earlier assessments prove incorrect, he should make haste to confess his error (which few men want to do) and put things back on the track. He should not report just "happy thoughts" or observations that he feels will conform to the "party line" then being pursued by Washington, with a consequent boost in his promotion and pay.

Before Senator McCarthy's anti-Communist "crusade" in the 1950's, certain foreign service officers, particularly in the Far East, had sent home reports about the gains or prospective gains of Communism. These dispatches were later interpreted to be, not factual reporting, but evidences of sympathy for the Communists. The veteran ambassador, W. Averell Harriman, testified in 1963, "I have seen men's careers set back and in fact busted because they held the right views at the wrong time, or for reporting accurately facts which were not popular at the time, or at some later time." [3]

Such pressures to report a "party line" are in the highest degree dangerous. The policy-makers in Washington have difficulty enough when they operate on the basis of an objective gathering of the essential facts.

PROLIXITY IS THE FOE OF CLARITY

The ambassador, no matter how small the country where he is stationed, is disposed to assign an exaggerated importance to his post. He is also tempted to prove his worth by drafting over-long dispatches.

Today, more than ever, brevity is a virtue which carries with it some assurance that one's reports will be read. By the mid-1960's the volume of "telegraphic traffic" between Washington and the embassies abroad was more than 400,000 words a day, or one large-sized printed book. This, of course, was in addition to the much vaster volume of nontelegraphic reportage. As Senator Henry M.

[3] *Administration of National Security* (1965), p. 53.

Jackson's subcommittee concluded in 1965, "The resulting flood of information swamps Washington's absorptive capacities." [4]

A constant complaint of the men in the field is that their dispatches are not read, or if read, ignored. This reaction is not surprising when we remember that the State Department is virtually drowned in words.

The frustration that flows from being ignored has prompted many envoys to go outside regular channels to get their messages through to high places. President Franklin Roosevelt encouraged some of his ambassadors to communicate with him directly through private letters or secret codes. Some write or have written directly to congressm n. But all these irregular approaches must be used with extreme caution and in the knowledge that they tend to throw the delicate diplomatic machinery out of gear.

THE AMBASSADOR SHOULD OBEY INSTRUCTIONS

Just as a general must loyally carry out the orders of his Commander-in-Chief, so must the warrior-diplomat carry out the orders of his superiors if overall strategy is to succeed. Otherwise chaos would prevail, whether on the military battlefield or the diplomatic battlefield.

The diplomat, like the general, may remonstrate and give his reasons for disagreement, often based on inadequate or localized information. But when overruled, he must carry out his instructions, both in letter and in spirit, without indicating dissent through facial expression, gesture, or voice. He must even defend his government's position loyally, even though disagreeing with it. If he finds he cannot do so, he should request a transfer or resign. Ambassador Arthur B. Lane, stationed in Warsaw from 1945 to 1947, not only resigned but published a book in 1948.[5] It sharply criticized the failure of the State Department to take a stronger stand against the Soviet absorption of Poland, contrary to Stalin's pledges at Yalta and Potsdam.

The classic case involves Walter Hines Page, Wilson's Ambassador to the Court of St. James. Pro-British, a noncareer man, and a journalist (hence an undisciplined soldier), he shamelessly sabo-

[4] *Ibid.*, p. 18.
[5] Arthur B. Lane, *I Saw Poland Betrayed* (1948).

taged his instructions.[6] Disapproving of a strong protest from Washington against British blockade practices, he took it to the Foreign Secretary Grey (as instructed) and avowed his disapproval of it (not as instructed). He then proceeded to collaborate with Grey in framing a reply. This type of sabotage was in fact a species of treason.

There are occasions when a circumstance occurs or when an atmosphere develops which seems to warrant a departure from orders. Minister Charles Francis Adams in London during the Civil War toned down some of Secretary Seward's more bellicose instructions, and Ambassador Josephus Daniels in Mexico in the 1930's on occasion declined to act as requested. In both of these cases the envoys escaped unscathed, but such free-wheeling is risky. If Washington disapproves, the headstrong subordinate may be recalled.

Above all, the ambassador must take orders from his superiors in the State Department and White House, and not from the Chairman of the Senate Foreign Relations Committee or some other member of Congress. The minister-historian John L. Motley, stationed in London (1869–1870), followed the policy line of the Chairman of the Foreign Relations Committee, Charles Sumner, rather than that of the Secretary of State, Hamilton Fish. President Grant, an ex-military man, resented this flagrant insubordination and finally sacked Motley.

Almost as indefensible as defying instructions is giving assurances for which there is no authorization. Andrew D. White, the able American Ambassador in Berlin, stumbled badly in 1898 when he encouraged the Germans to believe that Washington would not object to their having at least a foothold in the Philippines. These encouraging words were not only unauthorized but they ran counter to the policy being pursued in Washington. Ambassador White, though an immensely competent man, had his knuckles sharply rapped by the Secretary of State.[7]

[6] In 1914 Ambassador Page may have influenced the State Department when he threatened to resign if again requested to press Britain to adopt the navy-restricting Declaration of London. B. J. Hendrick, *The Life and Letters of Walter H. Page* (1923), I, 383. Critics complained that from 1914 to 1918 the British had two ambassadors: one in Washington, on their payroll, and one in London, on ours. Page's pro-British bias has often been forgiven because the war in which he sought to involve us became ours in 1917. It also became a righteous war for democracy which many Americans believed we should have entered much sooner.

[7] A. L. P. Dennis, *Adventures in American Diplomacy, 1896–1906* (1928), pp. 96–98.

REFER IMPORTANT PROPOSALS HOME

Just as the envoy should not act contrary to instructions in a positive way, he must not take negative action on the assumption that Washington will agree with him. For all he knows, basic policy has changed at home, or is changing.

In 1823 British Foreign Secretary Canning approached our Minister in London, Richard Rush, with a startling proposal. It was in effect that the two nations should form an alliance to prevent the European powers from restoring the revolted Spanish colonies to their former overlords. Rush had no instructions to cover this flattering proposition, so he quite properly referred it to Washington. The result was the independently declared Monroe Doctrine.

In 1845 the American Secretary of State suggested to the British Minister in Washington, Richard Pakenham, that the explosive Oregon boundary dispute be compromised along the line of the 49th parallel—the present frontier. Since London had already spurned a similar proposal three times, Pakenham evidently felt safe in rejecting it out of hand without referring it home. On this issue hung peace or war, and he presumed too much. British policy was shifting, and by this time London was more receptive to the proposed compromise line, which was agreed upon some months later.

DEVELOP AN EMPATHY FOR THE HOST NATION

No ambassador should ever be sent to a country whose people he dislikes. The American press reported that Ambassador Chester Bowles in India won the sympathies of the Indian people in the 1950's by his "you're as good as we are" approach. He even rode a bicycle through the streets of New Delhi and sent several of his children to Indian schools.

When the Salerno floods in Italy left a hundred or so dead and thousands homeless in 1954, Ambassadress Clare Boothe Luce arranged for United States army trucks to transport food and supplies. More than that, she spent two days in the wet and mud comforting the victims. This is clearly the kind of foreign aid that can pay rich dividends in good will and throw Communist propagandists on the defensive.

Empathy is helpful, but the ambassador must never let his attachment to a foreign people cause him to forget that he is there to promote the interests of his own country. In many cases sympathy is to the advantage of both nations, but in some spectacular instances it has been overdone. This was painfully true when in 1794 James Monroe, as American Minister to France, too enthusiastically identified himself in public—fraternal kiss and all—with the cause of the French revolutionists.

The envoy is not engaged in a popularity contest: he should be neither too popular nor too unpopular. He should steer a correct middle course and seek to command respect rather than adulation.

CULTIVATE FRIENDS BUT NOT INTIMATES

The ambassador should develop honest friendships with most persons but "entangling alliances with none," in Jefferson's phrase. If he becomes too friendly with certain factions, he may incur the hostility of their opponents and at the same time strain, if not undermine, his objectivity.

After Hitler overran France in 1940, the Roosevelt administration attempted to maintain correct relations with the unpopular Vichy regime, tool of the Nazi conqueror, despite vehement criticism from so-called liberal elements in America. By nursing such contacts, notably with the Vichyite Admiral Darlan, we were in a stronger position to induce the French to cooperate in the Anglo-American assault on French North Africa in 1942. Without such collaboration the American casualties would certainly have been much heavier, and the invasion attempt might even have failed.

As a rule, an envoy should avoid seeing too much of the opposition leaders. Joseph P. Kennedy, father of John F. Kennedy and himself the politically appointed Ambassador in London in the late 1930's, made this error. Dedicated to isolation and appeasement, he hobnobbed too freely with the isolationist Cliveden set.[8] Loudmouthed and indiscreet, he was also outspokenly disloyal to his chief, President Roosevelt.

The rule of nonfraternization is also relevant to the highest

[8] After appeasement failed in Britain and the German blitz came, Kennedy's violent pro-Germanism caused him to become *persona non grata*—a kind of Walter Hines Page in reverse. See Richard J. Whalen, *The Founding Father: The Story of Joseph P. Kennedy* (1964), Ch. 18.

levels. In 1966 President Johnson flew out to Honolulu, where he met and put his arm around the militaristic Premier Ky of South Vietnam, at a time when Ky's foothold was extremely shaky. This public affirmation that the Vietnamese quasi-dictator was "his boy" aroused the "Yankee Go Home" agitators in South Vietnam. Ensuing riots, whether triggered by the Honolulu meeting or not, almost brought the Ky regime down in ruins. President Johnson would have been on sounder ground if he had also invited to Honolulu other leaders of Asia and the far Pacific who were making token contributions to the war effort.

THE AMBASSADOR SHOULD MAINTAIN MOBILITY

The American envoy should not remain exclusively in the capital city, pleasant though living there may be, but try to visit as much of the hinterland as feasible ("diplomacy by jeep"). Paris is not France, and to form conclusions about the entire country after viewing only the metropolis can be dangerous. One of the handicaps from which American diplomats in the Soviet Union have suffered has been the severe limiting of their movements to restricted areas. The Washington government, having tried other forms of suasion, has been forced to retaliate with similar but seemingly childish restrictions on Russian representatives.

Social mobility should parallel physical mobility. The diplomatist ought to familiarize himself with the various strata of society, not just the upper crust among whom he most naturally moves. In the Russia of 1917 few, if any, of the American officials established contact with members of the lower classes, and this oversight does much to explain their singular blindness to what was about to erupt in that war-ravaged country. On October 4, 1917, Ambassador Francis (the grain merchant) cabled: "My sympathy with Russia deep, sincere and my conviction strong that the country will survive ordeal and be safe for democracy if we and other Allies are patient and helpful." [9]

Hardly a month had passed before the Bolsheviks seized control. The rest is history—unpleasant history for most Americans.

[9] *Papers Relating to the Foreign Relations of the United States, 1918, Russia* (1931), I, 203.

THE AMBASSADOR SHOULD AVOID "LOCALITIS"

The disease of "localitis" is easy to contract. A conscientious foreign service officer is apt to feel that his embassy is the navel of the universe, whether located in Mogadiscio (Somalia) or Ouagadougou (Upper Volta) or Tegucigalpa (Honduras).

"Localitis" flourishes in all climes. It is one more reason why the ambassador should be summoned home at relatively frequent intervals for a fresh briefing, and why he should endeavor to keep himself informed by studying trends in other countries as well as in his own.

One of the worst cases of "localitis" attacked General Douglas MacArthur. Best known as a strong-willed military hero, he occupied several quasi-diplomatic posts after 1945, including that of "Yankee Mikado" of Japan. Finally dismissed from his Far Eastern commands in 1951 by President Truman, he returned to the United States, which he had not visited for fourteen years. The nation that he then saw was not the same one that he thought he had been serving.

During the Korean War, General MacArthur found himself in a galling position. Placed in command of the United Nations forces, and understandably jealous of his reputation as an ever-conquering general, he became intolerably headstrong. He tried to shift the major emphasis from the line-holding European theater to the blood-letting Asiatic theater, despite the fact that Red Russia, not Red China, was the most formidable potential adversary. A famous Herblock cartoon of the era had Secretary of State Marshall saying to the General that the officials in Washington were using a round globe and not the square one, with Asia on top, that MacArthur was consulting.

THE DIPLOMATIST IS A WARRIOR FOR PEACE

The diplomatic establishment, not the military establishment, is the first line of defense. This fact of life is something that Congress often overlooks when it appropriates tens of billions of dollars for military hardware and tens of millions of dollars for the foreign service, normally in about the ratio of 50 to 1.

One of the most enduring myths is that white-spatted diplomats cause wars. Hence, if we could only get rid of the "cooky pushers," there would be no wars or, at any rate, fewer wars.

Inept diplomacy has no doubt often contributed to the coming of armed conflict. This was conspicuously true when President Jefferson, in the years prior to the War of 1812, overplayed his hand and tried desperately to wring unacceptable concessions on impressment from the British. But in general the explosives are already present when they explode in the hands of the diplomats, sometimes by spontaneous combustion.

Diplomatists are keenly aware that the outbreak of war means that their mission has failed, and that they have to go home. For this reason the Department of State has often been called the "Department of Peace." One of the ablest diplomat-warriors in our history was Minister Charles Francis Adams, in his lonely outpost in an unfriendly London during the Civil War. By nerve-wracking diplomacy he helped to dissuade Britain from intervening, at a time when such intervention probably would have widened the conflict into a world war. In such an eventuality the Confederates almost certainly would have won their independence.[10]

It is better that the diplomats should get ulcers than that the soldiers should get bullets.

PUBLIC LOQUACITY IS POOR POLICY

Traditionally the State Department has discouraged ambassadors from making too many public speeches. If they must speak, as on ceremonial occasions, they would do well to confine themselves to pious platitudes and harmless generalities. Above all, they should avoid detailed discussion of current political issues, unless specifically instructed to do so.[11] The danger is ever present that some innocuous remark will be misunderstood.

If the American envoy speaks the language of the host country

[10] Minister Adams, while valiantly upholding the interests of his own country, won the respect and admiration of his hosts. In 1868, when his name was mentioned in the House of Commons, that body broke into cheers. Martin B. Duberman, *Charles Francis Adams, 1807–1886* (1961), p. 330.

[11] Ambassador Joseph C. Grew's "straight from the horse's mouth speech," which jolted the Japanese by appealing over the head of the government to the people, had the prior approval of President Roosevelt and the State Department. Grew, *Turbulent Era*, II, 1212–1213.

fluently, he can often build up good will by speechmaking. This was conspicuously true of General Horace Porter, who served as Ambassador to France from 1897 to 1905.

In England, where there is no real problem with a foreign language, American envoys are sorely tempted to let themselves go. Joseph H. Choate, one of the most eloquent ornaments of the American bar, became "a British lecturer at large" at the turn of the century. In 1921 Ambassador George Harvey, a political appointee of Republican President Harding, delivered a violent harangue in which he presented the Republican case against the League of Nations. Although he spoke with President Harding's private blessing, he provoked a bitter outcry from Wilsonian Democrats, who were also Americans and who were helping to pay his salary. Not content with this brutal frankness, Harvey stirred up more animals when he indiscreetly tackled a less political subject: "Women's Souls." He facetiously but tactlessly tried to prove that they had none.

A DIPLOMAT SHOULD AVOID CRITICISM IN PUBLIC

The ambassador should not publicly criticize any nation, whether it be his own or the host country or neighboring countries. Nor should he create antagonism by overpraising his own nation. He should also remember that his largest audience is probably at home, and for this reason he should not condemn elements within his own constituency.

James H. R. Cromwell, a millionaire playboy-politician, is a case in point. A heavy campaign contributor to Democratic coffers, he received an appointment in 1940 as Minister to Canada, which was then at war with Hitler. He stepped badly out of line when, as a neutral envoy in a belligerent country, he openly took sides by condemning Nazi Germany. He also condemned those isolationist groups in the United States that were not anti-Hitler. He thus violated two rules of the diplomatic game, first by publicly discussing relations between foreign nations, and second, by publicly criticizing his own country.[12] Shortly thereafter his resignation was accepted.

[12] In 1947 ex-Prime Minister Churchill wittily declared that "when I am abroad I always make it a rule never to criticize or attack the Government of my own country. I make up for lost time when I come home." Kay Halle, ed., *Irrepressible Churchill* (1966), p. 276.

As a corollary proposition, the envoy should not wash dirty linen in public or "turn state's evidence" after leaving the service. In 1919, William C. Bullitt, a minor official on the American Peace Commission in Paris, resigned resoundingly when he found that the Treaty of Versailles did not measure up to the promised Fourteen Points. Then, when President Wilson was breaking himself down on a speaking tour for the Treaty, Bullitt appeared as a willing witness before the Senate Foreign Relations Committee, there to present damaging testimony from a private conversation with Secretary Lansing.[13]

In a number of instances conscientious men have convinced themselves that the national interest is so greatly jeopardized that conventional ethics must be compromised.

MEDDLING LEADS TO MUDDLING

The ambassador should confine his meddling, if meddle he must, to his own bailiwick—that is, foreign affairs. The French Minister Adet secretly and openly pulled wires in 1796 for the election of the allegedly pro-French Jefferson over the allegedly anti-French John Adams. He did not succeed, but his scheming had the unfortunate effect of stirring up much ill will and the fortunate effect of partially inspiring Washington's Farewell Address.

This type of interference is still used and abused to some extent. Sometimes foreign ambassadors in Washington, failing to win their point with the State Department, make contact with congressmen and try to prevail through the back doors.

Public lobbying is even more offensive. In 1945 the United States Ambassador in Argentina, Spruille Braden, vigorously opposed the rise of dictator Perón. Brought home to become Assistant Secretary of State, Braden was thought to be continuing his campaign when the State Department issued a Blue Book condemning Perón as a pro-Nazi. The Perónistas, then involved in a presidential

---

[13] Premier Clemenceau of France was wounded by an assassin during the Peace Conference. He was reported as remarking wryly, "I got my bullet at the Conference, but Lansing got his afterward." Bullitt later pooled his anti-Wilson prejudices with those of Sigmund Freud in a highly questionable psychoanalytical explanation of Wilson's failures, with emphasis on reactions to father-domination. Sigmund Freud and William C. Bullitt, *Thomas Woodrow Wilson* (1966).

election, raised the cry "Perón or Braden!" and swept to victory, no doubt aided by Yankee officiousness.

Sir Lionel Sackville-West, the British Minister in Washington, naively thrust a hand into American politics in 1888, when he penned a private letter indicating that a vote for President Cleveland was a vote for England. The blundering Briton not only violated the rule against meddling in local politics, but, worse still, he had been caught.

In sum, if one must meddle, meddle secretly, anonymously, and effectively. The British statesman Lord Palmerston once remarked that the ambassador might break all the commandments in the Decalogue except the Eleventh: "Thou shalt not be found out."

NEVER LIE FOR YOUR COUNTRY

Silence is golden but lies are leaden, and the diplomat is under no obligation to tell everything he knows. He can always duck the issue or change the subject. But if he makes a presumed statement of fact, it should be the truth, even though a qualified or partial truth. The common expression, "You're a diplomat, all right," usually means "You haven't told the entire story."

European diplomacy was traditionally more or less synonymous with duplicity: to lie and deny were among the envoy's first duties. He was not only a licensed spy but a licensed liar. Sir Henry Wotton, the English Ambassador to Venice, coined a famous pun in 1604 that has been polished to read: "An ambassador is an honest man, sent to lie abroad for the good of his country." The French King Louis XI instructed his envoys to fight fire with fire: "If they lie to you, lie still more to them." "Accredited mendacity" became so much the norm that Count Cavour, the nineteenth-century Italian statesman, reported, "I have discovered the art of deceiving diplomats. I speak the truth and they never believe me."

If a banker scores a financial *coup* in a crooked deal, he forfeits the confidence of the business community. If a diplomat scores a brilliant initial success by lying, he immediately impairs his future usefulness. His statements will thereafter be suspect all over the globe, his adversaries will be put on their guard, and he will not be believed even when telling the truth. The Russian Ambassador in Washington, Count Cassini, arrived there in 1898, fresh from diplomatic triumphs in China. He was notorious for his denial of the Cassini Convention, which he had negotiated while in Peking, and thereafter his every word was regarded with suspicion. Lying not only reveals that the diplomat is too lacking in skill to achieve his end by above-board means, but it arouses aggravation, a desire for vengeance, and even hatred.

Lying by the President or the Secretary of State—"lying in State"—may at times be defensible in the national interest. But these officials are operating on a different level from that of the career man in the field, who is looking forward to a lifetime in the service. As Socrates remarked, "The rulers of the State are the only ones who should have the privilege of lying, either at home or abroad; they may be allowed to lie for the good of the State." [14]

The Soviet rulers have notoriously followed the rule of Socrates, notably when they assured President Kennedy in 1962 that they were only supplying defensive weapons for Cuba at a time when they were sneaking in intermediate range missiles. But they were caught red handed, thus violating Palmerston's Eleventh Commandment.

HAVE NO TRAFFIC WITH SPIES

The ambassador has often been termed an "honorable spy," and that he normally is. One of his prime duties is to cast his eyes around the host country and report to Washington. The American attachés—military, naval, and air—also have this responsibility, and it is reciprocally tolerated by both nations, provided that it does not overstep the conventional bounds.

All great powers, and many of the smaller ones, engage in spying, which is sometimes called the second oldest profession. They must do so to insure their own security in this insecure world. But the American ambassador must remain aloof from cloak-and-dagger operations, or he will fatally compromise his position. His face is

[14] Plato, *The Republic*, Book III, Sec. 389. The rule about envoys not lying obviously has less applicability in wartime situations. Robert Murphy, acting under instructions, lied to the French about the size of the American force invading North Africa in 1942, and neglected to mention the British components. Robert Murphy, *Diplomat Among Warriors* (1964), p. 128. In 1962 President Kennedy instructed Press Secretary Pierre Salinger to deny that the United States was preparing for an invasion of Cuba at the time of the Cuban missile crisis. Elie Abel, *The Missile Crisis* (1966), p. 84.

too well known to escape detection, and he risks too much when he has to rely on traitors, some of them double agents, who are for sale to the highest paymaster. The "dirty work" of spying is left, at least supposedly, to the Central Intelligence Agency.

Soviet embassies, usually overstaffed out of all proportion to legitimate business, are notorious espionage centers. This is one of the reasons why many nations, as was true of the United States, have been slow to extend official recognition to the Soviet Union. In 1964 Moscow and Washington negotiated a treaty which would mutually facilitate the establishment of consulates. J. Edgar Hoover, head of the Federal Bureau of Investigation, badly hurt chances of ratification when he testified before a House subcommittee that the proposed pact would add to Soviet facilities for espionage and hence make more difficult the task of combating Communist sub-version in America.[15] He was no doubt correct, and the Senate had to weigh this disagreeable fact against the undoubted advantages that consular services in the Soviet Union would confer on the United States. The pact was narrowly approved in 1967.

SECRECY MUST BE SAFEGUARDED

A primary duty of the ambassador is to protect security. He must keep code books and all top-secret papers under lock and key when not in the hands of the most trusted employees. With professional spies and enterprising reporters everywhere under foot, this is no easy task.

In 1854 the American ministers to Britain, France, and Spain, acting under instructions, met secretly at Ostend, Belgium, to devise recommendations to the Secretary of State for the acquisition of Cuba. Their top-secret recommendation—seizure, if purchase was not possible—leaked out and made the land-grabbing Yankees the laughing stock of the civilized world. Redfaced, the administration in Washington was forced to repudiate the proposals of its diplomatic agents.

The ambassador, though a private citizen, is a public official, and in a sense can have no private life. Two of the most sensational incidents involving foreign envoys in Washington—the Englishman

---

[15] *Hearings Before a Subcommittee of the Committee on Appropriations, House of Representatives*, 89th Cong., 1st sess., pp. 328–333.

Sackville-West in 1888 and the Spaniard de Lôme in 1898 [16]—grew out of revelations that leaked out through private letters. Frederick Van Dyne, in a book on the foreign service published in 1909, concluded—brave man indeed—that one reason why so few women have risen in the service is their notorious inability to keep a secret.

If discretion was advisable in the nineteenth century, it is imperative today. Science has provided too many sensitive "bugging devices" and other eavesdropping instruments for picking up at long range the most confidential conversations. Moreover, there is the problem of leaky allies, of whom we now have some forty. There is pith in the Irish proverb, "It's no secret that's known to three."

[16] Minister Sackville-West wrote a letter advising an American voter to vote Democratic in the upcoming election; Minister de Lôme criticized President McKinley's weakness and lack of good faith.

PART II

Policy Formulation

CHAPTER VI

The Supremacy of National Interest

"I cannot forecast to you the action of Russia. It is a riddle wrapped in a mystery inside an enigma; but perhaps there is a key. That key is Russian national interest."

WINSTON S. CHURCHILL, 1939

PROLOGUE

What we condemn as selfishness in an individual, we condone as self-interest in a nation. When a statesman is pursuing goals that will promote the peace, security, and prosperity of his own people, the word "realism" would often be a better one to use than "selfishness." A diplomatist has been defined by an anonymous wit as "A person who can make his country's greed seem like altruism."

President Woodrow Wilson, in his famous Mobile speech of 1913, was referring to the Latin Americans when he said that it was "a very perilous thing to determine foreign policy . . . in terms of material interest." He ultimately learned that a wide gulf often yawns between the real and the ideal, and that his idealistic Fourteen Points of 1918 made better propaganda than policy. A statesman must deal with the world primarily as it is and not as he would like it to be. Adlai Stevenson, twice the Democratic presidential candidate, liked to think of himself as a "practical idealist" or a "sort of hard-boiled egghead."

SELF-INTEREST IS THE MAINSPRING
OF FOREIGN POLICY

If self-interest is not the primary motivation in shaping foreign relations, it ought to be. A government is not a charitable institution; it exists as the trustee of its people. Its first duty is to them, and it has no moral right to give away the assets of its constituency without at least some kind of equivalent.

This seemingly selfish conclusion does not rule out a certain amount of idealism or humanitarianism, which may also be in the nation's interest. Realism and idealism often complement each other. For example, the Washington government in the 1940's poured billions of dollars into Europe under the Marshall Plan. Some conscience-troubled Americans insisted that we owed such alms to these hungry and war-wracked people, many of whom had stood up against the monstrous forces that would engulf democracy, including our own. But the Marshall Plan appropriations could not conceivably have passed Congress on humanitarian grounds alone, as indeed they should not have. The overriding purpose was to avert a seemingly imminent takeover of Western Europe by Moscow-inspired Communism—a power grab that we regarded as menacing to our national interest.

Communist propagandists quickly pointed out that much of the Marshall Plan money would be used to purchase American implements and other commodities, thereby enriching our capitalistic economy. The Communists also declared that a revived and prosperous Europe would be a valuable market for our goods.

All this was true, and it further highlighted the fact that the Marshall Plan was bottomed squarely on self-interest. It represented a happy marriage between sentiment and selfishness, with a rehabilitated Western Europe the bouncing baby. Self-interest can often hide behind a mask of benevolence.

SELF-PRESERVATION IS PARAMOUNT TO ALL LAW

If self-interest is the overriding factor in formulating foreign policy, the preservation of the nation naturally takes priority over all other commitments and obligations. The ability of statesmen to find convenient excuses for breaking faith is a talent which Machia-velli recognized and described in classic form.[1]

During World War I, Germany was being slowly strangled by the British blockade, which Berlin insisted was illegal. The Germans had their choice between losing the war gradually and winning it quickly by breaking out of the iron encirclement by the unlawful use of the submarine. (The sinking of merchant ships without warn-ing and without providing for the safety of life was plainly contrary to international law as of 1914.) Unrestricted German submarine warfare dragged us into the conflict, and we tipped the scales of victory.

Perhaps Germany could have fought to a stalemate without resorting to unrestricted submarine warfare. But this is problemati-cal. When she was forced to choose between certain defeat with legal weapons and possible victory with illegal weapons, her leaders chose the latter.

Germany did what any other nation similarly circumstanced probably would have done. Certain British spokesmen later said that if the shoe had been on the other foot, Britain would have gone down to defeat like good sports, but the outspoken Admiral (Lord) Fisher expressed an emphatic dissent. A quarter of a century later, when we entered the conflict against Japan, we sank countless Japanese merchantmen without warning and without providing for the safety of passengers and crew—the very offense for which we had condemned Germany in 1915–1917. This was not the first war to be won with weapons that the victor had earlier denounced as illegal.

We can never expect a nation, especially when its life is at stake, to act contrary to what it regards as its vital interests. In time of war it can never be counted on to observe any more of international law than self-interest compels it to honor. Yet nations are restrained from wholesale violations of international law by fear of antagonizing

---

[1] "A sagacious prince then cannot and should not fulfill his pledges when their observance is contrary to his interest, and when the causes that induced him to pledge his faith no longer exist. If men were all good, then indeed this precept would be bad; but as men are naturally bad, and will not observe their faith toward you, you must, in the same way not observe yours to them; and no prince ever yet lacked legitimate reasons with which to color his want of good faith." *The Prince,* Ch. 18. Napoleon remarked in 1817 more succinctly, "Governments keep their promises only when they are forced or when it is to their advantage to do so."

neutral opinion or inviting crippling reprisals. Belligerents, for example, do not ordinarily resort to shooting prisoners; this is a gruesome game that two can play.[2]

ASCERTAIN WHAT OTHER NATIONS REGARD AS THEIR INTERESTS

Diplomacy resembles chess. Each player must make his key moves in such a way as to anticipate the moves of his opponent. In the game of diplomacy, self-interest is the only sound basis on which to predict the reactions of the other nation. Countermoves are difficult enough to foresee when presumed self-interest is involved; they become infinitely more difficult when idealism enters the picture.

Another pitfall is the assumption that the Soviet Union, for example, will act in a given situation just as we would. One of President Franklin Roosevelt's bitterest disappointments resulted from his conviction that the Soviet Union would simply have to cooperate with the Western world in the pursuit of a better tomorrow. He ladled out lend-lease largesse with a generous hand and made other concessions, at Yalta and elsewhere, on the basis of this belief. One of the mysteries of the postwar years is why the Soviets, while secretly committed to Communist world revolution, did not bilk us of millions in loans and gifts before slapping us in the face.

The Cold War era revealed that the Kremlin was infinitely cold-blooded. It evidently concluded that the interests of the Soviet Union (and world revolution) would be furthered by spurning the capitalistic Western world and promoting propaganda, turmoil, and wars of liberation. The avowed aims of the Soviets could be best served by discord; ours could be best served by concord. We erred in wishfully thinking that their interests paralleled our own.

A NATION OFTEN DOES NOT RECOGNIZE ITS OWN SELF-INTEREST

One of the most vexing problems confronting policy-makers is to determine what is best for their nation. A related difficulty is

[2] In 1966, during the undeclared war with North Vietnam, the North Vietnamese, suffering from aerial bombing, threatened to execute captured American aviators as war criminals. Washington strongly hinted that such action might bring an irresistible demand from the American public for nuclear bombing, which hitherto had been avoided. See *The New York Times,* July 16, 17, 1966.

to ascertain when a moth-eaten policy that once was viable is no longer valid. The international kaleidoscope is constantly changing; old formulas must be adjusted to new facts. America's rigidly isolationist and neutralist course of the 1920's and 1930's was, as we see it now, plainly not in the nation's interest. But that was what the masses shortsightedly demanded, and that was what they got. They believed that their own welfare demanded isolationism, insulationism, and abstentionism. So Uncle Sam played the ostrich.

The folly of such a purblind and misguided course is painfully illustrated by the abortive Security Treaty of 1919 with France.[3] Signed in Paris in 1919 by representatives of the United States and Britain, it pledged the signatory powers to come to the aid of the French in the event of another unprovoked German attack. But the American people were unwilling to abandon their century-old tradition of no entangling alliances, and the Senate shelved the pact. The first breach in the victorious coalition that had crushed Imperial Germany was thus made by the United States. If the Security Treaty had been ratified and honored, Adolf Hitler might have lived out his life ranting in the beer halls of an unbombed Munich.

SENTIMENT CHANGES BUT SELF-INTEREST PERSISTS

There are no enduring international friendships, only enduring interests. When the mutuality of interest fades, the friendship usually fades. The so-called traditional friendships that we enjoyed with Russia and Japan in the nineteenth century were all based on common interests. The traditional animosities that we harbored against Britain and Germany were based largely on clashing interests.

The so-called traditional friendship with France was largely fictional. When interests ran parallel, as they did during the American Revolution, we were drawn closely together. When they parted, as when Napoleon III invaded Mexico behind the smoke screen of the American Civil War, hostility developed. Given the opportunities for friction, our relations with France over the years have been about as vexed as those with any other great power.[4] The ultra-

[3] See L. A. R. Yates, *The United States and French Security, 1917–1921* (1957).

[4] This thesis is documented in Henry Blumenthal, *A Reappraisal of Franco–American Relations, 1830–1871* (1959).

nationalist aspirations of General de Gaulle, during and after World War II, did nothing to weaken this generalization.

The traditional nineteenth-century friendship with both Russia and Japan cooled sharply during and after the Russo–Japanese War of 1904–1905. In the case of Russia the change came because we sympathized with underdog Japan; in the case of Japan it came because President Theodore Roosevelt intervened to deprive her of what she regarded as her legitimate spoils of war. On America's side, a feeling of rivalry, not unmingled with fear, began to develop toward Japan, now that she had indisputably emerged as one of the Great Powers of the world by whipping the most populous white nation.

The friends of today become the enemies of tomorrow, and vice versa. All nations are potential friends or potential enemies.

In the nineteenth century the traditional foe was Great Britain. But in the twentieth century she became a comrade-in-arms in two wars, and a partner in the North Atlantic Treaty Organization.

In World War I we fought on the side of Italy and Japan; in World War II we fought against them, at the side of our traditional enemy of the nineteenth century, Britain. In World War II we fought by the side of the Soviet Union against Germany and Japan, both of which we defeated and disarmed. In the years after the war, we rehabilitated both Japan and West Germany, facilitated the rearmament of West Germany, and formed defensive alliances with both. We were determined to restore some kind of balance of power to halt the aggressions of the Russians, who had been our fighting allies during World War II.

IDEALISM CAN BE FATAL IN FOREIGN AFFAIRS

President Woodrow Wilson, the idealist and former teacher, undertook to teach the Latin American republics "to elect good men," not bloody-handed murderers. He directed most of his "teaching" at Mexico, where he was less than successful. His "missionary diplomacy" and "moral imperialism" finally degenerated into "moral meddling."

During World War II Franklin Roosevelt, imbued with Wilson's idealism, put pressure on his hard-pressed allies to liquidate their colonial empires. His heart went out to subject peoples. Thanks in part to Roosevelt's prodding during the war and after, Britain pulled out of India, with a resultant bloodbath and the creation of a geographical absurdity in Pakistan.[5] The British likewise abandoned their bases in Egypt, with the consequent ascendancy of Nasser and the Suez flareup of 1956, which came close to triggering World War III. The Dutch were squeezed out of Indonesia, with the subsequent rise of Sukarno and outbreaks of wholesale slaughter. The Belgians were forced out of the Congo prematurely, with frightful atrocities and more international time-bombs of a most explosive nature.

American policy in every case was largely motivated by a high-minded regard for the self-determination of colonial peoples. But in a number of instances a wholesome regard for realities might have dictated a more cautious approach. As we have observed, there is little room for do-goodism in diplomacy, except where it serves the national interest. In every one of the instances of de-colonialism just cited, our national interest was in some degree damaged.

The ideal must never be mistaken for the real, and wishful thinking is no substitute for hard-headed thinking. Preaching is not policy.

One additional danger lurks in idealism: the greater the idealism the greater the disillusionment. In 1917–1918 Wilson keyed the American people up for a tremendous crusade "to make the world safe for democracy" and "a war to end war." [6] When the conflict crashed to a close with wars erupting all over the world, and with democracy in many areas less safe than it had been before, we suffered a severe "slump in idealism." Content to let Europe stew in its own juice, we did not foresee that a generation later we would be back in the same old stewpot with the Europeans.

In World War II we paced ourselves better, and did our killing coldly, methodically, and devastatingly. We did not "slump" spectacularly from idealism because there was not much idealism to "slump" from. We helped to dispose of some of the mad dogs loose

[5] American policy-makers should remember that geographical monstrosities plant the seeds of future trouble, if not war itself. In 1919 President Wilson, dedicated to self-determination, consented to the division of Germany by Poland's Danzig corridor, and this grievance helped start World War II. At the end of World War II, Germany was again divided, and agitation for re-unification continued to inflame relations with Moscow.

[6] See James R. Mock and Cedric Larson, *Words That Won The War* (1939).

in the world, and then realistically measured up to our new responsibilities in a commendably adult fashion.

NAIVETY IS THE FOE OF REALITY

The Americans, though growing much more sophisticated in the harsh school of experience, have long been a sentimental, moralistic, Pharisaical people. We are prone to think of international relations in terms of a television Western. There are the "good guys" and the "bad guys"; and the "good guys" (100% pure) are the ones on our side, at least for the moment.

We have discovered to our sorrow that everything is not black or white, and that there are many intermediate shades of gray. We have learned that international politics makes for strange bedfellows and bedbugs, notably when we teamed up with the bloody-handed dictator Stalin in 1941 to fight the no less bloody-handed Hitler. Wartime propaganda portrayed good old "Uncle Joe" Stalin as a kind of foxy grandpa. When the war ended, and the veil of self-illusion was ripped from our eyes, we saw the ruthless Kremlinite in his true colors. In our efforts to halt Soviet Communism we found new and strange bedfellows in smaller-scale dictators, like Trujillo in the Dominican Republic and Franco in Spain.

The painful experience with Stalin should have taught us lasting lessons. We are naive indeed if we assume that all problems will yield to good intentions, as well as to the principles of justice and democracy. But we do not have to agree with the brutal cynicism of Adolf Hitler, who wrote in *Mein Kampf*, "Humanitarianism is the expression of stupidity and cowardice."

There is surely some kind of tenable middle ground between excessive soft-headedness and excessive hard-heartedness. And if we must sin, we can perhaps best sin on the side of humanity. We should rather be known as the nation that saved some 20 million Russians from starvation during the famine of 1921–1923 than as the maniac who murdered some 6 million Jews during World War II.

CHAPTER VII

The Shaping of Policy

"We want for other people what we want for ourselves, and I think that is the most effective foreign policy that we can carry out."

SENATOR JOHN F. KENNEDY, 1960

PROLOGUE

A common complaint about American foreign policy is that we do not have any. What such critics usually mean is that they do not approve of the policy or policies that Washington is pursuing, or that such policies, even if theoretically sound, are not producing the desired results. The truth is that from President Washington's day to the present we have always had policies, whether good or bad.

Much of the confusion flows from the fact that the word "policy" has a half-dozen or more connotations. It may, for example, be an objective, or it may be a course of action designed to attain that objective. For present purposes, the most useful homemade definition of policy is "a definite course or method of action, carefully selected by the Washington government from possible alternatives, and designed, in the nation's interest, to achieve well-established goals, such as peace, security, and prosperity."

POLICIES WITHOUT PURPOSE ARE POINTLESS

Many Americans cling to the naive idea that great nations must have policies, whether they need them or not, just as they have national debts, armaments, and other attributes of sovereignty.

Foreign policies are not, or should not be, an end in themselves. They should be instruments for achieving specific goals for the general welfare. If a given policy on balance subserves the national interest, it should be kept; if it does not, it should be reexamined or junked, especially if it runs counter to the national interest.

This is but another way of saying that policies are made for nations, by them, and in their own interests, rather than nations for policies. They spring from the soil of a country's needs and aspirations; they are (or should be) servants, not masters.

Beginning with President Washington's administration, the United States laid down a policy (not always successful) of neutralism, abstentionism, and noninvolvement toward the brawls and broils of Europe. This policy was bottomed on the sound concept that if small boys play rough games with big boys, the small boys will get hurt.

By the mid-twentieth century, and even before, the old philosophy no longer fitted. We were the biggest of the big boys, and the other boys were the ones most likely to get hurt. We therefore gradually but reluctantly forsook the no-alliance tradition, and in the years after World War II entered into some forty alliances with nations scattered all over the globe. This "pactomania" sharply reversed more than a century of traditional policy because, in this atomically supercharged world, such a change seemed to be in the national interest. Policies can be invalidated by events.

BASIC POLICIES SHOULD BE REEXAMINED PERIODICALLY

Thomas Jefferson once suggested that all laws and charters ought to terminate automatically after a predetermined period. If this were the case, we would reenact those that we needed, often with improvements, and permit the others to lapse. Countless laws, many of them unwise or outdated, remain on the statute books of the states and the federal government through the sheer power of inertia.

A wise Secretary of State, like a wise investment counselor, is constantly reviewing the portfolios of policies (stocks) entrusted to his care. He disposes of those that no longer look as though they might pay off, and perhaps strengthens those that look as though they might. In short, policies should be regarded as evolutionary and fluid, not static and frozen. Traditional concepts are not the Ten Commandments, and there is no need for us to bow down and beat our breasts at the mere mention of the Open Door or the Monroe Doctrine. The "spirit of the age" often repeals policies. The repeated landings of marines on the shores of the banana republics of the Caribbean, with consequent infringement on the sovereignty of these tiny nations, seemed increasingly out of step with the more enlightened internationalist outlook of the 1920's and 1930's. We therefore abandoned the old "gunboat diplomacy" and substituted the Good Neighbor Policy, so spectacularly proclaimed in 1933 by Franklin D. Roosevelt.[1]

FLEXIBILITY FACILITATES POLICY

One reason why the Monroe Doctrine has endured so long is that we can make it mean just about what we want it to mean. We have ignored it and we have invoked it; we have expanded it and we have contracted it. Like ivy on a tree, it has grown with our growth.

Inflexibility of policy virtually destroys the possibility of compromise. The United States was determined to stand firmly and uncompromisingly against the expansion of Japan onto the continent of Asia in the 1930's and early 1940's. We had already achieved our Manifest Destiny and our place in the sun on the continent of North America, but we were quite unwilling that Japan should achieve what she regarded, rightly or wrongly, as her Manifest Destiny.

The result of such rigidity was that various alternatives were choked off, and on the eve of Pearl Harbor the Japanese felt that they were confronted (whether correctly or not) with only two choices: to knuckle under or to burst out. They burst out at Pearl

[1] See Bryce Wood, *The Making of the Good Neighbor Policy* (1961). President Lyndon Johnson's landing of troops in the Dominican Republic in 1965 was a temporary departure from established policy.

Harbor. A debate still persists as to whether Tokyo or Washington delivered the so-called final ultimatum in 1941. But one moral to be derived from this humiliating catastrophe is that we should ordinarily avoid a line of policy which leaves freedom of initiative only to our adversary.

CONSISTENCY CLARIFIES POLICY

A nation should be consistent in fashioning its fundamental foreign policies, but not rigidly consistent. Ralph Waldo Emerson wrote that "A foolish consistency is the hobgoblin of little minds, adored by little statesmen and philosophers and divines." The makers of American foreign policy have taken his admonition to heart. Few nations knowingly pursue a course that is clearly contrary to their national interest simply because it is consistent.

Inconsistency in politics is soon forgotten, especially if the results are rewarding. The Louisiana Purchase fell into President Jefferson's lap in 1803, and he found that to keep it would fly into the face of his strict interpretation of the Constitution, to say nothing of other bothersome principles. But the bargain was so breathtaking that he wry-facedly accepted the windfall, and Congress and the people gladly supported his decision. To become the prisoner of rigid constitutionalism is folly.

Until two world wars shattered time-sanctified policies, the United States galloped down a three-lane highway. One was nonintervention in Europe, where we were not strong enough to work our will. The second was cooperation with the great powers in the Far East, where we were not strong enough to work our will alone. The third was intervention in Latin America, where we were strong enough to twist the arms of our little Latin brothers. All this was rather confusing to those European statesmen who tried to follow and comprehend the zig-zags of Uncle Sam.

Oddly enough, after emerging as a superpower from World War I and World War II, we essentially reversed these three policies. We intervened on a huge scale in Europe, where we were able to deploy formidable power. We went it alone or largely alone in Asia, notably Vietnam, where we were able to amass awesome strength. After 1933 we refrained from armed intervention in Latin America, where we had the power but where we decided unilaterally not to use it. A conspicuous exception was President Johnson's hasty and temporary landing of troops in Santo Domingo in 1965.

Domestic problems at home, much to our embarrassment, have often resulted in inconsistencies abroad. While denying first-class citizenship to American Negroes, we insisted that the white rulers of Rhodesia and South Africa grant greater equality to their "coloureds." While condemning dictators in some countries (Hitler, Mussolini, *et al.*), we played along with dictators in Latin America (e.g., Trujillo in the Dominican Republic) who would work hand in glove with the economic interests of the United States. As Franklin Roosevelt allegedly remarked, "They might be s.o.b.'s, but they are our s.o.b.'s."

MILITARY POWER SHOULD BE TAILORED TO SUPPORT POLICIES [2]

Military forces do not exist in a vacuum, or at least should not. A nation must first decide what policies it proposes to uphold in the national interest, and then amass the power that will make those policies effective. The military men should always be the servants of the policy-makers and the policy-executors, and not vice versa.

Only rarely can a nation have a cheap but effective foreign policy. As in the marketplace, one gets only what one is willing to pay for, unless one is immensely lucky. Proclamations and pronunciamentos are no real substitute for bullets and bombs. During the American Civil War, Spain reentered Santo Domingo, and Secretary of State Seward tried to force her out by invoking the Monroe Doctrine. Spain, recognizing that our hands were tied, at first refused to budge. Finally, and largely for internal reasons, she departed in time to avoid the wrath of the reunited United States.

In 1898 we entered the Far Eastern arena by picking up the Philippines from Spain, and by striving to uphold the Open Door Policy for foreign trade and investment in China. We did not possess the military might to defend the Philippines against the Japanese, and we were unwilling to go to the expense of building it up, even though we could have done so if we had regarded the islands as vital. Japan was in a position to seize them whenever she wanted to, and that she did in World War II, temporarily.

[2] See also Chapters XVIII, XIX, below.

A wise banker never takes on a financial commitment that he cannot reasonably expect to cover in a pinch. Overextension may produce disaster. The same is true of a wise statesman. At times the United States, when asked to put up or shut up, could do neither, especially in the Far East. We should tailor our commitments to our power, and if we are unwilling to increase our power adequately, we should reduce our commitments proportionately.

NATIONS THAT DRIFT WITH EVENTS MAY BECOME THEIR VICTIMS

Nations that are too weak to control international events, say Denmark, have little choice but to float along with them like driftwood. Sometimes, however, they are able to enter into alliances for their protection.

Following World War I, we had two choices. We could drift along more or less at the mercy of events, or we could use our immense power to control events in our own interest. By an active, aggressive, and farsighted course we might well have prevented Europe from falling under the iron heel of the dictators, and might well have headed off World War II. But fed up with Europe, we decided upon a policy of head-in-the-sands isolationism which in the end took a disastrous toll.[3]

Those nations that refuse to become the master of events, especially when they can do so, may wind up being their slaves. Not only that, but such chronic drifters permit others to dictate their foreign policy for them.

A policy of drift or do-nothingism is of course a policy of sorts, just as a policy of having no policy is a policy. Waiting for "the dust to settle" in China, during and after the Communist takeover of 1948–1949, had something to commend it. Unsolvable problems sometimes solve themselves if given time or if left alone. But such a policy is neither positive nor farsighted; it depends too heavily on pure luck. There is a time to move and a time to stand still, and a primary responsibility of statesmen is to make the right decision.

In the nineteenth century—when the Republic was smaller, and the oceans were wider, and the world was bigger—we could pursue isolationist or negativist policies with less risk to ourselves than we

---

[3] Robert A. Divine, *The Illusion of Neutrality* (1962).

could in the second and third decades of the twentieth century. Once shouldered, the burden of leadership cannot easily be laid down.

IMPROVISATION IS RISKY PROCEDURE

Policies should be formed in advance of the emergency, not just after disaster strikes. A statesman should strive for a long-range major gain (sometimes with incidental losses) rather than a short-range minor gain. The United States was notoriously shortsighted during World War I and World War II; it fought for quick military victory without proper regard for long-range political consequences. Too many Americans believe that once they have triumphed on the battlefield, all their troubles will be over. This attitude explains the psychology of "Whip the bullies and bring the boys home."

During World War II Winston Churchill and Franklin Roosevelt were repeatedly at odds over grand strategy. Churchill favored fighting the war with a weather eye to preventing a Russian takeover of Central Europe; Roosevelt was evidently more disposed to win the war as speedily as possible and then put some trust in the good faith of the Soviets. This philosophy explains in part why we permitted the Russians to capture Berlin and Prague and otherwise achieve dominance in their neighboring satellites. Hard pressed though they were, the Soviets fought throughout the conflict with a view to their postwar domination of Europe, if not of the world.

Napoleon once remarked that no battle is ever fought according to plan but that no general should ever engage the enemy without a plan. So it is with diplomatic affairs. One cannot look too far ahead with assurance, yet one should try to. But if a statesman peers too far into the future, he may fall into the ditch at his feet, as President Wilson did in his fight for the League of Nations.[4]

Improvisation also leads on occasion to cross-purposes. In some respects a statesman is better off with one poorish policy than with two or more good ones that he is trying to pursue at the same time in the same place.

---

[4] In 1945, following the Yalta Conference, Winston Churchill told the House of Commons, "It is a mistake to look too far ahead. Only one link in the chain of destiny can be handled at a time." Colin Coote and D. Batchelor, eds., *Winston S. Churchill's Maxims and Reflections* (1949), p. 164.

PERSONAL VENDETTAS ARE NO SUBSTITUTE
FOR POLICY

President Wilson started in 1913 with the lofty principle of working for the welfare of the Mexican masses against foreign exploiters. As time passed, he became more inflexibly determined not to extend recognition to their bloody-handed President-by-murder, Victoriano Huerta.

This idealistic policy degenerated into a personal vendetta between the stubborn Scotch–Irish Presbyterian and the no less stubborn Indian ruler of Mexico. Wilson finally helped to unhorse Huerta after a bloody intervention at Vera Cruz, in 1914, but his Mexican policy was generally judged a failure, or at best much less than an unqualified success.[5]

Wilson evidently did not learn from this encounter, nor from his later quarrel with Senator Lodge, that a statesman can hate what the man stands for without hating the man. In fact, Wilson's two armed interventions in Mexico helped to rally the Mexican masses behind their leaders against the *Yanqui* gringo. As David Lloyd George, the British Prime Minister of World War I, wisely remarked, "No quarrel ought ever to be converted into a policy."

CROSS-PURPOSES ARE POOR PURPOSES

With scores of agencies in Washington now having a finger in the pie of foreign affairs, directly or indirectly, we should not be surprised to find them working at cross-purposes. But this is perhaps more excusable than cross-purposes at the highest levels.

President Hoover is justly acclaimed for playing a considerable role in launching the Good Neighbor Policy, which was foreshadowed by his predecessors and carried forward flamboyantly by Franklin Roosevelt. Hoover had in fact headlined his interest in improved Latin American relations by the lengthy cruise that he took along the coasts of Latin America in an American battleship shortly after his election to the presidency in 1928. But in 1930, the year after his inauguration, Hoover both signed and supported the towering Hawley-Smoot tariff. It discouraged imports to the United

[5] See Robert E. Quirk, *An Affair of Honor: Woodrow Wilson and the Occupation of Vera Cruz* (1962).

States from Latin America and blighted the delicate plant of Good Neighborism that was just beginning to bloom.

Time and again we have built up a large bank account of good will in a foreign country, only to have it vanish after some clumsy or calculated affront. Such was the fate of Japanese–American amity in the 1920's. In 1923, following the great Tokyo earthquake, the United States, through official and private sources, sent a generous outpouring of aid to the sufferers. The Japanese were grateful. The next year Congress passed an immigration law that banged the door in the teeth of Japanese immigrants, not even permitting a hundred or so to enter on a quota basis. The resulting ill will helped pave the slippery path that led directly to Pearl Harbor.

In the mid-1960's the sincerity of President Johnson's peace overtures to North Vietnam was repeatedly called into question by simultaneous—or almost simultaneous—announcements by the Defense Department of a huge new arms buildup. The right hand should always know what the left hand is doing. If there are cross-purposes, the cost should be counted.

SOUND INFORMATION IS THE TAPROOT OF SOUND POLICY

If an effective foreign policy is to be formulated and executed, timely and accurate intelligence is needed. It should be drawn from all sides, not only the side we want to see win but also from the enemy or the potential enemy. A policy decision, unless blind luck is with us, is no sounder than the validity and completeness of the facts on which it is based.

In 1965 President Lyndon Johnson hastily decided to land American troops in the Dominican Republic, thus reversing the Good Neighbor pledge made by Franklin Roosevelt in 1933. On the basis of information fed to him by our embassy in Santo Domingo, he evidently believed that American lives were in grave danger and that the Communists were about to seize the country, as they had in Fidel Castro's Cuba. Critics have charged that Johnson's informants betrayed him by exaggerating the menace to American lives and the danger of a Communist *coup*.[6] Whatever the truth, the

---

[6] John B. Martin, *Overtaken by Events* (1966), pp. 656 ff. Martin, a former Ambassador to the Dominican Republic and a first-hand observer, is disposed to justify President Johnson.

result was a damaging blow to the prestige and good name of the United States, especially among "liberals" in general and Latin Americans in particular. But stability was restored to the Dominican Republic in 1966, all foreign troops were withdrawn, and considerable justification could be found for Johnson's intervention on the principle of "better safe than sorry."

On the other hand, too much intelligence can be worse than too little, as the shattering experience at Pearl Harbor illustrated. We had cracked the principal Japanese code and were secretly intercepting all messages between Tokyo and Washington. The American officials were simply inundated with a mass of data, some of which provided misleading leads.[7] President Roosevelt knew that a blow was about to fall, but evidently assumed that it would be somewhere in Southeast Asia, for Japanese troop transports were detected steaming in that direction. Here, in fact, was where the major blow did fall, but the gigantic surprise party at Pearl Harbor was costly and mortifying. The intercepting and decoding of an adversary's secret messages is not enough; we must know how to interpret them perceptively.

PRESENT DECISIONS ARE OFTEN PRISONERS OF PAST DECISIONS

Everything that happens in human affairs in some way results from something that happened before.

So it is with foreign policy. And this explains why a wise government should avoid becoming the prisoner of a previous policy, good or bad, or of its own propaganda, good or bad.

At Munich, in 1938, the British and French, fearing the menace and might of Hitler, sold out by appeasing him (temporarily) with a large chunk of Czechoslovakia. Prior to that time the word "appease" had been relatively colorless, but now it took on a lurid connotation; "Munich" became a synonym for "surrender on the installment plan." Thereafter, whenever reasonable concessions were necessary in the give-and-take of diplomacy, one heard the cries "appeasement" and "Munich," notably in connection with the Geneva settlement of 1954 regarding French Indo-China. So stri-

[7] See Roberta Wohlstetter, *Pearl Harbor: Warning and Decision* (1962).

dent were American voices against "appeasement" that the United States refused to sign this multination agreement. Instead we embarked upon a program of supporting South Vietnam which led us, perhaps inevitably, into the depths of the monsoon mud.[8]
Bogged down in the Vietnamese war, we found that any real moves toward peace were greeted with cries of "Munich," reinforced by the stereotype of "falling dominoes." The assumption was that if South Vietnam fell, all the other small nations of Southeast Asia would fall, and that ere long we would be "back on Waikiki beach" (another stereotype), desperately defending our liberties. One stubborn fact is that the biggest domino of all—China—fell in 1948–1949, but its neighbors have been a long time in falling.
The dangers of diplomacy-by-stereotype were further illustrated by Red China. Following the Communist takeover in 1949, we pursued a twin policy of nonrecognition of China and the nonseating of her representatives in the United Nations. This course was in response to potent public pressures, and it made considerable sense when adopted. But its reiterated justification by Washington finally became so convincing that public opinion would not tolerate a policy change nearly twenty years later. By this time the Red regime had apparently established iron-fisted control of its people and had become a power manufacturing fearsome nuclear weapons. But American elections had been repeatedly won on the basis of nonrecognition and nonseating, and few politicians in Washington who valued their political skins were going to buck the popular tide. In a sense we were the prisoners of our own propaganda.

POLICY PLANNING IS A COMPLICATED ART

Policy, as we have seen, is normally fashioned by the President, in close collaboration with his intimate advisers, in the State Department and out, and including the Department's Policy Planning

[8] Arthur M. Schlesinger, Jr., has suggested that the subsequent misapplication of the Munich analogy may have caused more harm than the Munich surrender itself. He further suggests that on occasion we should reverse Santayana's famous aphorism and make it read, "too often it is those who *can* remember the past [imperfectly] who are condemned to repeat it." *The Bitter Heritage* (1967), pp. 89, 91. We should note that the Communists, no less than the capitalists, have been able to cry "Munich" when faced with an undesired compromise.

Council. The official planners devise proposals for meeting all likely contingencies, except, as cynics have observed, those that actually develop.

Projected policies should be assessed for both their long-range and short-range impact. They should also be scrutinized by experts in the relevant fields, and the final evaluation should be made by officials other than their creators, who often suffer from pride of authorship.

A classic case of how policy should not be formulated and executed is provided by Washington's backing of the 1400 Cuban exiles in their ill-starred invasion at the Bay of Pigs in 1961. President Kennedy was dubious about the whole scheme, and his military experts were not enthusiastic about the landing site finally chosen. But the Central Intelligence Agency and other sponsors of the project had a strong voice in pushing for the final decision. Kennedy reluctantly approved what he thought was the perfected plan, but it turned out to be something quite different in certain important particulars. Another sin of the planners was not to anticipate fully all the costs if the invasion collapsed immediately or died slowly on the vine.

The cold gray dawn resulted in an unseemly hassle among Kennedy's advisers as to their individual blame for the blunder. Some of them should have spoken up when they remained silent; others should have remained silent when they spoke up. "There's an old saying," Kennedy pointedly remarked, "that victory has a hundred fathers and defeat is an orphan." [9]

CONFIDENTIAL DELIBERATIONS SHOULD REMAIN CONFIDENTIAL

An indecent ruckus developed in 1962, following the Cuban missile crisis. Adlai Stevenson, Ambassador to the United Nations, was publicly condemned as an appeasing "dove" by the warlike "hawks." He allegedly had suggested in secret conference that the United States might withdraw its obsolescent nuclear missiles from

---

[9] Arthur M. Schlesinger, Jr., *A Thousand Days* (1965), p. 289. This book contains an inside account of the Bay of Pigs disaster, as does Theodore C. Sorensen, *Kennedy* (1965).

Turkey and Italy, in return for a withdrawal by the Soviets of their ultramodern missiles from Cuba.[10]

The moral is that all such top-level discussions should be in the highest degree confidential. All possible and reasonable alternatives ought to be proposed and explored, even though they are all rejected. This is the best way to guarantee that the "bugs" in any given scheme will be exposed, and even then they may not all be discovered. But if a participant in these secret councils fears that his suggestions will be emblazoned in the newspapers a few days later, he will be inclined to hold his tongue at a time when all points of view ought to be tossed out on the conference table.

This is one of the times when silence is not golden.

[10] The Jupiter missiles in Turkey were deemed so ineffective that Kennedy had ordered their removal two months before the Cuban crisis, but his orders were not executed. To swap their removal for that of the Russian missiles in Cuba was thought unwise in Washington because of the adverse effect on Turkey, the eastern anchor of the NATO Alliance. Elie Abel, *The Missile Crisis* (1966), pp. 191–193.

CHAPTER VIII

The Power of Economic Interests

"Today, as never before, America needs a strong economy . . . to demonstrate to other nations . . . that the way of freedom is the way to strength and security—that their future lies with us and not with the Soviet Union."

SENATOR JOHN F. KENNEDY, 1960

PROLOGUE

"Man is what he eats," wrote Karl Marx. And when we remind ourselves that about two-thirds of mankind goes to bed hungry, we can better appreciate the importance of economic factors in the conduct of diplomacy.

We are naive indeed if we think we can readily teach democracy to the undernourished and undereducated masses of Asia who are more concerned with the next mouthful than with foreign ideologies, or with any ideology. Hunger knows no ideology, and "A hungry man," Adlai Stevenson remarked in 1952, "is not a free man." In Europe after World War II there were many "stomach communists"—human derelicts who would go along with Communism rather than starve. In many cases they did both.

As Woodrow Wilson told Congress on November 11, 1918, "Hunger does not breed reform; it breeds madness, and all the ugly distempers that make an ordered life impossible."

THE ECONOMIC IS OFTEN MORE POTENT THAN THE IDEOLOGICAL

When the American War of Independence ended, we felt bitter toward the British, who had fought us, and friendly toward the French, who had helped us. French statesmen assumed—and this was one reason for their intervention—that these sentiments would result in a switch of the lucrative prewar Anglo–American trade to Franco–American channels.

Such high expectations were dashed, even after the French monarchy was overthrown and American-inspired revolutionary ideas swept over France. Trade tends to slip back into well-worn grooves. The British spoke and wrote our language; the French did not. The British were accustomed to granting the colonials relatively liberal credit; the French were not. The Americans were familiar with British goods and trademarks, and the British were used to American imports, such as Virginia-cured tobacco. To the United States, the French, traditional foes in four intercolonial wars, were still largely strangers—and remained so.

Ideology again clashed with reality in 1933. The American people had long shown their distaste for bomb-and-whisker Bolsheviks by refusing to recognize the Moscow regime. But perhaps a billion-dollar trade with the Reds would help pull us out of the Depression morass, and the dollar sign loomed large among the arguments for recognizing the Soviet Union. Franklin Roosevelt gingerly extended the right hand of recognition in 1933.[1] But the anticipated trade did not flower, primarily because the Soviets were counting on Uncle Sam to extend billion-dollar credits. We had no intention whatever of adding to the debt of already untrustworthy debtors.

TRADE TENDS TO PROMOTE PEACE

A shrewd businessman makes it a rule not to quarrel with his best customers, or, in fact, with any customers. "The customer is always right" is a time-honored aphorism that also applies to foreign trade.

Nations have sometimes been restrained from fighting by the

[1] See Donald V. Bishop, *The Roosevelt–Litvinov Agreements: The American View* (1965).

realization that warfare might well result in a mutual cutting of economic throats. From the 1830's to the 1870's Anglo–American relations were almost always embittered, and often so severely strained as to threaten an explosion. But if war had come, each nation would have been fighting one of its best customers. The Americans bought large quantities of British manufactured goods, and England imported the bulk of the South's enormous cotton crop. Without it, the vital textile industry of the British Isles would have suffered from fiber-famine. A realization that an Anglo–American conflict would result in grave economic hardship was a potent restraint in keeping the two nations from each other's throats. In an almost literal sense, the dogs of war on both sides of the Atlantic were held back by threads of cotton. International trade is an ambassador of good will.

Now and then an exception proves the rule that good customers do not fight each other. In the 1920's and 1930's Japan and the United States were enjoying one of the most profitable two-way trades in history. Americans bought the bulk of Japan's critically important silk output, and the Japanese bought mountains of American cotton, to say nothing of scrap iron, much of which, in one form or another, was later returned in anger. Experts repeatedly said that this trade was so important to both sides, especially during the Depression-cursed 1930's, that neither would or could fight the other. But the fanaticism and desperation of the Japanese warlords proved that there were limits to the restraining power of thread, whether cotton or silk. Where national prestige and security are involved, economic profits may be shoved onto the back seat.

COMMERCE CEMENTS FRIENDSHIP AND VICE VERSA

In 1895 the Japanese government was building up its navy, and its British-trained engineers strongly favored buying from England the warships with which they were familiar. Our ambassador in Tokyo reported that pro-American influences in Tokyo were pushing for purchases in the United States. They were "desirous of testifying in some tangible manner their appreciation of the uniform friendliness of the United States towards Japan," and they realized that it was "good policy to buy where they sell the most. . . ." [2]

[2] Payson J. Treat, *Diplomatic Relations between the United States and Japan, 1895–1905* (1938), p. 14.

During the heyday of American imperialism in the Caribbean, roughly from 1898 well into the 1920's, we made enemies and alienated customers throughout all Latin America. American marines in Haiti, Santo Domingo, and Nicaragua could force a government to behave, but they could not force the people to buy American goods in competition with the British, Germans, and others.

Historically, the relations between the United States and Brazil have been the most friendly that we have enjoyed with any of the major nations of Latin America. The reasons are varied, but the most important one can probably be boiled down into a single word: "coffee." If Cuba was America's sugar bowl until Castro soured relations in 1959, Brazil was America's coffeepot. The great bulk of all the beans purchased by coffee-consuming America came from Brazil, thereby enriching that nation and enabling it to build up dollar credits with which to purchase our goods. One of the nightmares of Brazilians is the fear that the ingenious Yankees may come up with synthetic coffee, thus hitting Brazil below the trade belt and destroying a historic friendship bottomed somewhat shakily on coffee beans.

TARIFF WALLS ARE WAILING WALLS

It would be difficult to point to a major tariff revision in our history which did not in some way and in some place trample on the toes of foreign manufacturers or producers. Dislocations inevitably result, and the pinch is worldwide, whether in a button factory in Austria or a winery in France.

Two American tariff laws, both hurtful to foreign sugar, are intimately related to epochal events in Hawaii and Cuba. The McKinley tariff of 1890 produced great anxiety among the sugar barons of Hawaii. It contributed to the overthrow of the monarchy in 1893 and the ultimate annexation of the paradisiacal republic, after five years of mutual courtship. The Wilson-Gorman tariff barrier of 1894 created hardship among the already hard-pressed Cubans. It helped to trigger the revolt of 1895 and America's intervention in 1898, following the blowing up of the battleship *Maine*. The troubled events thus set in motion have not yet run their course. After Fidel Castro seized power, he claimed that the devilish

Americans had blown up the warship themselves so that they might have a pretext for fastening their greedy tentacles on Cuba. The Yankee intervention of 1898, in his Marxist view, was of, by, and for the American sugar interests.

The towering Hawley-Smoot tariff of 1930, signed by President Hoover, was motivated largely by politics and greed. Passed during the worldwide depression, it almost certainly worsened that depression. Economic warfare is a game that two or more can play, and governments should be careful when they hurl potential boomerangs. Many foreign nations threatened reprisals if the Hawley-Smoot tariff bill passed, and they carried out their threats in bitterness of spirit.[3] President Franklin Roosevelt's reciprocal trade agreements, which resulted in a piecemeal whittling down of the onerous schedules, did something to salve the resentment of foreigners. It started a trend which has brought the United States down into the category of low-tariff nations.

INTERNATIONAL DEBTS CHILL
INTERNATIONAL FRIENDSHIPS

Pity the poor creditor, at least in some degree, because he never can be popular. America in the nineteenth century borrowed huge sums from "the bloated British bondholder" with which to build roads, canals, banks, railroads, and other internal improvements. England had the capital but we had the continent—a raw continent. Some of the American states overborrowed, and in the panicky 1830's a half-dozen of them defaulted on their obligations or repudiated them outright. British enthusiasm for investing money in "debt-welshing" Yankeeland diminished. We resented the creditor when he lent money, and we resented him when he would not lend it.[4] We hated the noble lord who clipped coupons in his ancestral castle while we chopped trees in the American forest.

[3] See J. M. Jones, Jr., *Tariff Retaliation: Repercussions of the Hawley-Smoot Bill* (1934). Bilateral treaties, like unilateral tariffs, almost always have unfortunate side effects. The treaty of annexation in 1898, between the United States and Hawaii, directly concerned only these two nations, but it indirectly affected a number of other nations, notably Japan, which lodged a vigorous protest.
[4] In recent years the Canadians, fearing absorption by American investment capital, have experienced similar misgivings.

After World War I, America suddenly became the world's creditor, and our role as regards Britain was reversed. With more than a century of underdog experience, we should have appreciated better the debtor's point of view. We insisted on collecting the $10 billion or so in war debts incurred chiefly by our late Allies, but the only practicable way by which they could pay off this obligation was in goods. Yet we proceeded to erect formidable tariff barriers over which their goods could not clamber.

In retrospect, we would have been much wiser if we had cancelled the debts, which proved largely uncollectible anyway. A nation cannot collect debts by impoverishing its debtors, and often it has to forgive its debtors if it wants prosperous customers.[5] Trade is a two-way street, and if the traffic slows down on one side, it usually slows down on the other.

Debtors do not ordinarily love creditors, any more than cats love dogs. If nations become wealthy, they have to learn to live with this disagreeable fact of international life. Possessing surplus capital, they exploit foreign peoples by lending them the money they need, and in turn are exploited by them. Dr. Samuel Flagg Bemis has argued that the Latin American debtors borrowed hundreds of millions of dollars on which they defaulted in the 1930's, and that on balance they bilked the Yankees rather than being milked by them.[6]

ECONOMIC WEAPONS CAN BE TWO-EDGED

In 1807 President Jefferson rammed through Congress an iron-toothed embargo bill. It was designed to force Britain to make concessions regarding a free sea by prohibiting exports from the United States. Instead of bringing Britain to her knees, we brought ourselves to our knees by inflicting ruin on large segments of the country. The British, fighting for their life against Napoleon, stood firm, and the embargo was repealed in 1809, to be followed by milder economic reprisals. The stubbornness of a war-involved ad-

[5] President Calvin Coolidge showed no particular acumen when he reportedly remarked about the European war debtors, "They hired the money, didn't they?" Winston Churchill commented, "This laconic statement was true, but not exhaustive." Kay Halle, ed., *Irrepressible Churchill* (1966), p. 94.

[6] S. F. Bemis, *The Latin American Policy of the United States* (1943), p. 350.

versary, especially one fighting for its life, should never be underrated.

The Japanese warlords, without warning and in defiance of solemn treaty obligations, lunged into China's Manchuria in 1931. Many excitable Americans demanded that we join hands with the League of Nations or go it alone in an attempt to halt Japan's aggressive course. Less bellicose citizens urged an official economic boycott instead. But President Hoover, the Quaker who believed that economic warfare would lead inevitably to shooting warfare, threw the immense weight of his office against coercive schemes. More than that, he authorized a public statement to the effect that the United States would not resort to economic pressures. The Japanese militarists naturally took comfort from his hands-off policy.[7]

Several morals emerge. If possible, hold an ace or two in reserve. Keep your adversary guessing. And avoid proclaiming what you are *not* going to do, whether referring to economic sanctions or nuclear bombs.

In 1941 the United States, under President Franklin Roosevelt, imposed an embargo on fuel and other crucial supplies needed by Japan's war machine. Washington's spectacular assets-freezing order, proclaimed July 23, 1941, was in effect a declaration of economic warfare on the island kingdom. The Japanese militarists, watching the oil gauge slowly drop on their reserve tanks, were driven to the madness of Pearl Harbor.

One lesson is that we should never underestimate a hungry or desperate or fanatical foe. Another is that we should never tie down the safety valve unless we are braced for an explosion.

INTERNATIONAL BOYCOTTS ARE OFTEN SELF-DEFEATING

A successful economic boycott of one nation by another nation or group of nations is extremely difficult to bring off. More than a half-dozen large-scale attempts have occurred since the mid-1930's, but they have all proved ineffective, or at least disappointing.

The smell of profits invariably attracts chiselers or blockade runners or noncooperators. In 1935 the League of Nations formally imposed sanctions on materials going to Italy, as a consequence of

[7] Robert H. Ferrell, *American Diplomacy in the Great Depression* (1957), pp. 186–187.

dictator Mussolini's defiant and brutal invasion of Ethiopia. Certain members of the League, fearing Mussolini's presumably potent navy, and not wishing to drive him into the arms of Hitler, did not have the nerve to clamp an embargo on oil—the one key commodity that would have brought down his house of cards. They excused their lack of courage in part by pointing out that the United States and other nonmembers of the League either were supplying Italy with oil or were in a position to do so.[8] The result was that instead of bringing Mussolini's synthetic empire down in ruins, the League exposed its own impotence to the world and collapsed itself.

Noncooperators are always a problem. America's boycott of Communist China after 1949 proved futile, largely because China was backed up against a then friendly Russia. Other nations, including our own NATO allies, disagreed with Washington's policy and continued to sell enormous quantities of wheat and other essentials to the Red Chinese.

Much the same pattern was repeated in the 1960's, when the United States undertook to overthrow Fidel Castro in Cuba. The Soviet Union—our Cold War adversary—propped him up, and our NATO allies like Britain and France continued to supply him with critical commodities. After all, they had to keep their economies healthy; and being three thousand miles away, they were less worried about Castro than were the nearby Americans.

National boycotts have thus far conspicuously failed to produce internal political revolutions. On the contrary, they generally arouse the patriotic spirit of the people and persuade them to tighten their belts and hang on grimly. This was notably true of our sanctions against Castro's Cuba in the early 1960's. The bearded dictator was not only able to arouse the masses against the Yankee "oppressor," but he was also able to blame the obvious shortcomings of his own regime on the restrictions imposed by the Colossus of the North.

ECONOMIC ENTANGLEMENTS CAN BE DEEPER THAN POLITICAL ONES

In the 1920's, following the disillusionment of World War I, the United States attempted to pursue a policy of semi-isolation

---

[8] See *The Memoirs of Anthony Eden: Facing the Dictators* (1962), Ch. 16; Herbert Feis, *Seen From E. A.* (1947).

toward troubled Europe. Most dramatically, we refused to join or cooperate meaningfully with the League of Nations.

But the United States was not isolated politically from Europe, despite this avowed policy, and never has been. Few responsible American statesmen have ever argued that what convulsed that troubled continent could not conceivably concern us. Even during the isolationist 1920's the United States was represented at disarmament conferences, and in various ways edged more closely, if furtively, toward the League of Nations.[9]

If political isolation was only partially achieved in the 1920's and 1930's, economic isolation was widely disregarded. We were actively involved in an attempt, only partially successful, to force the European nations to pay their so-called war debts. To collect the money for these obligations, the Allied nations attempted to wring reparations from Germany, and to this extent we were deeply, though indirectly, involved in the reparations snarl.

While proclaiming political isolation, we became increasingly enmeshed in economic entanglements. Wall Street bankers loaned Germany hundreds of millions of dollars with which to build up her industries and (incidentally) to provide many of the wheels for Hitler's future war machine.

Economic entanglement is the deepest entanglement of all. A sovereign nation can always walk out of a conference or resign from a League of Nations or abrogate a treaty or terminate an alliance. But a factory, built in Germany with American dollars, simply cannot be shifted when policy shifts. This we subsequently learned to our sorrow, when the only way to remove the factory was to bomb it out of existence.

"DOLLAR DIPLOMACY" IS HERE TO STAY

Communist critics have habitually berated "dollar imperialism" and "dollar diplomacy" as though they were devilish schemes of rather recent vintage.

The United States, in an effort to protect its ocean-borne commerce, has from early days been defending the dollar and hence has been practicing "dollar diplomacy." President Jefferson, a Vir-

[9] See William A. Williams, "The Legend of Isolationism," *Science and Society*, XVIII (1954), pp. 1–20.

ginian, resented the cost of a navy that was used chiefly to protect New England shippers. But he was finally forced to employ that navy to defend American trade against North African pirates. As the twentieth century dawned, the dollar was under more compulsion to go abroad, for the nation was now highly industrialized and was blessed with surplus capital. The term "dollar diplomacy" was commonly and sneeringly referred to, notably during the administration of President Taft (1909–1913). His policy was twopronged. First, he would use American marines (supported by all the taxpayers) to protect American foreign investments from expropriation or local violence. Second, he would promote the national interest abroad by inducing American capitalists to pump dollars into key areas. He had specifically in mind Latin America and China, to which rival powers, such as Germany and Japan, were being attracted. Their presence might jeopardize our foreign policies, including the Open Door and the Monroe Doctrine.

President Taft, as events proved, was a small-time operator. The dollars that he was protecting or prodding were the *private* dollars of American investment bankers. After World War II the United States became involved abroad on an enormous scale in using *public* funds to promote the national interest, including American foreign policy. More than $100 billion was thus ladled out in economic aid and military aid, often more military than economic. We remember especially Truman's Marshall Plan for Europe and Point Four for backward countries. More recently, we have had the ten-year, multibillion-dollar Alliance for Progress in Latin America, launched with much fanfare under the aegis of President Kennedy.

This astronomical expenditure of the taxpayer's money has undergone heavy criticism at home. Much of the money was thrown away, as often happens with sour private investments, but much of it returned rich political dividends. It may, for example, have saved Indonesia from falling into the Communist camp in 1966, even though we had cut aid to that country in 1965.

Imitation is the sincerest form of flattery, and on the credit side of American foreign aid is the fact that the Soviets, noting our successes, embarked upon an ambitious program of "ruble diplomacy." The dollar and the ruble have locked horns in many a foreign land, and both have enjoyed successes or suffered failures. The Russians threw away the equivalent of some $3 billion in Indonesia prior to 1966. They learned, as the Americans had learned earlier, that large-scale foreign aid is a gigantic gamble. Substantial gains may be garnered but, on the other hand, one way to reap a rich harvest of ingratitude, resentment, and envy is to try to do good for other people in your own interest.

CHAPTER IX

The Domestic Front

"The United States cannot be strong in its foreign policy unless it is also strong domestically."

SENATOR JOHN F. KENNEDY, 1960

PROLOGUE

One of the major triumphs of the United States in foreign relations after World War II was the avoidance of another Great Depression. This achievement illustrates the increasingly close connection between domestic affairs and foreign affairs.

Specifically, the Kremlin was counting on a postwar depression to hamstring the United States so that we could not prevent the Communists from working their will in Europe and other key areas of the globe. In the normal course of events, such a depression might well have developed. But the Soviets outfoxed themselves. By embarking upon a menacing arms program that threatened to overturn the postwar balance, they forced the United States to rearm itself on a prodigious scale. This golden shot in the arm above all else was probably responsible for the prolonged prosperity in the decades after 1945. Indeed, the national economy became so tightly chained to war orders that any genuine disarmament might well have brought disaster.

DOMESTIC AND FOREIGN PROBLEMS ARE
OFTEN INSEPARABLE

There was a time in the adolescent years of the Republic when a citizen could speak of foreign affairs and internal affairs as though they were in no way related. That day has passed. The more powerful the United States has become at home, the more forcefully its domestic concerns have made themselves felt abroad.

Nothing would seem to be more of a domestic problem than the decision as to how many and what kinds of foreigners we would permit to enter our gates. Yet the Immigration Act of 1924, which discriminated offensively against the Japanese, profoundly disturbed foreign relations.

Nothing would seem to be more of a domestic problem than bolstering the price of silver in 1934 in the interests of the depressed American silver miners. Yet the side effects on foreign silver currencies added to the chaos in China and contributed to the grave disorders that paved the way for Communism.

Nothing would seem to be more of a domestic problem than for Congress to remove the tariff on imported sugar and authorize the federal government to pay a bounty to American producers of cane sugar and beet sugar. Yet this change in 1890 struck a body blow at the sugar planters of Hawaii and helped trigger the revolution of 1893, which eventually resulted in annexation.[1]

Domestic affairs, so-called, are increasingly but the reverse side of the shield of foreign affairs.

INTERNAL DISUNITY DEVITALIZES FOREIGN POLICY

A nation is no stronger abroad than it is at home. The Constitution of the United States was framed by men who, among other objectives, sought to strengthen the national government so that it could command the respect of the North African pirates and those European nations that were treating us with contempt. This immediate objective was achieved, but thereafter internal disunity periodically hampered the conduct of foreign policy.

The Republic of Texas, after winning its independence in 1836 with the aid of American volunteers, sought protection from Mexico

[1] See W. A. Russ, Jr., *The Hawaiian Revolution, 1893–1894* (1959).

by annexation to the United States. No nation in the world would normally spurn so rich a prize, but Uncle Sam kept the waiting Texan bride on tenterhooks for nearly nine long years. The basic reason was that the mounting protests of the anti-slavery elements, chiefly in the North, produced an uproar that caused the Washington government to tread the path of caution.

In the 1850's the sugar-rich island of Cuba was ripe for the picking. The pro-slavery expansionists of the South coveted it, while the powers of Europe, bogged down in Russia with the Crimean War, were in no position to arrest the hand of the grasping Americans. But the free-soil North would permit no more slave soil, and Cuba was saved by the acute indigestion of the colossus who would devour her.

The bloodiest quarrel of all—the American Civil War—is the most illuminating example of all. Taking advantage of the Republic's rupture, imperial France boldly challenged the Monroe Doctrine in Mexico, as Spain did in Santo Domingo. At the same time Great Britain permitted English-built Confederate commerce destroyers, manned by English crews, to ravage Yankee commerce. But a reunited United States finally vindicated the Monroe Doctrine, and the British ate humble pie when they paid damages, assessed in 1872 by the Geneva Arbitral Tribunal, for their sins of omission and commission.

INJUSTICE AT HOME WEAKENS DIPLOMACY ABROAD

Communist propagandists have long charged that a hypocritical Uncle Sam pursues a double standard: civil rights for foreign nonwhites but uncivil wrongs for his own Negroes. Self-determination, these critics insist, should begin at home.

In 1957 President Eisenhower felt compelled to send federal troops to Little Rock (Arkansas) to escort nine Negro pupils to Central High School, from which the local segregationists were trying to bar them. This rifle-backed intervention was a godsend to Communist propagandists the world over. It proclaimed anew that we were unwilling to practice at home the toleration that we were preaching abroad. Little Rock skyrocketed from obscurity into a prominent place among the best-known American cities.

Communist critics overlooked or chose to ignore the most significant point of these unsavory episodes. It was not that many Southerners were unwilling to permit Negro children to attend school with whites, but that the federal government, for the first time since Reconstruction days, was using its military muscle to uphold civil rights at home.[2]

The same was true in perhaps a more dramatic form when federal troops were sent to Mississippi in 1962. The issue was whether or not a lone Negro registrant, James H. Meredith, could attend classes with whites at the University of Mississippi. After a riot that cost two lives and injured many, Meredith finally graduated with a sheepskin that cost the national taxpayers about four million dollars.

Other episodes turned out less happily. During the 1963 "Battle of Birmingham" ("Bombingham"), fire hoses and police dogs were turned on Negroes demonstrating for their rights. Pictures of these savage animals attacking Negroes were distributed over the entire world. Such pictorial evidence generated further doubts as to the sincerity of the Washington government when it demanded that colored peoples, including Negroes in Africa under Portuguese sway, be given their basic rights.

As far as America's "image" is concerned, the locating of the United Nations in New York City has proved to be something of a blunder. Nonwhite delegates, many of them respected officials in their own lands, have suffered indignities, especially with regard to housing accommodations and service in restaurants. Such humiliations have implanted resentment in the hearts of nonwhite leaders whose support we need in the struggle for the survival of the free world.

DEMOCRACY BEGINS AT HOME

Defective products are hard to export successfully, and American democracy is not now, never has been, and never will be perfect. Winston Churchill remarked in 1947 that "democracy is the worst form of all government except all those other forms that had been tried from time to time."

Countless Americans believe or have believed that the Republic has a God-given mission to spread democracy all over the world.

[2] Dwight D. Eisenhower's own version appears in his autobiographical *Waging Peace* (1965), pp. 162 ff.

This obsession, in fact, was one of the mainsprings of Manifest Destiny, which became a kind of national disease in the 1840's and 1850's.[3]

During World War I, under President Wilson's inspirational leadership, one of the popular slogans was that we were fighting to "make the world safe for democracy." Wilson had in view creating such favorable conditions throughout the globe that our democracy, indeed any democracy, could exist without fear of being overrun by imperialistic aggressors. But this ideal was often subverted into a belief that we had a divine mandate to force democracy on the entire world.

The same fixation gained much currency after World War II, especially when we perceived that democracy was the chief foe of Communism. The most effective way to combat the Red virus, we concluded, was to shore up existing democracies or to create new ones. This conviction accounts for a large part of our enormous outlays for foreign aid, heavily military, after World War II.

The American people can best serve the cause of democracy if they make it work so well at home that other nations will demand the same blessings for themselves. Every time an American violates civil rights he is by that much blackening the national "image" and weakening the nation's foreign policy.

Nineteenth-century America was the lodestar of liberals the world over. But they were disenchanted when Americans chilled high hopes by debt repudiations, aggressions upon their neighbors, slave-mongering, lynchings, and other brutalities. At the same time the monarchs of Europe rejoiced over this ugly picture, for they could ask their people if the American way of life (and death) was what they really wanted. As President Kennedy bluntly told Congress on January 14, 1963, "We shall be judged more by what we do at home than what we preach abroad."

TAKE ADVANTAGE OF YOUR ADVERSARY'S DOMESTIC DIFFICULTIES

There is a hoary saying, "England's extremity is Ireland's opportunity." The implication was that whenever Britain found herself

---

[3] See Frederick Merk, *Manifest Destiny and Mission in American History* (1963).

in grave trouble, whether abroad or at home, the Irish should step up their agitation for independence.

The application of this axiom by a foreign office calls for a full understanding of the internal policies and pressures of one's diplomatic adversary. In 1898, when Washington was urging Spain to make concessions that would give rebellious Cuba partial or even full autonomy, the Spanish government found that it could not go far enough fast enough because of internal disorders. If the McKinley administration had been more fully aware of Spain's domestic difficulties, it might not have forced the Madrid regime so inescapably into a corner.

In 1931 the nations of the world were mired down in a depression, and Japan took advantage of their preoccupation to challenge the League of Nations by seizing China's Manchuria. None of the great powers was willing to beard the Mikado's minions alone or collectively, in part because of the debilitating effect of the Great Depression.

The United States, in the years after World War II, found itself involved in a desperate struggle to "contain" the worldwide spread of Soviet-fomented Communism. Droughts and crop failures in the early 1960's produced an acute grain shortage in Russia, at a time when American storage bins were bursting with surpluses. Was this not the time to spurn Soviet efforts to buy our wheat and force starvation upon that one nation above all others that had sworn to do us in?

Anti-Red critics in America were numerous and vocal. They quoted the statement, attributed to Lenin, that the capitalists would ultimately be hanged by the rope which they had sold to the Communists for a profit. But the Kennedy administration, breasting the waves of opposition, finally decided to sell vast quantities of wheat to the Soviet Union.[4] Humanitarians argued that it was obscene for Americans to sit on overflowing granaries while tens of millions of Russians went hungry or even starved. On the practical side, the surpluses were immensely costly to store, spoilage was occurring, and the payments by the Soviets would ease the alarming drain of gold from the United States. Besides, there was no convincing proof that a starving Communist was a more peaceful Communist. Nations that are driven to the wall sometimes resort to irrational acts, as the Japanese did at Pearl Harbor.

[4] See Theodore C. Sorensen, *Kennedy* (1965), pp. 741–742.

The Russian wheat famine presented a classic case where a grave internal problem threatened to weaken a powerful and unfriendly diplomatic adversary. In ordinary circumstances, the sale of food to a weakened enemy would be folly, but these were not ordinary circumstances. The national interest seemed to point to a path which combined humanitarianism with realism.

PARTISANSHIP AND FOREIGN POLICY DO NOT MIX

Politics is a queer game. Whatever happens during a given presidency is usually chalked up to the credit of that administration, whether the achievement came by accident or by design, or even as a result of support by the opposition party. Another quirk of politics is that the party out of power must prevent the party in power from getting too much credit, whether in the arena of domestic affairs or of foreign affairs. Democracy cannot function without parties, and such irrationality is the price, or one of the prices, that we must pay for misgoverning ourselves in our own way. Yet we should remember that good politics is often not good policy.

Constructive criticism is always needed if democracy is to work at its best, and the party out of power—"the loyal opposition"—is the only one that can provide that effective criticism without punches pulled. Thomas B. Reed, a prominent Republican politico of the 1890's, spoke sarcastically of his faith in the two-party system, under which one party ruled and the other party watched. He added that he preferred to have the Republicans rule while the Democrats watched.

The fight over the League of Nations is a classic case of a fateful injection of politics into foreign affairs. Although both houses of Congress were to be Republican as a result of the 1918 elections, the Democratic President Wilson assembled a peace commission of five members, only one of whom was a Republican—and he was a rather obscure one at that. The Republicans feared that if Wilson returned triumphantly from Paris with a League of Nations, he would have a potent feather in his cap. He might arrange to have himself reelected, despite the then inviolable two-term tradition, in order to get the League off the ground. He might then scheme to have himself elected again and again in order to keep it air-borne. If he had announced publicly that in no circumstances would he be a candidate for a third term, much of the partisan rancor would have evaporated. He presumably did not do so because he thought such an announcement presumptuous, and probably also because he craved the honor (as we now know) of a third nomination.

The Democrats under Wilson desired partisan credit for the League; the Republicans sought as much of the credit as possible by attaching Republican reservations. Wilson spurned all Republican reservations, although he was willing to accept certain Democratic reservations. The result was that both the friends and the foes of the treaty cooperated in engineering its defeat in the Senate. The half-dead League was forced to run as the major issue in the confusing presidential election of 1920—something that a foreign policy issue should never be forced to do. The resulting Harding landslide administered the death blow. When issues involving foreign affairs become a political football, they inevitably get kicked around.[5]

A dangerous type of partisanship occurred in 1952. The Republicans under Eisenhower were elected on the basis of slogans that seemed to promise "liberation" for the peoples of Central Europe who were "enslaved" in Communist chains. This appeal doubtless won many votes among Hungarian and Polish immigrants in America, but a premature uprising of these captive European peoples was the last thing that the Republican politicians really wanted. When the Hungarian revolt erupted in 1956, partly as a result of such false hopes, the inevitable slaughter did nothing to enhance the American image.

BIPARTISAN DIPLOMACY IS BETTER THAN PARTISAN DIPLOMACY

Politics, as we have seen, can never be completely divorced from foreign affairs. Recognizing this basic truth, Secretary Cordell Hull and other political leaders attempted during World War II to set up bipartisan consultations. They had especially in view averting a deadlock over the unborn United Nations such as had undone the League of Nations in 1919–1920. President Roosevelt, with an eye to Wilson's missteps, wisely chose Republican senators, as well as Democratic senators, to represent the United States during the drafting of the United Nations Charter in San Francisco in 1945.

[5] See Wesley M. Bagby, *The Road to Normalcy: The Presidential Campaign and Election of 1920* (1962).

The Senate subsequently approved the document by an overwhelming bipartisan vote.

This was bipartisanship, or rather nonpartisanship, at its best. But at times in subsequent years both Democratic and Republican administrations revealed a painful disinterest in bipartisanship. Noncooperation between the two parties seemed to be directly proportional to the proximity of the next election. When bipartisanship was employed, the general procedure was to inform rather than to consult—that is, to advise the other party in advance as to what decision had been taken, often without asking it to consider the issue while the discussions were going forward. Special problems were presented by the decisions to intervene in Korea (1950) and to force Russian missiles out of Cuba (1962). Time was pressing, so Presidents Truman and Kennedy consulted only with the leaders of both parties in Congress before taking their dramatic stands.[6]

But in many controversial instances, especially in the Far East after World War II, bipartisanship was a phrase rather than a fact. The opposition party in Congress all too often was presented with an irreversible decision. Many members, often with good reason, complained that they were consulted only on the crash landing, not on the takeoff.

Bipartisan dialogue *before* the takeoff, as well as at the time of the crash landing, is an ideal toward which we should work. The members of both parties are Americans; they pay taxes; and they die on the battlefield if the takeoff occurs at the wrong time or in the wrong place. The ultimate responsibility is, of course, with the administration in power, but prior consultation is advisable. It is not only good sense, but it blunts the edge of partisan opposition, which can sometimes be strong enough to wield a lethal knife. The fate of Wilson and the League of Nations continues to be instructive.

[6] Truman did not commit ground forces, though he did commit air and naval forces, before consulting with congressional leaders. Alfred Steinberg, *The Man from Missouri* (1962), pp. 377–378.

CHAPTER X

The Pressure of Public Opinion

"It is only governments that are stupid, not the masses of people."

PRESIDENT DWIGHT D. EISENHOWER, 1954

PROLOGUE

In an absolute monarchy, a dictatorship, or an oligarchy, the government is in the hands of a small group. Before the advent of Jacksonian manhood-suffrage democracy in the 1820's and 1830's, the electorate in the United States was limited by various qualifications. But once we had begun to count all white male heads as voters, we were forced to educate them so that they could run the government, *their* government, without courting disaster. Universal suffrage requires universal education.

The United States still suffers from the dragging anchor of millions of illiterates, dropouts, and semi-literate high school graduates. The overburdened schools are struggling to meet their problems, but the supremely discouraging fact is that the complexities of foreign affairs are increasing more rapidly than our faculties for comprehending them.

PUBLIC OPINION SHAPES FOREIGN POLICY
IN A DEMOCRACY

The government of a democracy is an *agent* of the people. The President and his bureaucracy cannot have, nor should they have, an independent or private policy of their own incompatible with the desires and aspirations of the voters. The Chief Executive should keep his finger more firmly on the public pulse than on the nuclear trigger. And he should make clear what his policy is, for whatever it is, it is ours.

On big issues, such as war with Spain in 1898, the Washington government receives guidance from the people, even though that guidance may be hysterical or shortsighted. On other issues, the guidance by the public is less clear. In these instances the officials in Washington must make assumptions, based on the national interest and on previous expressions of public opinion. The missile crisis in Cuba came with such secrecy and suddenness in 1962 that President Kennedy had no opportunity to sound out the people. So grave was the threat to our national existence that he enunciated a militant policy which he felt the masses would support—and they did.

In other conspicuous cases the administration has guessed wrong. President Franklin Roosevelt, speaking in Chicago in 1937, evidently went too far with his proposal for quarantining the aggressors. Recoiling in the face of the subsequent isolationist uproar, he retreated from his advanced position, and then endeavored to achieve his objectives in other ways, some of them devious.[1]

Sometimes small commitments, about which the public has little knowledge or no opinion, can lead to overwhelming commitments. This was tragically true in 1954, when the Eisenhower administration decided to back the Diem regime in South Vietnam with financial assistance, including military hardware. Most Americans probably did not know where the place was, but as they were

---

[1] There is evidence that the general reaction to the speech was more favorable than the isolationist outcry indicated. See T. B. Jacobs, "Roosevelt's 'Quarantine Speech,' " *The Historian*, XXIV (1962), pp. 483–502.

against Red China and fearfully anti-Communist, sending help to the South Vietnamese seemed like a wise precautionary move.

In short, a major policy that does not command public support is almost certain to fail. The statesmen-politicians in Washington know this, and since one of their basic aims is to be reelected, they will seldom adopt courses that fly in the teeth of public opinion or are likely not to win the support of a substantial segment of the voters. The public cannot make policy in detail, but it can direct the shaping of policy within broad channels. It can also, by voicing its displeasure, prevent a coherent policy from being proclaimed or an unpopular one from being pursued.

In truth, public opinion is often wiser than the policy-makers and the Congress.[2] In the dictator-mad 1930's, the polls showed that at times the people were more favorable to greater military preparedness than were the congressmen. This fact alone suggests that President Roosevelt should have used his persuasive powers of leadership more persistently. There is also strong evidence that the "I wanna go home" agitation, which caused the Truman administration to dismantle the American military machine after World War II with dangerously indecent haste, was supported by only a highly vocal minority. A series of opinion polls revealed that the public was willing to back a firmer stance against the Soviets than the administration evidently thought possible. The public often has to be "babied" less than many politicians think.

THE PUBLIC MUST BE EDUCATED
TO ITS RESPONSIBILITIES

Education is the primary task of the schools, the press, and other public agencies. When Washington embarks upon a "campaign of education" through its speechmakers, press releases, White Papers, and other media, it is accused of conducting a campaign of propaganda. The taxpayer-voter especially resents having his money used to propagandize himself; and he would be even more resentful if he were fully aware of how many hundreds of millions of dollars are involved.

Catastrophic events are the greatest educators of all. The down-

[2] Adlai Stevenson said in 1950, "I believe that in ninety-nine cases out of a hundred, the American people will make the right decision—if and when they are in possession of the essential facts about any given issues." Edward Hanna, *et al.*, eds., *The Wit and Wisdom of Adlai Stevenson* (1965), p. 29.

fall of France in 1940 was a crushing blow to American isolationism and America-Firstism. It enabled Franklin Roosevelt to gain sufficient public support to put over his fifty-destroyers-for-bases deal with Britain, followed by the epochal Lend-Lease Act for bolstering the embattled democracies.

A generation earlier President Wilson attempted to reverse more than a century of isolationism in favor of the internationalism that was embodied in the League of Nations. His campaign of education in behalf of this momentous shift was not launched soon enough, owing to preoccupation with World War I, and the Great Teacher himself collapsed while out on the platform. In the ensuing delay, drift, debate, and disillusionment, the public lost interest in the League of Nations and was content to let Europe work out its own salvation.

In certain critical periods, the government in Washington, assuming a "papa knows best" attitude, decides that what the people want is not good for them. John Adams, in the crisis of 1798–1800 with France, and Grover Cleveland, in the crisis of 1895–1896 over Cuba, courageously resisted the war hawks. In both instances a strident minority rather than a majority evidently favored war, and in both instances the President stood firm. Yet in 1898 President McKinley gave the people the war with Spain that they overwhelmingly demanded but probably should not have had. Many factors entered into his thinking, but presumably one of the most persuasive was a belief that in a democracy the people ultimately ruled, and that they should have what they wanted even if it was bad for them.[3]

DECEIVING THE PUBLIC IS UNDEMOCRATIC

President Franklin Roosevelt was caught in a world crisis in which he felt that he had to "do good by stealth." He warned the people repeatedly of the mounting danger from the dictators, but large segments responded lethargically or even resentfully, as in their reaction to his Quarantine Speech. A more forthright leader would probably have rung the alarm bell again and again and again. But Roosevelt, one of the less candid Presidents, believed

[3] In connection with the imminent hostilities with Germany in 1917, Colonel House reports a member of the Cabinet as saying that Wilson declared that "it did not make so much difference what the people wished as what was right." Charles Seymour, ed., *The Intimate Papers of Colonel House* (1926), II, p. 461.

that he could achieve his ends more quietly by easing the nation into a position of quasi-belligerency. As a consequence, we had the spectacular destroyers-bases deal, a daring lend-lease program, and outright misrepresentation, notably in his reporting of an attack which the U.S.S. *Greer* had provoked from a German submarine.

Roosevelt evidently concluded that since the people would not listen to him when he warned them of dire peril, he owed it to them to deceive them into an awareness of that peril.[4] He may have been right, but such a slippery course is paved with danger. It bespeaks a basic lack of faith in democracy and in a people who are "too damned dumb," as one wheel-horse politician put it, to know what is good for them.

OPINION POLLS CANNOT CONDUCT FOREIGN POLICY

Washington officialdom should not ignore the opinion polls, but it should not be unduly swayed by them. Oftentimes they merely reflect the abysmal state of public ignorance or indifference on complex issues. They are most useful when the question asked is open and shut. Secretary Dulles once remarked that he attached much importance to public opinion, but his primary responsibility was to choose the most beneficial policies. Sometimes he had to make such decisions before the public's views were known, and "often such decisions have to be based on circumstances so complicated that it's next to impossible for the majority of our people to understand them."[5]

Opinion polls are perhaps most reliable in ascertaining whether

[4] In my *The Man in the Street* (1948), p. 13, I unfortunately phrased this concept to mean that I was approving Roosevelt's course, not merely reporting it. Deliberate falsification is dangerous business. Republican Congresswoman Clare Boothe Luce charged in 1944 that Roosevelt had "lied us into a war because he did not have the political courage to lead us into it." (*New York Times,* Oct. 14, 1944, 9:2.) When being considered by the Senate for the ambassadorship to Brazil in 1959, she publicly regretted this statement.

[5] Andrew H. Berding, *Dulles on Diplomacy* (1965), p. 139. American public opinion strongly favored cutting off oil shipments during World War II to "neutral" Spain. Ambassador C. J. H. Hayes, an ex-history professor and a noncareer diplomat, favored increasing oil shipments so as not to drive Spain into the Nazi camp. He aroused much criticism at home by adopting the policy of doing what he thought best, and then hoping that public opinion could be changed, rather than letting public opinion govern. See his *Wartime Mission in Spain, 1942–1945* (1945), p. 148.

the public favors one political candidate over another. They are least useful when they require intimate knowledge of a foreign problem—a problem regarding which a small army of experts may be at odds.

The polls, moreover, have proved defective in measuring intensity of feeling. In the late 1930's, American opinion was pro-Chinese and anti-Japanese, and it overwhelmingly favored halting the shipment to Japan of all cargoes of aviation gasoline, scrap iron, and other war materiel. But such action would have involved cutting off similar though much smaller aid to China, and Roosevelt resisted this pressure for about four years. China was far away, and the opinion expressed was not intense. If it had been, the Washington government simply would never have dared to flout the wishes of the people.[6] Intensity of feeling by a majority of the people, or a lack of such feeling, constricts or enlarges the area of maneuver in which the policy-makers in Washington may operate.

Above all, the administration should never confuse public opinion with pressure-group opinion of an organized nature, especially form letters and telegrams. Pro-Franco Catholics in America, wielding political power out of proportion to their numbers, induced President Roosevelt to pursue a hands-off policy regarding the Spanish Civil War, greatly to the advantage of General Franco. For several decades the so-called "China lobby" in Washington kept up pressure on behalf of Chiang Kai-shek's anti-Communist regime, especially after it had fled to Formosa.

Policies dictated by minority groups are seldom in the interest of the majority. On several conspicuous occasions we have witnessed the absurdity of American longshoremen attempting to make or sabotage foreign policy by refusing to service the ships of certain foreign nations. In 1964 the International Longshoremen, partly for economic reasons, refused for nine days to load wheat onto ships for famine-threatened Russia, even though Washington had determined upon a hands-across-the-Baltic policy.

[6] Even dictators are concerned about public opinion, and propaganda is the tribute they pay to it. When Stalin asked at Yalta for concessions in the Far East in return for the use of his army, he declared that his war-ravaged people, while realizing why they were fighting Germany, "would not understand why Russians would enter a war against a country with which they had no great trouble." *Foreign Relations of the United States, Diplomatic Papers: The Conferences at Malta and Yalta, 1945* (1955), p. 769.

SECRECY CLASHES WITH DEMOCRACY
IN FOREIGN AFFAIRS

Sound policy must be based on public support. Yet the public cannot give its support, or cannot know what it is supporting, if it is kept in ignorance, partial or complete. Frequently all of the facts cannot be divulged because of possible international complications. This is but one of the many paradoxes of a democratic foreign policy.

The half-secret, half-open, in-and-out support that the Kennedy administration gave to the Bay of Pigs invasion in 1961 resulted in an abysmal abortion. The press got wind of what was going on, but "killed" the news so as not to undercut the government. Were these newsmen derelict in their duty in refusing to expose the whole dubious enterprise before it could be launched? Or did they have a higher obligation not to aid Castro? These questions are not easy to answer.

The "right to know" is becoming a sacred American principle, especially among journalists, to whom news is bread and butter. But the right to know clashes directly with the right of the government to govern effectively. On more than one occasion, conspicuously at the time of the U-2 spy-plane embarrassment of 1960, overwhelming pressure from the news hawks for statements resulted in slippery official denials. Freedom *from* the press can at times be as important as freedom *of* the press. The government has to learn to live with the newsmen, and be constantly on its guard not to be betrayed into fatal indiscretions.

Another problem is that the Washington officials must be careful not to educate the enemy while educating their own people. We are a nation of notorious blabbermouths. Through public media and official spokesmen we probably provide our adversaries with far more valuable information than they can secure through cloak-and-dagger espionage. During the hearings before the Senate Foreign Relations Committee on Vietnam, in 1966, Defense Secretary McNamara, in response to partisan criticism of shortages, gave out incredibly specific figures as to the number of bombs available.[7]

---

[7] *The New York Times*, April 21, 1966, 1:8.

NEVER RAISE PUBLIC EXPECTATIONS TOO HIGH

The "undersell" is better than the "oversell." If a policy falls short of expectations, there is disappointment; if it gains more than expectations, there is satisfaction. During World War I, George Creel and his Committee on Public Information grossly oversold Woodrow Wilson, his Fourteen Points, and his vision of a better tomorrow. Tens of millions of propaganda pieces raised up unrealizable hopes the world over, especially among oppressed minorities in Europe. When Wilson at Paris fell short of these ambitious goals, a sense of failure, not altogether justified, clung to his peacemaking labors.

A whole people, like a single individual, can be keyed up only so long without something giving way. The American masses, disappointed in Wilson and disillusioned by grasping Allies, experienced a fateful letdown. They not only turned their backs on Europe and Wilson but on the ideals for which he had stood.

An additional source of disillusionment was our failure to "hang the Kaiser"—a goal that had been widely proclaimed during America's "holy crusade." Wilhelm II appeared to be the Devil incarnate; and, with childish naivety, we blamed the whole war on him. (The public, which swallows simple and personalized explanations too readily, is inclined to accept the Devil Theory of history.) But during World War II we fought with much more sophistication. There was some loose talk about hanging Hitler, Hirohito, and Mussolini, but it never approached the volume and vindictiveness of World War I.

Fortunately, the American public is becoming more mature as its world responsibilities become weightier.

CRITICISM AT HOME WEAKENS POLICY ABROAD

Free speech is one of the prices that we have to pay for our democracy. (It is certainly not one of the burdens under which dictators labor.) Public criticism in time of peace cannot be suppressed, except by more or less subtle pressures. Criticism in time of war can be suppressed by law (e.g., sedition acts) and by public pressures (e.g., mob action). But such repression leads to grave abuses, as was lamentably true in America during World War I, when many pro-Germans were roughly handled.[8]

A diplomatic adversary can easily draw erroneous conclusions from the vocal criticism of a minority, which is often mistaken for a majority. On the eve of the War of 1812 London officialdom interpreted the abuse showered upon the Madison administration by Federalist New England as indicating paralyzing divisions. The British assumed that a regime so divided at home would not or could not fight abroad, and partly for this reason took such a stubborn stand against neutral rights as to force the United States into the abyss.

America's undeclared war in Vietnam during the 1960's encountered much opposition from "Vietniks" and other critics, who staged "teach-ins" and similar demonstrations. Beyond a doubt, these manifestations of disunity strengthened the determination of the enemy to hold on until public opinion could force a withdrawal of American forces.[9]

NEW POLICIES ARE MORE PALATABLE UNDER OLD NAMES

The Monroe Doctrine has endured partly because it became attached to an honored name of one of our more respected Presidents, a man who knew George Washington and other Founding Fathers. It must therefore be something of a sacred cow, whether we know what it means or not.

In 1904 President Theodore Roosevelt, faced with menacing European debt collectors in the Caribbean, decided to rewrite the Monroe Doctrine. The original concept meant: "Europe, you stay out of America and we'll keep out of Europe." The new principle meant: "We'll go into the Caribbean republics in order to keep you out." If this policy had been labeled the New Roosevelt Doctrine, it might have died aborning. But Roosevelt was fortunate enough to have it called the Roosevelt Corollary to the Monroe Doctrine. Un-

---

[8] See H. C. Peterson and G. C. Fite, *Opponents of War, 1917–1918* (1957).

[9] Similarly, the Filipino insurrectos under Aguinaldo, in their war against American troops (1899–1902), drew encouragement to resist from the outspoken opposition of the anti-imperialists in the United States.

der these hallowed auspices it had a long and rather inglorious life, highlighted by many landings of United States marines on Caribbean shores.[10] Freedom of the seas was a sacred principle to which we were wedded while a small-navy nation, especially during the early nineteenth century. It meant that the merchantmen of all neutral nations had the right to ply the high seas with noncontraband cargoes. In 1941, while implementing the Lend-Lease Act, Franklin Roosevelt clandestinely used American destroyers to shepherd merchant ships laden with American-donated weapons toward British ports. When German submarines, in response to hostile action by these destroyers, fired back, Roosevelt went on the radio and proclaimed that the historic principle of freedom of the seas had been violated by these "rattlesnakes" of the seas. This, of course, was a gross perversion of the original principle, but it commanded greater acceptance because it was attached to a popular and time-honored dictum for which we had fought Britain during the War of 1812.

Many people will lend their support to ancient doctrines, no matter how perverted, partly because they want to parade their patriotism, and partly because they do not want to confess their ignorance.

PERSONAL INTEREST INSURES PUBLIC SUPPORT

President Wilson commanded enthusiastic support for a limited time, from 1917 to 1919, when he preached idealism and self-sacrifice, while spurning the spoils of war. But the American people gradually lost interest in further do-goodism as they observed their ex-Allies running off with colonies, ships, reparations, and other booty.

The American public is shortsighted and short-memoried. It is impatient to see immediate returns, rather than returns ten years hence under an Alliance for Progress program of some sort.

The long-range Marshall Plan of 1947 was not easy to "sell" to the American people, even though they themselves would derive

[10] Niccolò Machiavelli, in *The Prince* (1532), argued that he who would reform a government must "retain the semblance of the old forms" so that the people will think there has been no change.

economic benefits from it. The necessary appropriations were lan-guishing in Congress when the Communist rape of Czechoslovakia in 1948 provided a brutal object lesson. The log-jammed funds were then approved, and the momentum of events propelled us into the multination North Atlantic Treaty Organization the following year.

Self-interest should, if possible, be kept to the fore. One recalls the words of an old-time Tammany politician, "What's in it for Mrs. Murphy and the children?"

WORLD OPINION IS A POTENT FORCE

Ever since its birth, the United States has worried about its "image" abroad. The Declaration of Independence sonorously de-clares that "a decent respect to the opinions of mankind" required some kind of explanation of the epochal break with Britain.

Lincoln issued the Emancipation Proclamation of 1863 with the European powers largely in mind. He sought to win their sympathy, if not their support, by avowing his determination to end the black blight of chattel slavery. In some respects the Emancipation Procla-mation was more important as a diplomatic document than as a domestic one; it elevated the moral cause of the Union to a higher plane.

President Truman, with immediate military objectives in mind, was evidently not much concerned about world opinion when he ordered the dropping of two atomic bombs on Japan in August, 1945. Foreign peoples in general, and Asiatic peoples in particular, have since then insisted that the war could have been won without the bombs; that the lethal effects of radiation may be found in the genes and bones of generations yet unborn; that the two atomic bombs were the only nuclear weapons ever employed in anger; that they were dropped on colored peoples; and that, if available in time, they would not have been used against the white Germans.[11]

Some of these conclusions have been challenged. But a stub-born fact remains; the reaction against the two monster bombs

---

[11] For the interesting but questionable thesis that the atomic bomb was dropped largely to impress Russia and keep her in line after the war see Gar Alperovitz, *Atomic Diplomacy: Hiroshima and Potsdam* (1965). There were other and more pressing reasons for using the bomb.

has been so unfavorable that the employment of such weapons was inadvisable in the Korean "police action" and then in the Vietnam war. World opinion has been and continues to be a powerful restraining force.

THE NATIONAL INTEREST IS PARAMOUNT TO WORLD OPINION

The United States, if completely hard-boiled, would attach little significance to the opinion of those countries that carry little weight. What African nations like Upper Volta and Mali think of us is of no vital consequence. We have few real friends in the world for the simple reason that a nation so big, so rich, and so powerful is universally envied, resented, or feared. President de Gaulle of France reportedly remarked that "A great country worthy of the name does not have any friends." We cannot hope to be loved; we can only hope to be respected and trusted.

About one-third of the world dwells in the Communist camp, which will routinely condemn much of what we do. The opinion thus expressed will not be that of the people but only that of the government and the propaganda machines that keep the masses in darkness. Obviously if the interests of the United States are best served by pursuing a course which they disapprove, they should be ignored.

The world reaction to nuclear testing was an eye-opener. In 1961 the Soviets, working behind a smoke screen of test-ban talks in Geneva, abruptly and spectacularly ended the informal moratorium on nuclear explosions in the atmosphere. But practically no condemnation came from the Communist world, surprisingly little from the uncommitted world, and a good deal from the free world.[12] When President Kennedy concluded that the Soviets would gain an intolerable advantage by their testing, he reluctantly and belatedly gave the order to follow suit. An outburst of condemnation came from the Communist world, a surprising outcry from the uncommitted world (much more than in the case of the Soviet testing), and a great deal from the free world.

The policy-makers in Washington must be realistic. When faced

---

[12] The General Assembly of the UN merely "noted with regret" the resumption of Soviet testing. Arthur H. Dean, *Test Ban and Disarmament* (1966), p. 90.

with any given problem engaging world opinion, they must decide whether on balance we have more to gain than to lose by pursuing a contemplated course. World opinion seemed to be strongly opposed to the Vietnam intervention in the mid-1960's, but Washington persisted. The Johnson administration reasoned, whether mistakenly or not, that the interests of this nation, not to mention those of the free world, would be best served by "containing" Communism in Southeast Asia.

The crushing of the Hungarian revolt in 1956 by Soviet tanks, though widely condemned in the free world, points up certain harsh lessons. First, such brutal episodes tend to fade into the past as other events, some no less brutal, crowd upon the world stage. Second, the quick and complete collapse of the Hungarian freedom fighters shows how fruitless it is to argue at length about a disagreeable reality established by overweening power. And finally, the free world, precisely because it is free, is far more sensitive to adverse criticism than are peoples of the Communist world. They are seldom told that their governments are being criticized.

PART III

Diplomatic Techniques

CHAPTER XI

Top-Level Diplomacy

"Diplomacy is primarily a matter of understanding and experience. It distinctly is not a matter of learning. You cannot teach diplomacy. You can teach many things it is useful for a diplomat to know—but that does not make a diplomat."

HUGH GIBSON, EX-U.S. AMBASSADOR, 1938

PROLOGUE

Diplomacy is defined by the veteran diplomat Sir Harold Nicolson as "the management of the relations between independent States by the processes of negotiation."

Secretary of State Dulles compared the art of diplomacy to that of sailing. The helmsman sees his destination straight ahead, but because of adverse winds or currents, he must tack and approach his landing obliquely, often many miles out of his way. "Sometimes, too," Dulles added, "you may be becalmed and unable to make any headway whatever. At other times you may have to trim your sails. Moving ahead in foreign relations calls for the sailor's attributes of patience, strength, endurance, and eternal vigilance." [1]

In brief, the delicate art of diplomacy calls not only for talents of the highest order but for hard work as well.

[1] Andrew H. Berding, *Dulles on Diplomacy* (1965), p. 164.

SUMMIT DIPLOMACY IS DANGEROUS DIPLOMACY

The highest peaks are the most windswept and snow-covered; they take human life, and missteps often occur in full public view.

The first President to attend a summit conference was Woodrow Wilson, an amateur diplomatist, as most Presidents have been. He journeyed to Paris in 1919 to do battle for the Fourteen Points in the hurly-burly of a noisy conclave. He returned a wiser and somewhat disillusioned man.

Franklin Roosevelt traveled to Quebec, Casablanca, Cairo, Teheran, and Yalta, among other far places. But the fruits, notably at Yalta, were not always sweet. Harry S Truman tangled with Stalin at Potsdam in 1945, and he was so badly shaken by the experience that he resolved to attend no more summit conferences, and he never did.

General-President Eisenhower, a seasoned warrior, likewise grew gun-shy. He could not be induced to go abroad until he went to the summit at Geneva in 1955. The temporarily happy "Spirit of Geneva" evaporated as the Soviets quickly junked certain principles that they presumably had accepted. Eisenhower reportedly remarked that "this idea of the President of the United States going personally abroad to negotiate—it's just damn stupid. Every time a President has gone abroad to get into the details of these things, he's lost his shirt." [2]

Eisenhower learned even more about summit conferences when he flew to Paris in 1960, following the U-2 spy-plane mishap, only to be upbraided by Premier Khrushchev of Russia. He did not lose his shirt, but he almost lost his temper. One lesson was reaffirmed by this experience: nations cannot negotiate from frozen positions, especially when taken publicly. Prior to the abortive Paris conclave, both the U.S.S.R. and the U.S.A. had proclaimed their inflexible stand on the explosive Berlin deadlock. In these circumstances there was little point in holding a summit conference, except as a propaganda sounding board for the Soviets, and even in this capacity it backfired.

The presumption is strong that the Soviets clamored for summit conferences during the Cold War years primarily for propa-

---

[2] Emmet J. Hughes, *The Ordeal of Power* (1963), p. 151.

ganda purposes. They could pose on the world stage as sole guardians of the dove of peace; their leaders could gain stature by being photographed with the American President and other eminent leaders. This was evidently true at the Geneva Conference of 1955, where photographs were taken of a smiling President Eisenhower beaming on a smirking Premier Bulganin of Russia. These pictures, with the other members present cleverly cropped out, were distributed wholesale by the Soviets in their satellite countries. The obvious purpose was to make these subject peoples more subservient by proving pictorially that the United States applauded the wardens who had enchained them.

SUMMIT DIPLOMACY IS INEFFICIENT DIPLOMACY

Many critics contended that President Wilson would have done better as a peacemaker in 1919 if he had remained in Washington, far from the Parisian pressures of personal contact. There, unhurriedly, and unfatigued he could have made crucial decisions when fresh and clear headed. After a top negotiator in a man-to-man conference has repeatedly said "no" to the chief representative of another state, the pressure mounts to say "yes" occasionally, whether an affirmative answer is wise or not. A normal man dislikes to offend his host repeatedly. Friendships not only form but antipathies deepen, such as Clemenceau's contempt for Wilson, and tend to deflect the negotiator from a single-minded pursuit of the national interest.[3]

The President, as the Chief of State with many other responsibilities weighing on his mind, simply does not have the time and energy to bone up on all complicated international problems. On the other hand, the professional diplomat can devote full time to his task. A sickly and exhausted President Roosevelt journeyed to Yalta with stacks of briefing papers, but he clearly gave them little more than a somewhat perfunctory thumbing. Moreover, the absence of the Chief Executive slows down the machinery of government at home, not only in other important phases of foreign policy but in domestic affairs as well.

Ex-Ambassador George F. Kennan and other professionals have

[3] The "realistic" Clemenceau allegedly growled that the "idealistic" Wilson talked like Jesus Christ but acted like Lloyd George, the British Prime Minister.

long argued that the summit is the wrong spot for pressing problems. The gestation of a successful conference, declared the experienced Sir Harold Nicolson, is about as long as the gestation of a baby elephant (twenty-one to twenty-two months). After the experts have gone to the bottom of a problem and carefully worked out recommendations, the President can go to the top in an effort to achieve these goals. This is the proper procedure if the adversaries are striving for a fair understanding, involving reciprocal concessions, rather than a prolonged propaganda circus. In truth, each side should give convincing evidence of seriousness of purpose in lower-level discussions before they are taken to the summit for "instant diplomacy" or "diplomacy by loudspeaker." As Dean Rusk has pointed out, "The direct confrontation of the chiefs of government of the great powers involves an extra tension because the court of last resort is in session." [4]

STATESMEN SHOULD NOT LEAN
TOO HEAVILY ON LUCK

During the early years of the Republic we were perhaps the most fortunate of nations. We had weak neighbors north and south, vast oceans east and west. In Europe, which constituted the only real threat, the monarchies were bogged down in their own wars, or the balance of power quivered in delicate equipoise. No one nation felt completely free to tackle the upstart Yankees, lest it be stabbed in the back by neighbors who were powerful, envious, greedy, or vengeful—sometimes all four.

During the first flush of our youth we were able to grow and expand, thanks to these fortuitous circumstances. The convulsions of Europe shook rich diplomatic plums into our basket, notably the French alliance of 1778, the Paris Peace Treaty of 1783, the Pinckney Treaty of 1795, and the Louisiana Purchase treaties of 1803. Many Americans wrongly attributed these triumphs primarily to the skill of our "militia" diplomats or to the justice of our case. If we could achieve such dramatic successes with only diplomatic skill and a righteous cause, why bother to go to the trouble and expense of

[4] Dean Rusk, "The President," *Foreign Affairs*, XXXVIII (April, 1960), p. 365. This article was read by John F. Kennedy and evidently had something to do with Rusk's being offered the Secretaryship of State. Arthur M. Schlesinger, Jr., *A Thousand Days* (1965), p. 141.

creating potent armies and navies? Why enter into entangling alliances? The twentieth century, especially after World War I, provided a harsh corrective. Increasingly the distresses of Europe and Asia became our distresses; if we let these peoples "go to pot," we were likely to be sucked into the pot with them, as was distressingly true in 1917 and again in 1941. We could no longer count on the British navy, when the policies of Britain and America ran parallel (as they often did not), to provide an oaken bulwark behind which we could enjoy so-called "free security." [5] We were forced to build an enormous army, navy, and air force of our own. Some Americans began to feel a degree of sympathy in the 1960's for President de Gaulle of France. He contended that, when the chips were down, we would not come to the defense of Europe if we had to risk losing all of our cities to nuclear attack. Accordingly, he undertook to build up a small nuclear capability of his own.

TAKE CALCULATED RISKS

While luck is a fickle ally, it can on occasion prove to be a fruitful ally. Diplomatic tactics are like military tactics, and the able statesman, like the able general, must leave something to chance. Napoleon's maxim was not to risk more than one-third on the iron dice. All life is a gamble, and one seldom has the chance to bet on sure things. Where nothing is ventured, little is usually gained, except where blind luck comes into play.

But this does not mean that one must throw caution overboard and not give the most careful thought to the consequences of any proposed action. Good precepts to keep in mind are "When in doubt do nothing" and "Doing nothing is better than doing the wrong

[5] "Free security" was presumably provided by geographical location, buttressed by three thousand miles of ocean. But "free security" is like free love; it can be costly in the end. The fixation of "free security" caused Americans to be grossly unprepared for all of their wars, especially to 1917. The cost of supplementing "free security" with adequate military and naval defense was probably less than that of the wars we might have stayed out of if we had possessed such deterrent arms, notably the War of 1812 and World War I. The total cost would include physical destruction (the burning of Washington), the loss of tens of thousands of lives (a loss beyond calculation), the treatment of the wounded and crippled, and pensions for the war veterans. For a contrary view on "free security," see C. Vann Woodward, "The Age of Reinterpretation," *American Historical Review,* LXVI (Oct., 1960), pp. 1–19.

thing." [6] Time, as we shall see, will often solve problems without having a diplomat rush in with both arms waving. We fought vainly against impressment in the War of 1812, but as the so-called "Peaceful Century" came to Europe, the British navy ultimately gave up this brutal practice in favor of more humane and more efficient enlistment techniques.

The element of chance can often be reduced by sounding out one's adversary in advance as to his reactions. In 1909 Secretary Knox bluntly proposed to both Russia and Japan that they arrange to turn over their vital railroad holdings in Manchuria to the Chinese. The response was a stinging rebuff from Tokyo and St. Petersburg. This reaction, which could easily have been anticipated, might well have been avoided by some judicious preliminary feelers.

President Kennedy's partial Nuclear Test-Ban Treaty of 1963 is a prize example of risk-taking diplomacy. The signatories, including the Soviet Union, agreed to refrain from nuclear testing in the open air or under water, while retaining the right to conduct their experiments underground. Many suspicious Americans feared that the Russians might secretly "cheat," and thereby gain an intolerable advantage over the United States. But the devices for detecting such illegal tests were so sophisticated that the element of risk was virtually eliminated, especially in view of the right of any signatory to withdraw after giving three months' notice.

The gain from a purer atmosphere seemingly outweighed the possible fruits of faithlessness, and as a consequence the United States Senate took the risk, albeit with much reluctance.

TROUBLE CREATES OPPORTUNITIES

A statesman should capitalize on the opportunity "to fish in troubled waters."

The United States in the nineteenth century was often the fish, conspicuously during the Civil War, when Napoleon III frontally challenged the Monroe Doctrine. Taking advantage of the death grapple between the North and South, he propped up a puppet

---

[6] A sound practice is to put a protest on record, even if one expects to do nothing. Having established the claim, one may later press it. The United States belatedly reserved its rights following the highly irregular mining of the North Sea by the British in World War I.

emperor on the throne of the Montezumas in Mexico and supported him with strong contingents of French troops. His luck ran out when the sands of the Confederacy ran out.

A corollary maxim is that a statesman should always leave his hands free to exploit these openings as they develop. In the mid-1960's an ideological quarrel produced a momentous rift between Red Russia and Red China. But we were so deeply bogged down in the mud and muck of Vietnam that we could not take full advantage of this opportunity to widen the rift. On the contrary, the strong-arm policies to which we committed ourselves in Vietnam had a strong tendency to drive the two name-calling allies back together.

KEEP THE DIPLOMATIC INITIATIVE

The best defense is often an unexpected offense, whether militarily or diplomatically.

During the Cold War freeze after World War II, the Soviet Union seemed to be enjoying the offensive most of the time. The actions of Washington were often merely reactions to Moscow's actions. This kind of diplomacy is purely negative and defensive, though often necessary and usually better than nothing.

But the amount of American negativism has often been exaggerated by partisan critics. On a number of occasions we seized the initiative and threw Moscow off balance. A prime example occurred at Geneva, in 1955, when President Eisenhower unveiled with much fanfare his "open skies" proposal.[7] In the interests of reducing the tensions in the current arms race, he proposed that the Soviets and Americans permit mutual aerial inspection to guarantee that there was no alarming buildup of armaments.

In view of Russia's age-long obsession with secrecy, President Eisenhower could hardly have expected the Soviets to embrace his scheme. They spurned it out of hand. But the result was to put the initiative temporarily in the hands of the Americans, produce some confusion in Soviet ranks, and improve our image as keeper of the dove of peace. All this probably was about as much as Eisenhower really hoped to gain.

---

[7] See Dwight D. Eisenhower, *Waging Peace* (1965), p. 470.   .

EXPECT THE UNEXPECTED

In diplomatic warfare, as in armed warfare, one should be prepared for all possible eventualities. One should never completely rule out what may happen if everything goes wrong. The astute diplomatist should be braced for confusing power shifts, and then try to take advantage of them. We readily recall the complexities created by the turnabout Russo–German pact of 1939 that was the curtain-raiser for World War II; by Hitler's bewildering attack on Russia in 1941; and by the sudden invasion of South Korea by the North Koreans in 1950.

Never underestimate an opponent's daring or overestimate his stupidity. At the time of the Pearl Harbor blowup we assumed that the Japanese, even if they had the capability, would not be so fool-hardy as to unite the American people by the one act best calculated to achieve that end. Similarly, at the time of the Cuban missile crisis in 1962 we assumed that the Soviets were not daring enough or foolish enough to provoke us by turning nearby Cuba into a missile launching pad.[8]

In sum, the diplomatist should anticipate all probable counter-moves, and some improbable ones to boot. In 1956, when Secretary Dulles withdrew the offer to Egypt to finance the High Dam on the upper Nile, he should not have been surprised, as he evidently was, by Egypt's response in nationalizing the Suez Canal. Indeed, this was the most predictable countermove, given President Nasser's need to save face.

One should not only expect the unexpected but also keep one's adversaries guessing. As a rule fuzziness is not desirable in diplo-macy, but occasionally purposeful ambiguity will serve the national interest.[9] In 1955, when Congress passed the Formosa Resolution empowering the President to come to the defense of Chiang's exiled regime, the authors deliberately left vague any intention of defend-ing the tiny offshore islands of Quemoy and Matsu. To have included or excluded them would have reduced flexibility.

[8] For perceptive comparisons of the two incidents, see Roberta Wohlstetter, "Cuba and Pearl Harbor: Hindsight and Foresight," *Foreign Affairs*, XLIII (July, 1965), pp. 691–707.

[9] As the Yalta and Potsdam disputes demonstrated, the Soviets like agree-ments of such ambiguity that they can interpret them their own way while professing to abide by them.

PEACETIME DIPLOMACY INVOLVES TIT FOR TAT

At the end of a war, the victor may hold his pistol to the head of the vanquished and force him to sign on the dotted line. This in effect was what the Allies did to Germany at Versailles in 1919. In time of peace, one has to give up something to get something, unless one is prepared to seize it with arms, as President Polk seized California. Negotiation without concession is doomed to failure, or, as Napoleon Bonaparte put it in 1802, "To negotiate is not to do as one likes." [10] But concession should normally come at the end of a negotiation, rather than at the beginning; and if the agreement is a fair one, there should normally be about equal satisfaction and dissatisfaction on both sides. Diplomacy may even be defined as the art of avoiding extremes.

Give-and-take inevitably involves compromise, and this practice has led to much misunderstanding. The Munich "surrender" of 1938 proved to be a one-sided compromise, but a compromise nonetheless: the yielding of a large part of Czechoslovakia to Hitler in return for his promise to take no more of it. In this way the desperately unprepared British bought a year of time. But Munich turned out badly, and thereafter many people thought that any peaceful accommodation with aggressors was folly, that is, if one read aright the "lessons" of history. One is reminded of Mark Twain's cat, which sat down on a hot stove lid. It learned its lesson so well that thereafter it would never sit down on any stove lid, hot or cold.

A corollary maxim is that one should never surrender a bargaining piece without exacting an equivalent. By late 1962 the Washington government had secretly decided to withdraw its obsolescent Jupiter nuclear missiles from Turkey and Italy, all pointed at the Soviet Union. Critics insisted that wise diplomacy would have extracted a concession for a move that was in the cards anyhow. When the missiles were finally withdrawn some three months after the nerve-racking Cuban crisis, the rumormongers declared that this was all part of a secret bargain with the Soviets in regard to Cuba.

[10] J. C. Herold, ed., *The Mind of Napoleon* (1955), p. 170. In fact, peacetime treaties ordinarily involve some yielding of sovereignty, or denying one's self certain rights in return for others. The twelve-nation Antarctica Treaty of 1959 bound the signatories, including the U.S. and the U.S.S.R., to exclude warfare from the region and to preserve it for scientific research.

Where a *quid pro quo* is involved, a nation should not forget what it received while lamenting what it lost. At the Washington Conference of 1921–1922, the United States induced Japan to accept the small end of a 5–5–3 ratio in capital ship tonnage, in return for a pledge not to fortify further our holdings in the Philippines and Guam. In later years we berated ourselves for having made this concession, conveniently forgetting that without it there might not have been any agreement whatever on armaments.

We should also remember that a hard bargain is a bitter bargain, especially when we are dealing with weak countries. A rich nation can afford to be generous, and the wise negotiator would usually be well advised to give the other side a face-saving bauble to take home.[11] The one-sided treaties with Panama over the canal zone and with Cuba over Guantánamo were hard bargains, and the United States has reaped a rich and continuing harvest of resentment.

THE BEST IS THE ENEMY OF THE GOOD

The Treaty of 1783, by which Britain granted us our independence plus a princely domain, was not a complete treaty. Ideally, it should have contained provisions for regularizing commerce with the young Republic. Yet the territorial advantages offered were so great, and the possibilities of their being withdrawn were so disturbing, that the three American negotiators in Paris settled for a generally satisfactory treaty rather than the best possible one. They hoped that the commercial pact would come later, as it did in Jay's Treaty of 1794.

In 1945 the United States, bitter against a "treacherous" Japan, held out for her unconditional surrender. This sloganized policy appealed strongly to vengeance-minded America. But here the seemingly best conditions (unconditional surrender) proved to be the enemy of good conditions (conditional surrender). The United States finally agreed to back down and accept a surrender condi-

---

[11] This rule can be applied to treaties at the end of wars. In 1848 the United States seized about half of Mexico, and then paid the Mexicans $18,250,000. The Mexican leader Santa Anna could claim that he had won, because the victor seldom pays an indemnity.

tioned upon the Japanese keeping their emperor. If this concession had been offered sooner, the war in the Far East might have ended months earlier and without the horrors of atomic bombing.

Diplomats should take care not to cling stubbornly to a lesser advantage at the cost of a greater, or spurn a fair settlement in the hope of getting an impossibly good one. In 1806 the British negotiated a treaty with the United States under which they made important trade concessions, and were prepared to give *unofficial* assurances regarding the impressment of our seamen. But President Jefferson refused to approve the treaty because it contained no *official* renunciation of impressment, and the result was that we got nothing—except a steady drift toward the War of 1812.

A quail in the hand is worth two in the thicket.

COME TO TERMS WITH THE INEVITABLE

A prudent statesman learns to tolerate or acquiesce in what he cannot possibly prevent, or prevent at too high a price, even though he may not approve of it.

At Yalta in 1945, President Roosevelt acquiesced in Soviet control of much of Eastern Europe and partial control of China's Manchuria. These were two key areas where the Soviets were determined to assert their power and where they had large armies already on the ground. We could not conceivably have halted them except by inviting another war at a time when World War II was yet to be won. By consenting to these takeovers, Roosevelt was able to win an important concession—or what seemed to be an important concession at the time—namely a promise from Stalin that he would enter the Far Eastern war with his army in time to help crush Japan.

In brief, accept what you cannot avert, and trade your acquiescence for a concession or at least good will. This is substantially what President Theodore Roosevelt did in 1905 when he consented to Japan's absorbing Korea. The Japanese, on their part, reciprocated by disavowing aggressive designs on the American-held Philippines.[12]

[12] R. A. Esthus, "The Taft–Katsura Agreement—Reality or Myth," *Journal of Modern History*, XXXI (1959), pp. 46–51.

DIPLOMACY IS A FIRST LINE OF DEFENSE

It is obvious that in this Atomic Age diplomacy is cheaper than fighting, for the cost of a world war in one day is far greater than that of the entire diplomatic service for one year. The frock-coated warriors are no less essential than grenade-bearing warriors. The typewriter is often mightier than the machine gun, as President Wilson demonstrated when he personally drafted his formidable Fourteen Points.

Diplomacy is a species of warfare to which many military maxims are applicable. One is "Never lose contact with the enemy," because of lack of contact multiplies the possibilities of a sharp surprise.[13] America's policy of quarantine against Communist China after 1948–1949 resulted in a self-imposed handicap on our diplomacy. We almost certainly would have known better what the Red Chinese were cooking up if we were not forced to get so much of our information at second hand through questionable sources.

Another relevant military maxim is "Never wittingly or willingly give hostages to a potential enemy." Canada during the nineteenth century was a hostage unwittingly given by Britain to the United States for her good behavior. But in 1899 we took over the Philippines, in Japan's backyard, and shortsightedly gave to Japan a hostage, which Theodore Roosevelt called an Achilles' heel.

A useful diplomatic-military guideline is "Divide and conquer," or "Play both ends against the middle." During the nineteenth century the powers of Europe tried this tactic against America by propping up an independent Texas and by encouraging the Confederacy to stand fast. All this was in pursuance of the principle, "Stay in with the outs," especially if there is some real hope of their winning.

Another related military precept is "When two of your enemies fall out, support the weaker." This explains our backing of Stalin after Hitler turned against him in 1941. We played the same game with some success after 1948, when we began our expensive support of Marshal Tito's deviationist Yugoslavia. The success of this policy was attested by the speedy collapse of Communist guerrilla warfare in adjoining Greece, and by further defections from the Soviet

---

[13] The Soviets could have vetoed the UN intervention in Korea if they had not boycotted the sessions of the Security Council at this time.

camp. In fact, much of the foreign aid program of the United States after World War II was bottomed on the principle of divide and conquer. It seems also to have paid dividends in Indonesia, with the collapse of the abortive Communist takeover in 1966.

Still another military-diplomatic maxim is "Get the big ones first," whether warships in a naval battle or objectives in a diplomatic battle. This rule explains why the United States, in the years after 1945, poured billions of dollars into Europe, where the stakes were enormous, and only millions into Latin America, where the stakes seemed minor or at best secondary.

Likewise relevant are the admonitions, "Keep your adversary off balance" or "Don't tip your hand too soon." President Kennedy was tempted to confront the Soviets with the evidence as soon as he discovered that they were sneaking missiles into Cuba in 1962. If he had done so, they could have blunted his strategy by various defensive maneuvers. But by holding back until he was fully prepared to establish his naval "quarantine," he caught the Kremlin off guard and rather bewildered and indecisive.[14]

A final diplomatic principle with military overtones is "Beware of too little and too late." The obvious example is the Bay of Pigs botch in Cuba, where President Kennedy followed a course of half-in and half-out. Either we should have gone in to win or we should have stayed out altogether.

GREAT POWERS CAN AFFORD TO LOSE FACE

Diplomacy, like other forms of politics, is the art of the possible, of the attainable, often of the second best. Nations simply have to learn to live with some situations, provided that the cost is not intolerably high.

The United States lost much face at Cuba's Bay of Pigs in 1961, but the incident soon faded from the headlines. It certainly was eclipsed by President Kennedy's handling of the Cuban crunch

[14] Elie Abel, *The Missile Crisis* (1966), pp. 101–103 *ff.*

Occasionally a statesman can gain ground by accepting something not offered, as Secretary John Hay did in 1900 when he treated Russia's virtual rejection of his Open Door note as an acceptance. President Kennedy did somewhat the same thing in 1962 when he ignored Premier Khrushchev's "tough" letter of October 27 and used the more reasonable one of October 26 as the basis for negotiation. He thereby accepted a proposition that Khrushchev never formally offered. *Ibid.*, pp. 198–199, 204.

of 1962. Here the Soviets lost much face, but they put the best possible complexion on what was left by boasting that since they had wrung assurances from Washington not to invade Cuba, they had won a great victory. (These assurances were contingent on an on-the-spot inspection which never occurred.)

The experience of the French in recent years is instructive. After losing much face in a seven-years' war in Indo-China, and after losing even more in another seven-years' war in Algeria, France emerged under de Gaulle richer and more powerful than ever.

In the mid-1960's we became deeply involved in what had once been Indo-China, and wanted desperately to extricate ourselves as gracefully as possible. National pride (another name for "face") prevented us from taking initial steps that held some promise of success. The French proved that sometimes it is better for a country to lose face than its life blood.

The American story is one of the world's great success stories, and we do not take kindly to failure. We believe that we have "won" all of our wars, although we clearly did not "win" the War of 1812 or the Korean War in a military sense. A slogan of the United States Army Air Forces in World War II ran: "The difficult we do immediately. The impossible takes a little longer." A persistence of this unrealistic belief in our supernatural powers may help win wars, but it can hamper the conduct of rational diplomacy. We should never confuse national pride with the national interest, nor regard ourselves as omnipotent or omniscient.

KNOW THINE ADVERSARY

A diplomatist should be familiar with the foreign policy and the domestic problems of the nation with which he is dealing, just as he should be acquainted with those of his own. Only in this way can he properly interpret or anticipate the moves of his opponents. But he must not make the mistake, as we did in dealing with Hitler and other dictators, of assuming that their reactions will be as rational or logical as we regard ours in a given situation.[15]

---

[15] Official Washington could not understand why President Ho Chi Minh of North Vietnam would not consent to peace negotiations in 1965–1966, when it seemed obviously to his advantage to permit the Americans to negotiate a face-saving agreement and leave South Vietnam.

One should never overrate the diplomatic skill of one's opponent, or underrate it either. He is often less clever or more clever than he seems. There was a tendency during the Cold War years to regard Soviet diplomats as creatures ten feet tall. It is true that they scored some spectacular successes, but they made some monumental blunders, notably in the Congo and in their dealings with Indonesia and Communist China. The latter they shortsightedly built up into a kind of Frankenstein's monster.

We should note well what a leader has to say about himself, whether he be a Chiang Kai-shek or a Charles de Gaulle. Adolf Hitler laid bare his dreams of world conquest in *Mein Kampf*, which he wrote in prison and which sold millions of copies. Leaders of the Western world were prone to sneer at the little man with the Charlie Chaplin mustache and to ignore his literary effort as the fantasies of a madman. The Greeks said, "Know thyself." Today we might say, "Know thine adversary." If the statesmen of Europe (and America) had gone to the trouble to take *Mein Kampf* seriously, the tragedy of World War II might conceivably have been averted.

NEVER SLAM DOORS

When rejecting the other nation's proposals, the skilled diplomat will keep the door ajar for further discussion. There can be no compromise without dialogue. He can say that the issues should be discussed further or that they could better be postponed for further consideration. But in no circumstances should he cause his opponent needlessly to lose face.

Secretary Dulles, when he withdrew America's offer to finance the Egyptian High Dam in 1956, violated this elementary rule. To be sure, President Nasser of Egypt had been annoying, and pressures were converging on the State Department from American cotton growers and outraged Jewish groups. But presumably Dulles could have delayed the blunt and final decision until it sank in the sands of the Egyptian deserts. Certainly he showed a genius for procrastination, after Nasser had seized the Suez Canal, in holding back the British and the French from two-fisted action.

Presenting counterdemands is a time-honored way of keeping doors open. In 1964 mobs in Panama attacked American forces in the Canal Zone, with considerable loss of life on both sides. The Panamanian government immediately demanded that the lopsided treaty of 1903 be renegotiated. The usual response of a major power to this kind of indignity is to present demands for monetary indemnity and to insist on assurances of good behavior in the future. Yet the Johnson administration adopted an apologetic tone, even though the blame for the incident rested with both sides.

But this turn-the-other-cheek approach was one that squared with the image the Johnson administration was trying to project. Power speaks for itself, and oftentimes only the powerful can afford to be humble.

AGREEMENT IN PRINCIPLE MAY MEAN
DISAGREEMENT IN PRACTICE

During and after World War II, we learned to our sorrow that agreements "in principle" with the Communists could be disillusioning or downright dangerous. When the time came to carry out terms, the Communists would often renege on promises that they had given, or had presumably given.

The classic case was the fate of Poland in 1945. After much haggling at Yalta, Churchill and Roosevelt believed that they had extorted from Stalin a pledge that the Polish government would be so reshaped as to give considerable political freedom to the large non-Communist population. But after the Yalta Conference, democracy in Poland (Western style) was speedily done to death.

Agreement in principle may occasionally be used to save face. In 1963, prior to the negotiation of the partial Nuclear Test-Ban Treaty in Moscow, the Soviets were pressing for a nonaggression pact between the Western NATO allies and the Communist Warsaw Pact countries. The West would not give way, so the Russians inserted in the Moscow communique the following face-saving language: ". . . The three delegations discussed the Soviet proposal relating to a pact of nonaggression . . . [They] have agreed fully to inform their respective allies in the two organisations concerning these talks and to consult with them about continuing discussion on this question with the purpose of achieving agreement satisfactory to all participants." [16] The Russians thus managed to make their point. Of course, nothing came of all this double talk.

[16] *Department of State Bulletin*, XLIX (Aug. 12, 1963), p. 239.

AVOID HAVING THE RIGHT POLICY
AT THE WRONG TIME

Adlai Stevenson declared in 1952, "Timing—timing with respect to change—is an important as change itself." A policy may be launched prematurely, and fall on its face. This was true, as we have seen, of Secretary Knox's scheme in 1909 for the neutralization of the Manchurian railroads. A policy may be launched prematurely, and later achieve success. Often a diplomat will insert an idea into the pipeline and get it into circulation, as was notably true of the Root–Takahira agreement with Japan in 1908 for guaranteeing the status quo in the Pacific and elsewhere in the Far East. When first broached in 1907, it was spurned by Tokyo. But after the air-clearing which followed the visit of the Great White Fleet to Japan, the proposal was accepted by Tokyo. Premature may later spell mature.

In connection with Laos and South Vietnam in the 1960's, Washington was often one jump too late with its proposals and concessions. Again one is reminded of Theodore Roosevelt's maxim that the great virtue of being right is being right in time. Repeatedly we were willing to make concessions which, if made earlier, might have been acceptable but which were no longer palatable to our foe. In 1965, in a nationwide television speech, President Johnson offered to dump the whole Vietnam mess into the lap of the United Nations. But by that time the North Vietnamese and their Chinese backers, probably scenting complete military victory, spurned outside interference.

TIME IS THE GREAT SOLVENT

Relatively weak nations that are fast growing stronger would generally be wise to avoid a showdown on a critical dispute with a powerful adversary. At a later date "something may turn up," in Disraeli's phrase, and they can press their case more advantageously. The United States played this game with spectacular success in the nineteenth century. Time was on our side, and patience and persistence brought rich rewards.

Time also cools tempers and creates changes in perspective. Adlai Stevenson, speaking in San Francisco on the twentieth anniversary of the founding of the United Nations, said, "There is not a single dispute in this world . . . which will not look different two decades from now, after time and change have done their erosive work on the sharpest corners of the conflict." [17] Time may not heal all wounds, but it certainly heals many and salves more.

Today time is on the side of those nations that make the best use of it. The United States is no longer a young nation on the make, and the stalling game is not generally advisable. On occasion we try to hurry history. With the Nuclear Club expanding fearsomely, and with the mounting danger of a nuclear war either by accident or calculation, time is no longer the precious diplomatic ally of yesteryear.

ARBITRATION FAVORS THE WEAK

In 1794 John Jay negotiated a famous treaty with Britain—"infamous," said its foes—which is hailed as a landmark in modern arbitration. Certain controversies were settled, but the negotiators could not agree on two disputes relating to financial claims and the location of two of our northern boundary lines. These issues were therefore referred to joint arbitral commissions.

Postponement favored the United States. We were growing wondrously in population and power by the month, and the longer we waited the stronger we became. The arbitral awards might take many years (as they did), and if we saw fit to reject them, we would be in a stronger position to assert our original claims.

Now that we are a superpower, arbitration is less attractive to us. A true arbitration means that the solution is placed entirely beyond our control, and in the hands of foreigners. These outsiders are presumably neutral, but they may have an unfriendly bias. Arbitration also means that we have an excellent chance of losing, for arbitrators sometimes have a tendency to split the difference.

A weak country cannot ordinarily force its will upon a great power, and arbitration is therefore more attractive to the powerless than to the powerful. The strong are in a better position to twist arms to achieve their ends without resort to outside judges.[18] This

---

[17] Edward Hanna, *et al.*, eds., *The Wit and Wisdom of Adlai Stevenson* (1965), p. 53 (June 26, 1965).

[18] This is particularly true of interpreting disputed points in bilateral treaties; such a treaty is usually more binding on the weaker than the stronger

explains why the United States, since becoming a great power, has seldom been willing to submit to arbitration any issue of crucial importance—such as the Canal Zone, the Monroe Doctrine, or Asiatic immigration. Most of the varied arbitrations to which we have been a party have involved secondary issues or minor squabbles that were not worth the expense and trouble of even a victorious war.

Some arbitrations have involved us with nations of relatively equal strength, such as the Geneva arbitration of 1872 with the British. England was finally assessed $15.5 million in gold for the ravages of Confederate commerce destroyers which she had unneutrally permitted to be built or operated under her protection. In this case, an Anglo–American war, which seemed to be heating up, would have been far more costly in treasure alone than the monetary damages finally paid.

Fair arbitral awards, despite the normal dissatisfaction on both sides, are more likely to endure than solutions imposed by arms. Broadly speaking, a successful arbitration is to diplomacy what a military victory is to war. And a half-loaf is usually better than no bread or a shooting war. It is better to lose in the courts, especially when the issues are relatively minor, than in the foxholes.

---

party. In 1903, while supporting the independence of revolting Panama, the United States interpreted (misinterpreted?) the treaty of 1846 with Colombia in a way that would have been inconceivable to the Colombians when they signed it. The United States refused to arbitrate the issue. See D. C. Miner, *The Fight for the Panama Route* (1940).

CHAPTER XII

Ethics and Morality

"The established rules of morality and justice are applicable to nations as well as to individuals. . . ."

SECRETARY ALEXANDER HAMILTON, 1791

PROLOGUE

Niccolò Machiavelli, a prominent Florentine statesman and Renaissance author, is best known for his small treatise *The Prince* (1532). It describes how a calculating and amoral ruler may gain and retain power, and it is supposed to have influenced latter-day dictators, including Benito Mussolini. The adjective "machiavellian" has come to mean unscrupulousness, duplicity, and bad faith. But when Machiavelli's most outrageous statements are read in context, they are somewhat softened. Certainly the cynicism and realism that he recommended are descriptive of much that passes for diplomacy in our era, when we feel, whether correctly or not, that Communist fire has to be fought with fire.

Ethics in statecraft often operate at a different level—perhaps a lower level—than ethics in private life. The point was well put by Count Cavour, the unifier of Italy, who reportedly said, "What scoundrels we would be if we did for ourselves what we are ready to do for Italy."

HONESTY IS USUALLY THE BEST POLICY

The employment of honorable techniques is especially advisable for a democratic nation, where dishonest practices may be exposed in the press and recoil upon their authors. But complete, cards-on-the-table candor is to be used with caution. As in poker, a diplomat never unintentionally exposes his own cards; he sometimes peeks if he can discreetly; he often plays for higher stakes than his hand or his finances warrant; and he can always try to engineer a bluff.

Secretary of State Dulles, who was given to holier-than-thou pronouncements, believed that the Soviets debased the currency of diplomacy. They were constantly presenting long-winded notes so as to spin out a propaganda argument, to put their adversary in the wrong, to give the outside world a false picture of their strength, and to sow seeds of dissension among our democratic allies. "Diplomacy must be based on honesty," Dulles remarked. "Therefore, messages between heads of governments and diplomatic notes between governments should be honestly written to reach agreement, to express a protest, to state or clarify a position, and the like. They should be honestly written to achieve an honest objective." [1] Thus spoke the devout Presbyterian layman.

A good rule of thumb for nations, especially democracies, might well be, "When in doubt, do right." One of Harry S. Truman's favorite sayings was Mark Twain's admonition, "Always do right. This will gratify some people, and astonish the rest."

The United States did right when it remitted to China the excess of its share of the Boxer indemnity, which the Western powers had imposed upon Peking after crushing the Boxer outburst in 1900. This fair-minded concession created a reservoir of good will, and the Chinese government used the funds to educate hundreds of its brightest young men in American colleges and universities.[2]

[1] Andrew H. Berding, *Dulles on Diplomacy* (1965), pp. 54–55.
[2] The British government likewise remitted a substantial part of its share of the Boxer indemnity. By the agreement of 1930 the funds were used for philanthropic and other enterprises in China for the mutual benefit of both nations. Irving S. Friedman, *British Relations with China, 1931–1939* (1940), pp. 15–16.

The United States did wrong when it used a show of force to prevent Colombia from crushing the Panama revolution in 1903. The wrong was finally admitted by inference when the United States Senate approved a treaty with Colombia in 1921 that would pay the aggrieved nation an indemnity of $25 million. Yet belated justice is only partial justice.

MORAL JUDGMENTS CAN OBSCURE
THE NATIONAL INTEREST

President Wilson, the stern Presbyterian, at times made the mistake of putting what he regarded as international morality ahead of a realistic foreign policy. The result was an involvement in the quicksands of Mexican politics, as we have seen, and then involvement in World War I. Rather than bend with the hurricane, Wilson insisted on the undoubted right of our citizens and our ships to sail into submarine-infested waters, should they choose to do so. These venturesome American voyagers had international law on their side, but, when killed, they were just as dead as if they had been wrong.

Foreign policy should not be thought of as a crusade against sin but a clear-headed and honorable pursuit of the nation's best interests. Excessive holier-than-thouism leads to rigidity and unreality. Evangelism is not a satisfactory substitute for realism. To paraphrase an American political proverb, a diplomat sometimes finds it advantageous to rise above principle.[3]

We have learned the hard way that neither good nor evil is total. No one side, not even the American, has a monopoly on the right; there are good Germans and good Japanese, as well as bad ones. Our adversary has his point of view, and he is sometimes more right than we are, given his premises. In 1962 the neutralist world thought it hypocritical that we could threaten the Soviet Union with rockets, some emplaced in Italy and Turkey, while denying the Soviets the right to emplace rockets in Cuba. One nation's "containment" is another's "encirclement."

There are times when the ends seem to justify questionable means, even though this is the doctrine of totalitarian dictators.

[3] "Never stand so high upon principle," remarked Winston Churchill in 1902, "that you cannot lower it to suit the circumstances." Kay Halle, ed., *Irrepressible Churchill* (1966), p. 50.

In 1783, contrary to our solemn treaty pledge to France not to make a separate peace with Britain, we did essentially that, greatly to our advantage. The American negotiators in Paris, with good reason, believed that France was supporting certain Spanish interests against ours and that the United States was completely justified in double-crossing the double-crossers.

If we could only assume that our diplomatic opponents were as honorable as we self-righteously regard ourselves, the game would be simpler. But in diplomacy, as in any other rough game, one is almost certain to lose if one abides religiously by narrow rules while the other side hits below the belt.

EXPEDIENCY IS SOMETIMES BETTER THAN CONSISTENCY

When the stakes are high enough, international law and morality tend to be thrown into the ashcan. Principle frequently bows to expediency, as the Germans demonstrated in 1917 when they resorted to unrestricted submarine warfare.

The United States has often shifted positions when the shoe was on the other foot. Prior to 1812, 1917, and 1941, we championed neutrality toward the wars of "wicked" Europe and preened ourselves, like the Pharisees of old, on our superior morality in not plunging into such bloodbaths. But after we were sucked into World War I and World War II, we lost much of our sympathy for those nations, like Sweden and Spain, that were fortunate enough or farsighted enough to remain on the sidelines.

During the Cold War years after 1945, we frowned upon the uncommitted nations, especially India under Prime Minister Nehru. Steeped in our post-1789 tradition of neutralism, we should have been able to appreciate better the so-called "Nehrutrality" of India.

American leadership has often resorted to questionable tactics to gain desirable ends. President Polk made an underhanded deal with Santa Anna in 1846, in the vain hope that the exiled Mexican dictator would return from Cuba and sell out a large part of his country. (Santa Anna double-crossed his seducer.) Before 1941, Joseph Stalin was a bloody-handed dictator; after 1941, when he was fighting on our side (and the side of the angels) he became good old "Uncle Joe."

Nations, like individuals, seldom can indulge in the luxury of avoiding all compromise with evil. We have learned that one price we have to pay for overwhelming power is an uneasy conscience.

MORALITY COVERS A MULTITUDE OF SINS

An ingenious statesman, if he wishes, can usually find a moral cloak for selfish deeds. Misled by the mirage of imperialism in 1898–1899, we found that we had a moral obligation to take up the White Man's Burden in the Philippines and civilize and Christianize and uplift these "backward" peoples. At the same time we could exploit their natural resources and induce them to buy American calico for their naked loins. Morality tends to fly out the window when profits come knocking at the door.

As late as the mid-1960's the United States found itself deeply involved in a Vietnamese war on grounds that were partially moral. The initial intervention was motivated basically by a desire, presumably in the national interest, to prevent the potential spread of Chinese Communism throughout Southeast Asia. But as time wore on the Washington spokesmen stressed the moralistic sugar coating. We were there, they said, to honor our commitments (to a puppet government long since defunct); to uphold American-style self-determination the world over (an impossible task); and to preserve faith in America's promises to allies and others in Southeast Asia who were living under the shadow of China's nuclear bomb.

Some of these moralistic motivations were no doubt valid. But what had been the primary motivation was played down, especially after Red China became less of a menace following her noisy falling out with the Soviet Union.

HONOR ALL COMMITMENTS

A good rule, though not a completely inflexible one, is to honor all commitments, not just those that are convenient and mutually profitable but those that are inconvenient and unprofitable.

The President of the United States should always remember that when he signs a treaty he creates a presumption that it will be ratified. When Woodrow Wilson went to Paris in 1919, a centuries-old European tradition held that the negotiating of a pact by the agents of sovereign states honor-bound the signatories to carry through ratification.[4] This was not true in the United States, where the Constitution enjoins the Senate to provide advice and consent, often advice and dissent. The Europeans either did not read the American Constitution or were persuaded by Wilson's eloquence not to take it seriously.

When the Treaty of Versailles fell under the senatorial hatchet, America's late Allies, especially the French, charged bad faith and betrayal. Their displeasure could not amend the American Constitution, but the President should take warning from this experience. He should be ultracautious in committing the nation on crucial issues unless he is reasonably sure of success with the Senate, and unless he has emphatically warned the other parties of the possibility of a senatorial veto. Apparently one reason why Wilson fought so stubbornly and uncompromisingly for the Treaty of Versailles was his realization that both his own honor and that of his nation were involved.

MAKE REASONS REALISTIC
AND PRETEXTS PLAUSIBLE

Some cynic has said that every man has two reasons for what he does: a good one and the real one.

After 1783, the British continued to occupy a half-dozen or so forts on American soil, contrary to the plain stipulations of the recent peace treaty. Their real reason was to keep the Indians in line (and retain the fur trade), but their sound excuse was that the Americans were not carrying out their obligations under the treaty.

After World War II, the Soviets applied to Washington for a postwar credit of a billion dollars. They received no answer, and this snub may have had something to do with their embarking on a bellicose course which heated up into the Cold War. The official reason later given in Washington was that the request had been mislaid for six months.[5] This is hard to believe, even though much postwar confusion existed in the State Department. The probability is that some anti-Communist underlings, unfriendly to the proposal, managed to have the request pigeonholed.

[4] Sir Harold Nicolson, *Diplomacy*, 3rd ed. (1964), p. 45.
[5] *New York Times*, March 2, 1946, 1:2–3.

A related rule is that a diplomatist should refrain from publicly giving his reasons for some action, unless circumstances demand such a statement. If he delays publishing his reasons, he may think of better ones later. President Johnson hurriedly landed troops in Santo Domingo in 1965, alleging that American and other foreign lives were in grave danger and that (later) the Communists were assuming leadership. Both of these allegations were stoutly challenged in later weeks. Johnson would have been on sounder if less tactful grounds if he had declared publicly what he evidently believed privately, namely, that we could tolerate no more Castro-like takeovers in the Caribbean.

ONE MIGHT AS WELL BE HANGED FOR A RAM AS A LAMB

The Bay of Pigs blunder in 1961 caught President Kennedy in a tangled web of deception, betrayal, and wrong-doing. Added to these misdeeds was the crime of failure. The moral seems to be that a statesman should not sin. But if he is forced to sin in what he conceives to be the nation's interest, there is something to be said for sinning in the grand manner. Nothing succeeds like success, and success would have blurred in some degree the illegality and immorality of the Cuban invasion.

Nearly two years later, at the time of the Cuban missile crisis, President Kennedy was still concerned—and more successfully—with morality. Some of his advisers favored a surprise bombing attack on the Cuban installations. But Robert F. Kennedy objected passionately to a Pearl-Harbor-in-reverse, saying, "My brother is not going to be the Tojo of the 1960's."[6]

A half century earlier, in 1903, a canal-minded President Theodore Roosevelt took action that was ethically vulnerable in connection with the so-called "rape" of Panama, but he carried it off. Subsequent generations in North America, but not so much in Latin America, have praised him for having started the dirt flying.

In 1956, after President Nasser had seized the Suez Canal, Egypt was assaulted by our NATO allies, Britain and France. But President Eisenhower and Secretary Dulles took the morally high ground of backing the United Nations and our peaceful commit-

[6] Elie Abel, *The Missile Crisis* (1966), p. 64.

ments to it as against the interests of our friends. The British and French, bending to such pressures, were forced to suspend their blow against Egypt in midair. The history textbooks (at least those in the United States) probably will continue to give Theodore Roosevelt more acclaim for his morally questionable course than they do to Eisenhower for his unquestionably moral course.[7] "Success, like charity, covers a multitude of sins," wrote A. T. Mahan in 1911.

TO ACQUIESCE IN GREAT WRONGS IS TO BE AN ACCOMPLICE

Washington officials during the 1930's and 1940's were hostile to the dictators of Europe, while generally friendly to those of Latin America. This was especially true if the latter "played ball" with our policy-makers and our investors. Unlike Hitler, these despots were generally small-time operators, and hence no real menace to the hemisphere, much less to the world.

The United States was forced to walk a tightrope in Latin America. If we intervened to overthrow these junior-league Hitlers, we would be denounced throughout Latin America for returning to the old "gunboat diplomacy" that Franklin Roosevelt had renounced in 1933. Yet if we established amicable relations with them, we would be guilty of collaborating with oppression.

During the 1950's the iron rule of dictator Batista in Cuba was acceptable to the Washington government and American investors. Subsequent events, including Fidel Castro's *coup*, revealed that we paid a high price for having been more friendly than necessary. When the Castroite firing squads began to mow down Batistas, a storm of protest arose from the United States. Castro responded, not unreasonably, that no comparable outcry had followed Batista's less publicized executions of the oppressed people.

The Latin American policy pursued by Washington during these years was clearly vulnerable to criticism. In 1953 and 1954 President Eisenhower presented the Legion of Merit to the dictators of Peru and of Venezuela, respectively. Such bemedaled approval

[7] Machiavelli observed that any means used by a prince for the successful maintenance of his state will be "accounted honorable, and will be praised by everybody; for the common people are always taken by appearances and by results, and it is the vulgar mass that constitutes the world." *The Prince*, Ch. 18.

of torture-chamber tyrants won us few friends in Latin America, especially among the liberals and the forgotten masses. We should have realized that there was a better way to deal with the Latin American rulers as they came into power. For the dictators, there could be a cold and not overhasty nod; for the democratically elected leaders, there could be a warm, arm-on-the-shoulder *abrazo*.

THE BIG LIE IS OFTEN THE CREDIBLE LIE

We have already noted the folly of lying at the ambassadorial level but observed that the President is differently circumstanced. He occupies office temporarily and will not ruin a lifetime career in the foreign service by gaining a reputation for untruthfulness.

A number of Presidents have evidently regarded occasional mendacity as in the national interest. Woodrow Wilson remarked to Colonel House shortly before taking office that a falsehood was justified in two circumstances: where the honor of a woman and public policy were involved.[8] He himself lied (or had an unaccountable lapse of memory) when he twice denied before the Senate Foreign Relations Committee in 1919 that he had ever heard of the notorious secret treaties among the Allies before going to Paris. The presumption is that he was trying to put the best possible face on the Treaty of Versailles, including its precious League of Nations. Franklin Roosevelt, as we have seen, repeatedly deceived the American people in his attempts to persuade them to bolster the embattled democracies.

Adolf Hitler discovered that people will disbelieve little lies of the kind that their own petty minds invent, but will swallow lies that are outrageously big. They are unable to dream up such whopping fabrications, or are ashamed to use them, and therefore assume that others would be so restricted, especially where repetition increases credibility. Hitler built a fantastic career partly on the basis of this belief.[9] And he was little concerned when the deception was

[8] House Diary, February 14, 1913, cited in G. L. Anderson, ed., *Issues and Conflicts* (1959), p. 199.
[9] Prime Minister Chamberlain evidently accepted Hitler's terms at Munich in 1938 in the belief that statesmen are gentlemen and that gentlemen do not lie to one another. Winston Churchill remarked that such "high belief in the perfection of man is appropriate in a man of the cloth, but not in a Prime Minister." Kay Halle, ed., *Irrepressible Churchill* (1966), p. 143.

exposed, for, as he wrote, "the victor will never be asked if he told the truth." Success seems to sanctify falsehoods, and the short memory of the masses is one of the greatest assets of their leaders. All this does not mean that the United States should adopt Hitlerian tactics, but at least we should know of them and be on our guard against them. The head of a great democratic nation cannot afford to be known as a chronic purveyor of lies, whether small or big. President Lyndon B. Johnson's uncandid reports on the Vietnam war in the mid-1960's definitely weakened his position as a world leader by creating the "crisis of credibility" or the "credibility gap."

DIPLOMACY ORDINARILY INVOLVES DECEPTION

Diplomacy by its very nature normally involves some guile, even if no more than concealing certain information of value to the other party. The diplomat is engaged in selling something: the point of view of his country, the basis for an agreement, a proposal for a treaty. The real estate agent does not point out all the defects in the house he is selling any more than the diplomat points out the defects in the cases he is presenting. When one is approached by either a diplomat or a real estate agent, the ancient rule applies: "Let the buyer beware."

In a democratic society, the elected officials usually want to stay in office, and hence are under pressure to tell the public what they think it wants to hear. In 1964, as we later learned, the North Vietnamese put out peace feelers, but they were quietly rebuffed by Washington on the alleged grounds that they were not sincere. How could one read the minds of the supposedly inscrutable Orientals? The probability is that President Lyndon B. Johnson, then a candidate for election in his own right, did not want to be embarrassed by charges of "appeasement."

In 1917 British secret agents intercepted the famous Zimmermann telegram, dispatched from the Berlin foreign office to the German minister in Mexico. This was on the eve of America's entry into World War I. Germany, among other feelers, proposed that Mexico join with Germany and retrieve Texas and other territory lost to the Yankees under the treaty of 1848. A rumor about a British forgery was beginning to gain momentum when Berlin, with incomprehensible candor, admitted the authenticity of the telegram.[10]

This was one of those instances when an outright lie, so shocking to the moralists, would probably have been better than an outright admission. Washington had received the message in secrecy from the British, who had secured the German code. In these circumstances the State Department could not offer proof of authenticity without betraying a confidence and revealing to the Germans that their code was in the hands of their enemy.

The general rule that democratic governments would be well advised to respect the truth applies most forcefully in peacetime. During a war an honest man feels freer to deceive his enemy by every possible ruse, sporting or unsporting. At the end of the Teheran Conference of 1943 with Stalin and Roosevelt, Winston Churchill remarked, "In wartime, truth is so precious that she should always be attended by a bodyguard of lies." He later wrote that Stalin and his cohorts "greatly appreciated" this observation, and that the session came to a gay end.[11]

REALITY AND NOT MORALITY SHOULD
GOVERN RECOGNITION

In 1793 Thomas Jefferson, then Secretary of State, foreshadowed the traditional recognition policy of the United States. We would recognize *de facto* governments, whatever their antecedents, that established themselves in power and were in a position to speak for their people. On this basis we extended the right hand of fellowship to the Revolutionary government of France, despite protests from American conservatives that it had come into power by pillage and murder.

A sense of propriety requires that we defer recognition of a new regime until the evidence is clear that it is in control. Indeed, the premature recognition of a rebellious colonial government has long been regarded as a legitimate cause of war by the mother country. In 1778 France brought down on her head hostilities with

[10] See Barbara W. Tuchman, *The Zimmermann Telegram* (1958). President Eisenhower might well have profited from this experience when he acknowledged full responsibility for the U-2 spy-plane affair.

[11] Winston Churchill, *The Second World War: Closing the Ring* (1951), V, 383. Stalin reportedly remarked elsewhere, "Sincere diplomacy is no more possible than dry water or iron wood."

Britain when she recognized the thirteen revolting colonies and made an alliance with them.

President Wilson, the devout Presbyterian moralist, could not bring himself to recognize the murder-elevated President Huerta of Mexico. As the event proved, Wilson would have spared himself infinite pain and anxiety if he had hewed to the line of tradition and had not attempted to go behind the returns and scrutinize moral antecedents. Since then, we have generally returned to the traditional formula laid down by Jefferson. Many of those nations that we now recognize could hardly qualify as charter members of a Good Boy's Club. President Kennedy, speaking in the Mormon Tabernacle at Salt Lake City in 1963, remarked that "If we were to have diplomatic relations only with those countries whose principles we approve of, we would have relations with very few countries in a very short time." He concluded that the purpose of foreign policy was not to vent indignation or preach "self-righteous sermons" but "to shape real events in a real world." [12]

NEVER BASE RECOGNITION SIMPLY ON PREJUDICE

The Washington government steadfastly refused to recognize Communist Russia from 1917 to 1933. We claimed that the Bolsheviks were engaging in worldwide propaganda (which they were), and that they had repudiated debts incurred by the Tsarist government (which they had). But the basic reason why we did not recognize the Moscow regime was that we did not approve of it. We feared it as an incendiary example to the capitalist world and as a subversive revolutionary agency. We felt that if we recognized it, we might give it sufficient moral standing to permit it to survive, and we prayed for it to collapse. We rather hoped that if we averted our gaze, it might go away. But closing our eyes to disagreeable realities is a dangerous practice; these are the realities that we should most carefully watch.

The absurdity of refusing to have official dealings with a nation that occupies one-sixth of the earth's land surface became increasingly evident. In 1933 Franklin Roosevelt and the New Dealers came into power. Hoping to pull ourselves out of the Depression by

[12] *Public Papers of the Presidents: John F. Kennedy, 1963* (1964), p. 736.

means of Russian trade, we hesitatingly and with strings attached granted official recognition. The trade did not materialize, but a vast amount of mutual name-calling did.

Red China posed a more complicated puzzle in 1949, but one that was essentially the same. We simply did not approve of Communists, and we were still putting our money, hundreds of millions of dollars of it, on the exiled regime of Chiang Kai-shek on Formosa. To recognize Communist Peking was in effect to de-recognize Chiang, and this was contrary to a policy that had persisted since 1928. The British, who had enormous investments in China, quickly extended the warm hand of recognition.[13] They got a cold shoulder in return, for the Red Chinese did not reciprocate to the extent of sending a full-fledged ambassador to London.

We had good reasons for not recognizing Red China, including the physical abuse inflicted upon American representatives in the early days of the regime. Why extend a friendly hand if the chances are good that it will be bitten off? Yet the anomaly remains of not recognizing a nation that boasts about one-fourth of the world's population, especially a nation that has now become a nuclear power with infinite capacity for mischief.

Nonrecognition of Peking has produced an odd twist. We have continued it so long on the basis of disapproval—for about twenty years—that to recognize now would in some measure indicate approval. Such a gesture would be demoralizing to those nations of Southeast Asia that live in mortal fear of the Red Chinese dragon.

REFRAIN FROM RUSH-ORDER RECOGNITION

If the Washington government has sometimes been conspicuously stubborn in withholding recognition, it has on occasion been conspicuously hasty in extending it.

In 1903 a successful revolution occurred in Panama against Colombia, thanks to intervention by United States warships and troops. President Theodore Roosevelt, on fire to start a canal, waited

[13] On November 17, 1949, Winston Churchill said in the House of Commons: "Recognizing a person is not necessarily an act of approval. . . . One has to recognize lots of things and people in this world of sin and woe that one does not like. The reason for having diplomatic relations is not to confer a compliment, but to secure a convenience." Kay Halle, ed., *Irrepressible Churchill* (1966), p. 289.

only three days before according *de facto* recognition. The precipitancy of his action, combined with open American connivance, caused eyebrows to rise abroad, especially among those to whom we had long preached about our superior national morality.[14]

Washington has often been overhasty in recognizing Latin American dictators who have seized power by military *coups*. Such action has involved some curious but understandable contradictions. We have spurned Communist dictators like Castro in Cuba; we have supported fascist-like dictators who would protect American investments and parrot Washington's policies. A prime example is Cuba's Fulgencio Batista, whose brutal regime paved the way for the Castro takeover in 1959. Chickens have a queer way of coming home to roost.

SECRECY IS THE SOUL OF NEGOTIATION

After World War I burst upon the world in 1914, many Americans were convinced that the catastrophe had resulted from secret diplomacy. This conviction grew out of the popular confusion of policy with diplomacy. Diplomacy is the technique by which policies are carried out, and in the case of Europe in 1914 the villain was secret policy rather than secret diplomacy.

President Wilson, reflecting this popular misunderstanding, called for "Open covenants of peace openly arrived at" in one of the most famous of his Fourteen Points.[15] Upon more mature reflection he modified this preachment to mean "Open covenants unopenly arrived at." In short, he did not want the birthpangs of the peace to be exposed from the rooftops.

The blunt truth is that meaningful diplomacy must be conducted in private or it is not diplomacy. Bargainers almost invariably ask for more than they expect to receive, so that there can be mutual concessions prior to agreement. If they publish their extreme claims and then back down, they will be pilloried in their

[14] In the 1930's, when a Japanese spokesman was asked when Tokyo proposed to recognize its puppet government in Manchukuo, he reportedly replied that Japan was in no hurry: she did not plan to build a canal there.

[15] The original Point I was unfortunately worded: "Open covenants of peace, openly arrived at, after which there shall be no private international understandings of any kind but diplomacy shall proceed always frankly and in the public view."

home country for a base surrender. If their shifting demands are publicized at every stage, they will inevitably reflect public pressures, and accommodation will become more difficult.

Treaties normally have to be negotiated in secret. But the final texts should be published so that the peoples of the nations involved, whose lives may be at stake, will know where and in what way they are bound. Secret or unpublished treaties, notably the notorious Treaty of London (1915), proved to be one of the most vexatious headaches of World War I. Wilson won a battle when he forced into the Covenant of the League of Nations the proviso (Article 18) that every treaty and "international engagement," to be binding, had to be registered "forthwith" with the Secretariat of the League of Nations and "as soon as possible published by it." The same rule, almost verbatim, was later included in the Charter of the United Nations (Article 102).

Completely open or "housetop" diplomacy is liable to be not diplomacy at all but pure propaganda. Livingston Merchant, an American foreign service officer, recalls that at the Berlin Foreign Ministers' Conference in 1954 the Soviets tipped their hand. They refused to negotiate in secret on German reunification or on the proposed Austrian treaty, and this, of course, meant that they were not seriously concerned about a settlement. They were seeking not agreement but a "propaganda carnival." [16]

SECRETS WILL OUT

Secrecy is hard to preserve in a free-press democracy, as the Bay of Pigs debacle demonstrated. It cannot always be preserved in a dictatorship. Hitler's clandestine preparations for an attack on his accomplice Stalin in 1941 were well known outside Russia, even in Washington, but warnings relayed to Moscow were evidently not believed.

A useful rule is that if you cannot afford to be found out, do not engage in activity that will cover you with shame when it comes to light. Presidents Jefferson and Madison, in their zeal to

[16] In E. A. J. Johnson, ed., *The Dimensions of Diplomacy* (1964), p. 126. A former Ambassador to Moscow, Charles E. Bohlen, is quoted as having said, "In dealing with the Communists, remember that in their mind what is secret is serious, and what is public is merely propaganda." *New York Times,* January 2, 1966, 12 E, col. 5.

acquire the Floridas, became involved in underhanded dealings
that reflect scant credit on their illustrious names.

When the American U-2 spy plane was shot down over the
Soviet Union on May 1, 1960, it was not engaged in anything particularly wicked. All major powers, especially the Soviet Union,
spy on one another, and this particular exploit was actually a spectacular triumph for American technology and espionage. The Russians had known about such aerial forays for some two years, and
had been enraged by their inability to shoot down aircraft flying
at such a high altitude. The most disquieting aspects about the
whole affair were the initial lying and denying and defying. When
the U-2 fell out of the skies, America's reputation for integrity also
plummeted.[17]

From a diplomatic standpoint President Eisenhower committed an unpardonable blunder by assuming full personal responsibility for this espionage foray. Premier Khrushchev had recently made
his jolly (at times) propaganda visit to the United States, and now
the Soviets were given ample justification for cancelling President
Eisenhower's scheduled countervisit. He probably would have
made a most favorable impression, and could have won a significant battle in the Cold War.

SECURE YOUR ADVERSARY'S SECRETS
IF YOU CAN DISCREETLY

An upright statesman may have qualms about international
larceny, but he should remember that his adversaries are trying to
steal his secrets, and may well have succeeded. During and after
World War II the Russians, through agents like Klaus Fuchs, stole
valuable information about the atomic bomb. Scientists have estimated that the Soviets gained a year or more through such back-
door methods.

The United States, with its anti-monarchical and pro-Puritani-
cal background, has been somewhat Boy-Scoutish about this whole
unsavory business. By the time of the Harding administration a
cryptographer named H. O. Yardley had set up a code-cracking
agency (The Black Chamber) in the State Department, and it
proved highly useful at the time of the so-called Washington Dis-

[17] See David Wise and Thomas B. Ross, *The U-2 Affair* (1962).

armament Conference. He later wrote that he made available to the American delegates, before their "morning coffee," translated intercepts of instructions from Tokyo to the Japanese delegation. "Stud poker," he added, "is not a very difficult game after you see your opponent's hole card." [18]

Secretary of State Stimson, who took office under President Hoover in 1929, summarily shut down the Black Chamber with the cryptic comment, "Gentlemen do not read each other's mail." But later, through sheer necessity, the United States went back into the code-cracking business, and in 1940 achieved a signal triumph by cracking the main Japanese diplomatic code.[19] During the anxious months before Pearl Harbor, Washington officials were intercepting the official communications between Tokyo and its embassy. They knew that the blow was about to fall somewhere, but they did not suspect that it would be in Hawaii.

Continued interceptions of Japanese secret messages proved to be vital. They enabled us to concentrate what naval and aerial strength we had at Midway in 1942, and the subsequent victory proved to be the major turning point in the Pacific War.

Code-cracking is admittedly sneaky business. But now that we are in danger of blowing up the world, the gentlemanly standards of a Lord Chesterfield seem as outmoded as a horse-drawn cab. And if American consciences are troubled by our having cracked the Japanese code, they may be eased by the knowledge that the Japanese had previously cracked our code and were intercepting top-secret communications to and from Washington.[20]

[18] H. O. Yardley, *The American Black Chamber* (1931), p. 221.

[19] The story is told in great detail in Ladislas Farago, *The Broken Seal* (1967).

[20] Waldo H. Heinrichs, Jr., *American Ambassador: Joseph C. Grew and the Development of the United States Diplomatic Tradition* (1966), p. 263.

CHAPTER XIII

Allies and Alliances

"[The Utopians] never enter into any alliance with any other state. They think leagues are useless things, and reckon that if the common ties of human nature do not knit men together, the faith of promises will have no great effect on them."

THOMAS MORE, *Utopia*, 1516

PROLOGUE

"Tis our true policy to steer clear of *permanent* alliances with any portion of the foreign world," declared President Washington in his Farewell Address of 1796. He quite evidently had in mind the French Alliance of 1778. At no time since then have we ever made "permanent" alliances, and probably never will. But we have definitely abandoned the misleading misinterpretation of Washington's address that we should never make any alliance of any kind with any nation for any purpose. In 1947 we linked arms in an alliance with our numerous Latin American neighbors in the Rio Pact, from which the Organization of American States stemmed. In 1949 we planted both feet formally and firmly in Europe by ratifying the North Atlantic Treaty (NATO), which then embraced twelve nations. The menace of Soviet Communism thus forced us, in the national interest, to toss overboard a century and a half of tradition and embark upon a period of wholesale pact-making.

SELF-INTEREST IS THE CEMENT OF ALLIANCES

The best alliances are based on mutuality of interest. When self-interest dissolves, the alliance disintegrates. And no alliance is dependable, especially among democratic nations, that does not enjoy broad popular support. Sometimes a catchall coalition may be as effective as a conventional two-power alliance, notably the multination Allied coalition which, despite many differences, finally overthrew Napoleon at Waterloo in 1815.

In 1778 the newly born United States negotiated its first entangling alliance, that with France. The Americans needed help in winning their independence from Britain; the French needed help in defeating Britain and regaining their ascendancy in Europe.[1] As long as the two allies were fighting for the common goal of victory over Britain, the alliance held together fairly well. But when we won our independence, we lost interest in the alliance, and ultimately were able to wriggle out of it in 1800.

In 1966, more than a century and a half later, we were treated to some curious reverse irony. President de Gaulle of France, pursuing a nationalistic lone-wolf course, partially dissolved the fifteen-nation NATO Alliance. He argued that the danger of a Soviet attack on Western Europe—a danger that had welded the alliance together—no longer existed.

Emergencies make strange alliances, in conformity with the adage, "Any port in a storm." America's first alliance, that with our hereditary foe France, was not the last unnatural one in which we became enmeshed. When the rats are loose we are not unduly concerned about the social acceptability of the rat catchers. So it was that in 1941 we clasped hands with the Communist dictator Stalin to overcome the Nazi dictator Hitler. In the same spirit Prime Minister Winston Churchill remarked that "If Hitler invaded Hell,

[1] The French did not actively intervene until after the Americans, by their victory at Saratoga in 1777, had demonstrated that they had a good chance of winning. Giuseppe Mazzini, the Italian revolutionist, complained in 1840 that foreign governments were never really willing to give aid "until you have shown that you are strong enough to conquer without them." Winners can pick up allies more readily than losers.

I would make at least a favorable mention of the Devil in the House of Commons." [2]

Yet bullies can make embarrassing buddies. Churchill later wrote in his history of the war, "How much easier it is to join bad companions than to shake them off." [3]

ALLIANCES SHOULD HAVE TERMINAL DATES

Every long-term alliance should have a clause permitting the signatories to end it after a stipulated period. In the case of the North Atlantic Treaty Organization, joined by the United States in 1949, the stipulation was that any one of the signatories could give notice of termination after twenty years, effective one year later. One of our many complaints against President de Gaulle was that he undertook to pull out of the alliance, at least in part, before the twenty years had ended.

What is a good rule for alliances is a good rule for other pacts. The one-sided treaty of 1903 with Panama granted canal rights to the United States "in perpetuity," which is a long time. Friction inevitably developed, and it continues despite subsequent modifications of the original pact. The Nine Power Treaty of 1922, signed during the Washington Conference and designed to uphold the Open Door in the Far East, was open-ended—that is, without time limit. When the Japanese imperialists decided to seize China's Manchuria in 1931, they were not free to terminate the treaty; they could only tear it up.

ALLIANCES GENERATE FRICTION

Alliances with nations of fundamentally different interests and policies should be entered upon with the utmost caution, for even under the best of circumstances trouble ordinarily results. During the wartime heyday of the Franco–American Alliance of 1778, the two ill-matched partners could not completely forget that they had

[2] Kay Halle, ed., *Irrepressible Churchill* (1966), p. 179. Churchill had earlier remarked (1940), "There is only one thing worse than fighting with allies, and that is fighting without them." *Ibid.*, p. 157.

[3] *Ibid.*, p. 232 (1951).

long been enemies. Ugly incidents occurred, involving some slight bloodshed. They grew out of misunderstanding, suspicion, resentment, or a feeling that one ally or the other was not faithfully living up to his part of the bargain.

Alliances are supposed to confer benefits while imposing obligations. If the obligations heavily outweigh the presumed benefits, the alliance is in trouble. The "entangling alliance" of 1778 with France did not really "entangle" until the United States had derived from it about all the benefits it could hope for and was under heavy pressure to defend the French islands in the West Indies "forever."

Nations that negotiate alliances usually borrow trouble. Some of it is generated by the friction created within the alliance itself. Some of the rest comes from inheriting the burdens of one's ally. In the American War of Independence, for example, the United States was allied to France, while France was allied to Spain. As a consequence, the Franco–Spanish problem of wresting Gibraltar from the British became by indirection our problem.

Friction and resentment are most likely to develop when the strength of the two partners is grossly disproportionate. This proved to be the case in the Franco–American Alliance. When two men ride a horse, the weaker one usually rides behind; and when Hitler teamed up with Mussolini, the Italian dictator was relegated to the rump end. As Representative Fisher Ames observed in 1800, weak nations that seek a protector will not lack a master. If they have more to gain than to lose by a go-it-alone policy, they would be well advised to ride by themselves.

Ordinarily partnership is a poor ship to sail in, and he travels fastest who travels alone. Secretary John Q. Adams, who was aware of these truths, pressed for a go-it-alone course in enunciating the Monroe Doctrine in 1823 and in spurning joint action with Britain.

A corollary proposition is that the more allies one has, the more limitation there is on one's freedom of action, and the more friction there is. In the Korean War, there were sixteen allies (plus South Korea), most of them contributing only tiny forces. The addition of new allies increased problems by geometrical rather than arithmetical progression. Many red-corpuscled Americans were eager to blast Chinese bases north of the Yalu River, but the bombers were held back in the face of heated opposition from

Britain and other token-force allies. Alarmed by reports that President Truman was about to authorize atomic bombing, the British Prime Minister Attlee made a hurried trip to Washington late in 1950.

American critics repeatedly complained that the influence of our Korean allies in decision-making should be proportioned to their contribution to the common cause. Yet allies can hardly be allies unless, whatever their strength, they are treated more or less as equals. Coalition warfare, which involves ticklish coalition diplomacy, is the most difficult kind of warfare because it constitutes multi-alliance warfare. Not surprisingly, the partners in Korea experienced difficulty in getting all sixteen clocks to strike the hour simultaneously. The fewer the allies the more decisive the action.[4]

Further friction develops when allies in one part of the world do not cooperate in another. In the mid-1960's the United States was fighting North Vietnam, while its French and British allies, partners in the North Atlantic Treaty Organization, were profitably shipping supplies to war-torn North Vietnam.

DISTRUSTED ALLIES ARE UNDEPENDABLE ALLIES

Soviet Russia, though a wartime partner of the United States from 1941 to 1945, was pathologically suspicious of its capitalistic associate in the "Strange Alliance." The Kremlin evidently looked upon the Americans as future enemies in the next war, which would be fought to the death between the capitalists and the Communists.

As a rule, allies cannot be trusted without some reservations, even in the best of circumstances. But the Russians, who were desperately beating off the German invader with American help in World War II, tipped their hand. If they betrayed such acute suspicion and distrust in their hour of direst need, we could hardly expect them to cooperate with the United States when the Hitlerian menace had collapsed in ruins.[5] Many optimistic Americans, con-

[4] The twenty-one nation alliance between the United States and the nations of Latin America ran into similar problems when unanimous action was desired against Communist infiltration. In World War II we were forced to make unpalatable concessions to our allies, notably Russia in connection with Poland, in order to retain their cooperation at critical junctures. For the problems of coalition warfare against Napoleon, see Gordon A. Craig, *War, Politics, and Diplomacy* (1966), Ch. 2.

[5] See John R. Deane, *The Strange Alliance* (1947).

spicuously President Franklin Roosevelt, wishfully concluded that the Soviets simply had to cooperate with the Western world after the war in the building of a brave new world. What was unthinkable during World War II became quite thinkable after World War II.

Constancy, as well as self-interest, is the lifeblood of alliances. If you cannot support your ally when inconvenient, you can hardly expect him to support you when inconvenient. President Eisenhower, as we have seen, turned against the French and British NATO allies when they attacked Egypt in 1956, thereby shaking the alliance to its very foundations. President de Gaulle of France, as if to return good for evil, proclaimed his support of the United States during the Cuban missile crisis of 1962. But, in so doing he probably discounted, with calculating eye, the probabilities of a nuclear Armageddon.

In the 1960's de Gaulle attempted to expel American influence and forces from Europe, arguing that the Continent should not be dependent on the United States for defense that might not come in a crunch. His position was certainly a tenable one. It was probably due in part to his knowledge that while we shared our nuclear secrets with our British ally, Congress forbade us to share them with our French ally.

A nation cannot play favorites among its allies and expect to retain their full confidence. We most certainly invite trouble when we are no more candid with our ally than we are with our adversaries.

UNHAPPY ALLIES ARE POTENTIAL ENEMIES

When war convulsed Europe in the late summer of 1914, there were two sets of alliances: the Central Powers (Germany, Austria–Hungary, Italy) and the Entente Powers or Allied Powers (Britain, France, Russia). The Germans and the Austro–Hungarians expected Italy, under the terms of their Triple Alliance, to enter the fray on their side. But Italy held aloof until 1915, alleging that she was bound to declare war only if the Central Powers were attacked— and they were the ones who had done the attacking. This was an excuse. The real reason apparently was that the unredeemed territory claimed by Italy was held by Austria–Hungary, an ally. And allies do not ordinarily seize one another's possessions. The result was that Italy, after receiving secret and easy-to-make promises of Austrian territory, entered the conflict on the side of her presumed enemy, the Allies. Likewise, in World War II, the Italians were not happy allies of the all-conquering Hitler. After the Allied invasion of Italy in 1943, they switched sides and tried to drive their former German comrades-in-arms out of the Italian boot. Hitler's troops naturally fought doggedly in resisting eviction by their turncoat hosts.

In 1956, when enchained Hungary rose against Russia, the Western world was worried about the huge army amassed by the U.S.S.R. and its satellites. The latter, which included restive Hungary and Poland, were bound to Moscow by the Warsaw Pact. The Soviets reportedly had about 160 divisions, plus the 40 divisions of their uneasy allies, for a grand total of about 200. The uprising of 1956 in Hungary, combined with anti-Soviet demonstrations in Poland, changed the statistics dramatically. The satellite divisions were obviously not reliable in a showdown, so the effective total fell to about 160. The satellite divisions would have to be watched by Soviet divisions, presumably about 40. Hence the grand total of available divisions dropped roughly from 200 to 120.

These are realities that statesmen must take into account as they assess the strength of a coalition of potential enemies.

A COMBINATION OF WEAK ALLIES IS OF LIMITED VALUE

When Catherine the Great of Russia formed her Armed Neutrality of 1780 against the formidable naval might of Britain, she privately and realistically dubbed it the "Armed Nullity." It consisted of Russia, Denmark, Norway, Sweden, Prussia, the Holy Roman Empire, Portugal, and finally the Two Sicilies. The wolf is never frightened by the number of sheep, and the whole lot of these could not muster enough naval strength to overawe the British.[6] The more nations in a coalition, the less unity there usually is and the less available power there is concentrated in a single hand.

[6] The fifteen-nation NATO Alliance (begun in 1949) embraced many weak members, including Iceland, Norway, the Netherlands, Denmark, Belgium, Portugal, and Greece. The looser Southeast Asia Treaty Organization (SEATO), launched in 1954, boasted eight members, including such relatively weak states as New Zealand, Pakistan, Thailand, and the Philippines.

The more allies there are, the less secrecy there is bound to be, because affairs of mutual interest must be discussed in many capitals. When Stalin, Churchill, and Roosevelt met at Yalta in 1945, they deliberately withheld decisions from Chiang Kai-shek as to the bartering away of China's assets, even though China was an ally of Britain and America. The conferees feared that these arrangements would leak back to the Japanese, who in alarm might attack Russia prematurely from the rear.

The more allies there are, the more likely they are to have conflicting claims. The Turks and the Greeks, partners with the United States in the NATO Alliance, began to quarrel alarmingly over the fate of the Turkish minority on the Greek island of Cyprus. At one time, notably in 1964, there was imminent danger that the eastern wing of the alliance would crumple by going to war within itself. By attempting to mediate as the senior partner, the United States incurred the wrath of the Greeks and Turks, both of whom we presumably had saved from Soviet domination by the Truman Doctrine of 1947.[7] A cynic may be tempted to say, "Who needs enemies when he has allies?"

Small allies, or small nations not allied but in effect covered by an alliance, can involve their big brothers in global wars. Assassins from tiny Serbia murdered the Archduke Francis Ferdinand of Austria in 1914, and an aroused Austria–Hungary attempted to crack down on Serbia. Russia, essaying the role of a quasi-ally and protector of Serbia (a sister Slavic nation), began to mobilize in her defense. The chain of events continued in motion that brought on the horrors of World War I.

The misdeeds of one ally also tend to taint the other allies. The United States, even though it had renounced imperialism with the freeing of the Philippines in 1946, is tarred with the brush of imperialism in the eyes of the anti-colonial "backward" nations. Britain, France and the Netherlands—our NATO allies—were once foremost imperialists. Portugal, also a NATO ally, retains an immense colonial empire in Africa, the largest still in existence. Allies, like ordinary mortals, are generally known by the company they keep.

[7] The Greeks erected a bronze statue of Truman in Athens in 1963; the next year it was daubed with whitewash and a warning, "Go home, Yankee!"

AVOID MEDDLING IN THE INTERNAL
AFFAIRS OF ALLIES

Twisting the arms of weak allies is not the way to build up good will or constancy. In 1962 President Sukarno of Indonesia, after making warlike noises at the Dutch, secured their East Indian possession of West New Guinea, the last large remnant of a once-fabulous Eastern empire. The Washington officials twisted the arms of the Dutch authorities and persuaded them to yield to this bare-faced threat of aggression. The Netherlanders have not forgotten this needling, nor the pressure that the United States (a wartime ally) put on them after World War II to free what became Indonesia.

The French, our touchy ally, likewise resented outside meddling with their colonial empire, especially Algeria. With Gallic logic on their side, they insisted that the Algerian war for independence, waged bloodily between 1954 and 1961, was a purely internal affair. They opposed the efforts of American spokesmen to have the United Nations intervene, and they particularly resented a speech in 1957 by John F. Kennedy, then a United States Senator, that was outspokenly sympathetic to the rebels.

Born of a rebellion, the United States in the eighteenth and nineteenth centuries developed a tradition of siding with revolutionists. We ran true to form when we expressed sympathy for the Algerians in their war for independence against France, even though France was a NATO ally which more than a century and a half earlier had helped us win our independence. Someone has said that we have favored everybody's revolutions except our own, namely the attempt of the Southern Confederacy to achieve nationhood in 1861–1865.

In recent years we have forsaken our ancient traditions in the face of the Communist threat. Once a revolutionary force in a conservative world, we now appear to be apostles of the status quo in a world torn by revolution.

PART IV

The Fragmented Globe

CHAPTER XIV

The Role of the Foreigner

"In Great Britain, for instance, the ordinary man or woman has not yet realized that foreign affairs are *foreign* affairs, namely that they concern, not our own national interests only, but also the interests of other countries."

HAROLD NICOLSON, 1939

PROLOGUE

From earliest times the individual foreigner has been an object of suspicion, if not outright hatred. Foreign nations themselves are no exception. Ways that are different annoy us. Ralph Waldo Emerson wrote of an English lady who, while visiting the Rhineland, overheard a German resident refer to her party as foreigners. She burst out, "No, we are not foreigners; we are English; it is you that are foreigners."

Ignorance is frequently the mother of suspicion, and oftentimes the more we see of some people, the better we like them. Yet the reverse may be true. Familiarity can breed not only contempt but hatred.

Getting along together is a problem as old as the Biblical Adam and Eve, whose son Cain slew his brother Abel. This is true whether in marriage, in the family, in the neighborhood, in the community, in the state, in the nation, or among nations. At times we seem to be no more civilized than the children of Adam, for the scientific man has far outstripped the sociological man.

FOREIGN COUNTRIES HAVE FOREIGN WAYS

Different countries have different outlooks, and there is a built-in antipathy among many of them. We cannot see their problems clearly because we view them with our own eyes, not theirs. We sometimes regard Arabs as Americans in flowing robes.

We fail to comprehend fully the traditions, aspirations, and needs of other peoples. A virtual continent unto ourselves, we have had difficulty in understanding that maritime trade is the bread and butter of many less favored nations. We have seldom extended to the British complete sympathy when their foreign trade, which is their lifeblood, has been jeopardized. When President Nasser of Egypt held the razor to the jugular vein of Britain's oil supply by seizing the Suez Canal in 1956, we sided against the British, our allies, and found ourselves strange bedfellows with the Soviet Union in backing Egypt.[1] We fall into grave error when we measure all other peoples by our own yardsticks.

We could have comprehended better the go-it-alone course of President de Gaulle of France in the 1960's if we had known more of French history, especially the faded glory of Louis XIV and Napoleon Bonaparte. De Gaulle, a kind of male Joan of Arc, was determined to regain the *grandeur* of yesteryear, even if it meant dashing all hope of political and economic unity for Europe or smashing the NATO Alliance so laboriously forged in 1949.

Americans should not only see themselves as others see them, but they should put themselves in the other fellow's place and try to understand the feelings of the poor, the weak, the sensitive, the indebted. We ought to succeed in this endeavor more than most peoples because in the early decades of our national existence we were all of these.

THE OTHER SIDE ALWAYS HAS
SOME KIND OF CASE

Americans will generally concede that there are two sides to every international dispute: our side and the wrong side. We tend to see complicated problems in terms of simple blacks and whites, rather than in terms of the intermediate grays. This one-way tunnel-

[1] See Herman Finer, *Dulles over Suez* (1964) for a view strongly sympathetic to the British and bitterly hostile to Secretary Dulles.

vision is a common human failing, not unique with the United States. Pascal, in referring to France's relations with Spain, wrote, "Truth on this side of the Pyrenees, error on the other side."

In scrutinizing the events leading up to our major foreign wars, historians have found a British side, a Mexican side, a Spanish side, a German side, an Italian side, and a Japanese side. Other nations, when viewed from Mars, are entitled to their place in the sun. We achieved ours in the nineteenth century, partly by force, but we were quite unwilling that Japan should achieve hers by force in the twentieth century. Yosuke Matsuoka, who led the Japanese delegation out of the League of Nations in 1933, once remarked that "the Western Powers had taught the Japanese the game of poker but that after acquiring most of the chips they pronounced the game immoral and took up contract bridge." [2]

This is not to say that the other side always had the better case. But there was a case, and a fuller understanding of it in all these instances might have led to less misunderstanding.

The adversary, say the U.S.S.R., often appears to us as slippery and double-dealing. We do not realize that in Russian eyes we frequently stand condemned of the same faults, and in some cases with good reason. *We* know we are nice people and have no intention of attacking the Soviets, but the nagging question is, do they know it?

TREAT ALL NATIONS FAIRLY FOR YOU MAY ONE DAY NEED THEM AS FRIENDS

There is a cynical saying in show business, "Be kind to those you meet on the way up for they are the same people you will meet on the way down."

No nation is so small or weak that it cannot conceivably be useful to the United States at some time in the future. During the Cuban missile crisis of 1962, both Senegal and Guinea were approached by Washington, and both gave assurances that they would deny Russian aircraft transit rights, including refueling privileges.[3] To this extent they strengthened President Kennedy's hand.

---

[2] Frederick Moore, *With Japan's Leaders* (1942), pp. 38–39.
[3] Elie Abel, *The Missile Crisis* (1966), p. 137.

The case of General de Gaulle is distressingly instructive. A haughty and virtually unknown brigadier general in 1940, this self-crowned representative of a prostrate France was cold-shouldered by Prime Minister Churchill and especially by President Franklin Roosevelt, partly because de Gaulle's pretensions were so grotesquely out of proportion to his power. When he subsequently became the powerful President of a resurgent France, he probably found much solace for these slights by cracking down on the United States in the 1960's, notably in draining away America's precarious gold supply and in forcing American NATO troops out of France.

If we treat nations as outcasts, as we did Red Russia and Red China, we should not be surprised if they develop the neuroses of outcasts. A good rule is to treat inferior nations as equals and relatively equal nations as superiors. A superpower as muscular as the United States can afford to be gentlemanly.

ABSENCE PROMOTES AMICABILITY

Relations between America and Outer Mongolia have on the whole been untroubled because they have been virtually nonexistent. In politics, as in physics, friction generates heat, and there can be no friction without contact.

Relations between Britain and America during the nineteenth century were for many years deeply troubled. Geography played a cruel joke on these two proud peoples by forcing them to be next-door neighbors. Much of the more than 5000 miles of border between Canada and the United States was hotly contested, in places by armed invaders from each side in two wars.

But the test of character is the presence of temptation rather than the absence of it. If we maroon a man on a desert island for fifty years, we can hardly praise him for eschewing wine, women, and song. The fact that Britain and America were able to iron out their persistent differences with only two wars is in considerable measure a tribute to the good sense that prevailed in both nations.

America's relations with Russia in the nineteenth century were on the whole untroubled, basically because the two nations seldom came into direct contact.[4] In the twentieth century, and particularly

[4] This theme is developed at length in Thomas A. Bailey, *America Faces Russia* (1950).

during the Cold War years, relations were badly strained, primarily because the two nations were now ideological rivals and ran headlong into each other in many parts of the globe.

A general rule of political physics, but not an invariable one, is, the closer the contact the greater the friction.

OTHER NATIONS CAN SOLVE THEIR PROBLEMS BETTER THAN WE CAN FOR THEM

So-called "backward nations" can be helped onto their feet. But they will not stay there unless they have the will to stand, any more than an alcoholic can be cured unless he has the will to be cured.

Americans should bear this in mind when they try to ram democracy—"instant democracy"—down the throats of impoverished peoples who have never experienced it. Many of them do not know what it is, do not want it, and probably could not make it work if they had it. The military regimes in Latin America and Africa in the 1960's that successively took over dying democracies, some of them recently born, should be a grim reminder.

The United States, under President Wilson's leadership, tried to solve many of Europe's age-old political and economic problems by a treaty settlement that included the League of Nations. The Treaty of Versailles was not one that Europe really wanted, but the exhausted victors did not wish to offend a rich Uncle Sam, who was counted on to help finance the brave new world. When we finally crawled back into our isolationist shell, many Europeans complained bitterly that they knew their problems better than we did. They further complained that if we had only stayed out (since we were not going to stay in), they could have worked out more satisfactory and more lasting arrangements. This post mortem may have been correct.

POLITICS MAKES STRANGE YOKEFELLOWS

In 1778 France, the traditional enemy of the revolting British colonists in America, made a treaty of alliance with them against Britain. Many naive Americans regarded this intervention as an act of friendship, as indeed it technically was—for selfishly realistic reasons. France was seeking both restitution of her prestige and revenge against her traditional foe.

Later generations of Americans cherished the legend of French friendship for the United States, as symbolized by the youthful and glamorous General Lafayette. They ignored the experience of Troy with the Trojan horse and the subsequent lesson, "Beware of Greeks who leave going-away presents." Nations do not enter upon ruinous wars in support of other nations simply because they love them.

During America's morning years, the Hamiltonian Federalists were anti-French and pro-British, while the Jeffersonian Democratic–Republicans were anti-British and pro-French. The pro-French sympathy was inspired largely by the memory of America's debt to France for help in securing independence. Political passions rose to a fever pitch as the Hamiltonians and the Jeffersonians attached their fortunes to the tails of rival foreign kites. But as Washington sagely observed in his Farewell Address, those people who hate or love some foreign nation too ardently become in some degree its slave. Antipathies and attachments color the public's assessment of the facts, as was notably true during 1914–1917, when American public opinion was overwhelmingly pro-British, pro-French, and anti-German.

Strange bedfellows are thrown together by the workings of a simple rule: The enemy of my enemy is my friend. During much of the nineteenth century democratic America and despotic Russia drew relatively close in an "historical friendship," which was actually hollow. Russia, with a weak navy, was the traditional foe of the big-navy British, and she sought to build up small-navy America as a counterweight against Britannia's overweening power.

Crisis friendship is usually only skin deep. After Pearl Harbor, Uncle Sam courted the Latin American nations like an ardent lover; he needed their copper, nitrate, and other products. When the war ended, the suitor grew inattentive and the Latin Americans resentful.

These experiences reinforce the conclusion that the friends of today are not all good, and that the enemies of today are not all bad. The ties that bind can easily unwind.

PARALLELISM OF POLICY IS NOT
NECESSARILY FRIENDSHIP

Technically, a friendly nation is one that we may not like but with which we have conventional diplomatic dealings, even though, as in the case of de Gaulle's France, with much bitterness. Friendship among nations is not the same thing as friendship among persons.

Personal friendships between the leaders of nations can help promote policy, but such intimacies cannot endure. Even American Presidents, under the Twenty-second Amendment, cannot constitutionally be elected for more than two terms. Franklin Roosevelt established a friendly working basis with Prime Minister Churchill, though subsequent revelations show that they often differed sharply on policy, military and otherwise, especially during the later years of their association.[5]

During the Suez Crisis of 1956, when President Eisenhower abandoned his British ally to support the United Nations, relations with London became seriously strained. (We reversed the rule: "Stand by your friends if you expect your friends to stand by you.") The ailing Prime Minister Eden resigned, to be succeeded by Prime Minister Macmillan, who finally established a cordial relationship with Eisenhower. Transatlantic tensions greatly eased.

During the nineteenth century relations with Britain were vexed by hereditary Anglophobia, recurrent friction, and a series of diplomatic crises. But in 1823, when Monroe issued his famed Doctrine warning the powers of Europe to keep their hands off Latin America, Britain's policy happened to coincide with ours. In this sense, and for limited periods, the British navy helped uphold the Monroe Doctrine. The legend took root that the British navy was *always* the chief buttress of the Doctrine. The truth is that the British themselves repeatedly violated the Doctrine in the nineteenth century; that they permitted violations which they could have stopped with their potent navy; and that during the half-dozen or so near-war crises of the nineteenth century, the British

[5] This note runs through *Churchill: Taken from the Diaries of Lord Moran* (1966).

navy was the one instrument of destruction most dreaded by the United States.[6]

Nations in peril tend to exaggerate the significance of gestures that are regarded as friendly. The classic case occurred during the American Civil War. Russia, on the verge of war with both Britain and France over Poland, sent two fleets to America, one to San Francisco and one to New York. Many naive Americans assumed that these movements were designed as a blunt warning to Britain and France not to intervene on behalf of the Confederacy. But the truth is that the Russians wanted to get their warships out onto the high seas, away from their easily blockaded inner seas. They could then ravage British and French shipping, after the manner of the Confederate commerce destroyers, in the event that the then current crisis over the Polish rebellion against Russia blossomed into a general war with Britain and France.

Appearances are not always what they seem to be, and self-deception is one of the commonest of human failings. Often in history the important thing is not what is true, but what people think is true.

GREAT NATIONS CANNOT EXPECT
TO BE LIKED BY EVERYONE

The rich and powerful banker, who lives in a mansion on the hill and who rides in a chauffeur-driven Rolls-Royce, excites the envy and even hate of the lowly folk who live below. This is one of the prices that one has to pay for enjoying such privileges.

Great Britain used to be the top-dog nation in wealth and power, and we greatly resented her arrogance and her far-flung empire, with its exploited peoples. After two blood-draining world wars, she and her empire fell upon evil days, and we almost pitied those snobbish Britons whom we had once envied. And pity can be more annoying to the pitied than envy.

The United States, with fabulous wealth and power after World War I, inherited Britain's mantle as the most-hated nation. Normal people, especially Americans, like to be liked. But if con-

[6] On these points see the remarkable letter of Theodore Roosevelt in E. E. Morison, ed., *The Letters of Theodore Roosevelt* (1954), VIII, 1407–1409 (Nov. 30, 1918).

tinuing to be wealthy and powerful is the price we have to pay for being disliked, then we are willing to bear this burden. We should remember that almost nobody likes Big Brother.

International friendships are fragile, and the masses are fickle. When President Wilson visited Rome in 1919, the multitudes hailed "Voovro Veelson" as a Messiah, for they expected him to uphold Italy's claims to the territory of Austria–Hungary. At the subsequent Peace Conference in Paris, Wilson blocked such demands as contrary to self-determination. The same Italians who had acclaimed him in January damned him in April.

When friendship and self-interest clash, friendship usually takes the back seat.

CHAPTER XV

Foreign Aid Programs

"The world will not live in harmony as long as two-thirds of its inhabitants find difficulty living at all."

U THANT, SECRETARY GENERAL, UN, 1962

PROLOGUE

Large-scale foreign aid, from the United States and from other nations as well, is a relatively recent development. As one of the most conspicuous battle fronts of the Cold War, it involves a struggle for men's minds through their stomachs. It provides a classic example of what is known as "enlightened self-interest." Whatever may benefit the recipient nations also benefits the United States, or in general it ought to if it is to be continued. President Kennedy reminded Congress in 1963 that the aid program was not only the "right thing to do" in accepting our "international responsibility," but that it was "clearly in our national self-interest." He then went on to say, "That our aid programs can be improved is not a matter of debate. But that our aid programs serve both our national traditions and our national interest is beyond all reasonable doubt." [1]

[1] *Public Papers of the Presidents of the United States: John F. Kennedy, 1963* (1964), p. 295.

194

FOREIGN AID SHOULD BE IN THE NATIONAL INTEREST

Pure governmental philanthropy, as we have seen, begins at home and ends there, or should. Philanthropy abroad is an extension of conventional diplomacy by other means. A stitch in time, such as the $400 million under the Truman Doctrine for the salvation of Greece and Turkey in 1947, may head off a war that could cost a thousand times as much, in money alone.

Secretary of State Dulles emphatically objected to the phrase "give-away program" in connection with the Mutual Security Program of the Eisenhower era. "What people who use the phrase don't stop to consider is that not having this program would 'give away' a large part of the world to international communism. The United States would end up encircled and fighting for survival."[2]

Many criticisms were voiced in America against the more than $100 billion "squandered" on foreign aid after 1945—"too much money with too little thought." One of the most pointed accusations was that a large part of it was self-defeating and therefore not in the national interest. Critics charged that it was too much, of the wrong kind, and in the wrong place.

The charge of "too much," at least for some countries, seems fully justified. Ex-Ambassador Robert Murphy notes that when Americans decide on a policy, they characteristically "go all out and damn the cost." He cites specifically the case of Yugoslavia after its break with Stalin in 1948. We showered so much aid on this sturdy little country that we aroused its suspicions as to our motives and created resentment when we did not maintain the frantic pace.[3]

The charge of "the wrong kind" can likewise be supported. Roughly one-third of foreign aid has been in military services and hardware, presumably to fight Communism. But the arms have often fallen into the hands of the Communists, as in Chiang's China. Sometimes they have been shipped directly to dictators, notably Marshal Tito in Yugoslavia, who have used such weapons to perpetuate their iron-handed rule. Why press tanks on people who desperately need tractors, even old-fashioned plows, especially

[2] Andrew H. Berding, *Dulles on Diplomacy* (1965), pp. 137–138.

[3] Robert Murphy, *Diplomat Among Warriors* (1964), p. 425. Murphy also tells of a Soviet major in Berlin after World War II whose pride was hurt when the Americans declined payment for some penicillin. *Ibid.,* p. 289.

when they slap you with one hand while holding out the other for handouts?

The charge of "to the wrong nations" is perhaps less damning. Even so, a substantial fraction of our aid has gone to countries like Poland, and particularly Yugoslavia, which were already under Communist domination. Why put guns into the hands of foes who presumably are sworn to destroy our capitalistic system?

The answer from Washington is that support for countries already Communist lessens their dependence on Moscow and helps promote schisms within the so-called Marxist monolith. In Yugoslavia, American aid bolstered Titoism or deviationism from the Soviet line and set off a chain reaction that brought further confusion into the Communist camp.

FOREIGN FRIENDSHIP CANNOT BE BOUGHT

Mutual respect, not the lavish handout, is the most solid foundation for any international relationship. In the years after 1945 the United States poured more foreign aid into French coffers than into any other country, for a total of about $9 billion. Yet by the 1960's a resurgent France, led by the formidable President de Gaulle, was deliberately kicking the United States in the shins.

Presidents Nasser of Egypt and Sukarno of Indonesia both accepted large quantities of aid from us, while pursuing antagonistic policies and publicly condemning their rich benefactor. In 1964 Nasser, resenting Washington's protest against the shooting down of an American-owned aircraft, invited us to "drink from the sea," which was the Egyptian equivalent of saying "go to hell" if we did not like his actions. But mature nations like the United States cannot afford the luxury of giving way to primitive emotions, and with considerable foot-dragging Congress continued to vote appropriations for Egypt. The reasoning behind the be-nice-to-Nasser movement was that the poverty of the Egyptians might become so desperate that in the long run our national interest would suffer more from withholding than from continuing foreign aid.[4]

[4] American food for India in the 1960's saved millions of Indians from starving, but the Communist-leaning Krishna Menon denounced the shipments as arrogant, immoral, and unjustified. See Paul H. Douglas, *America in the Market Place* (1966), p. 310.

America's attempts to "buy" friendship have resulted in a number of "nonaffluent" nations resorting to ill-concealed forms of blackmail. By threatening to go Communist if foreign aid was not granted or maintained or even increased, various small countries have been able to "shake down" rich Uncle Sam for hundreds of millions of dollars. Some of their spokesmen have openly suggested that if they did not have Communists, they would do well to create some.

One nasty byproduct of such blackmail is evident. Well-behaved nations friendly to the United States are encouraged to twist Uncle Sam's beard in the hope of getting that dollar-wrapped attention which bad conduct may bring them. Riots are sometimes richly rewarded, even when they involve the defiling of our flag, the damaging of our embassies, and the burning of our information libraries. We should not be diverted by such superficial outbursts from a close look at underlying discontents.

EXPECT NO GRATITUDE FROM FOREIGN AID RECIPIENTS

Many Americans are naive enough to think that the recipients of our aid ought to be groveling in gratitude for our generosity. "Gratitude is a word only fools use," wrote Balzac. "You can find it in the dictionary, but not in the human heart."

Gratitude, like friendship, is not only perishable but nonpurchasable. The so-called backward nations do not like being called backward, and such gratitude as they demonstrate is often only "dollar deep." A prominent Colombian journalist wrote bluntly in 1945, "The more favors we receive from the Yankees, the less we like them."

Nations that have seen better days also deplore being forced into a position where they have to plead for alms. The proud British, after having been bled white by two world wars, sought a large gift, or at least an interest-free loan, from the United States in 1945. After much haggling, Congress appropriated nearly $4 billion in 1946, at the nominal interest rate of two percent and with some bothersome restrictions attached. This was a "soft loan," which many Americans assumed would turn out to be a gift. But it came after protracted debate and other delays, as well as much resentment from the British, who felt that Uncle Sam had driven too harsh a bargain. The once-richest nation in the world did not like to be cast in the role of a beggar rattling a tin cup.

All too often the beneficiaries of American foreign aid have reacted with fear and envy rather than gratitude. Gift-receivers have frequently turned into ingrates, and those denied handouts have turned into enemies. Overseas critics have repeatedly alleged that such aid, much of it in the form of goods manufactured in America, is essential to sustain our economy. Congress is not unaware of this enrichment, without which such appropriations would be inconceivable. In the mid-1960's about eighty percent of the foreign aid appropriations went to purchase American goods and services, thereby providing more than a half million jobs at home and a large domestic constituency.[5]

The American foreign aid program has suffered failures but has also rung up triumphs. By 1966 five nations, including Taiwan, had "graduated" from the nonmilitary phase of overseas assistance, and to that extent cut themselves off from both American purse strings and apron strings. The Soviets, envious of our limited success, have embarked upon competitive schemes of their own. But they have learned to their sorrow what we had long since learned, that handouts can produce jealousy, envy, resentment, hurt pride, and ingratitude. They also discovered that entering a bidding contest with Uncle Sam has enabled the nations being suitored to play one off against the other, like high-salaried football stars being approached by rival leagues.

Flood victims in America will accept money from the Red Cross without qualms, but they would in many cases be embarrassed to receive it directly from private individuals. Far-visioned critics have repeatedly proposed that all foreign aid should be disbursed through the United Nations or some other impersonal agency. This procedure would eliminate the venom of ingratitude, and it would also reduce, if not terminate, international rivalry in give-away programs.

One barrier to this reform is that many Americans continue to believe that gratitude is purchasable, and they want full credit abroad for their generosity. We like to have "U.S.A." printed on our overseas boxes and bags. We feel that the resultant good will is

---

[5] Paul G. Hoffman (former Marshall Plan administrator), "The Rich and the Poor: 1966," *Saturday Review*, XLIX (Sept. 17, 1966), p. 25.

an important weapon in the war against Communism. Foreign aid is indeed a major weapon in the Cold War, but if it brings the stability to "backward" nations that enables them to fend off Communism, then we shall have received a substantial reward.

There is one almost insuperable obstacle to de-nationalizing foreign aid. As we have seen, the only real justification for an American "give-away" program is that it subserve the national interest. United States dollars disbursed by the United Nations, and hence under foreign control, might easily be diverted to Communist or pro-Communist countries. There they could be used to strengthen collectivist or other Communist programs that the American people would regard as inimical.

NATIONS THAT ACCEPT FAVORS
COMPROMISE THEMSELVES

An old rule still has much validity: "He who pays the piper calls the tune." Weak nations that accept expensive gifts from powerful nations are to a degree the slaves of their benefactors. We learned this lesson the bitter way, as earlier noted, when we became the junior partner of monarchical France in 1778.

A rich nation, say the United States, seldom hands out hundreds of millions of dollars to another nation, say Laos, without strings attached, visible or invisible. If the purpose is to stem the Red tide, the string, whether announced or not, is that the "client nation" must hold the dyke against Communism. If the aid is forthcoming from the Soviet Union, as in the case of Castro's Cuba, then the string is that the beneficiary must promote the aims of Moscow.

The presence of American "strings," whether overt or covert, inevitably provokes the cry of "dollar imperialism," especially from Soviet propagandists. The same charge may also be voiced in the recipient nation by the opposition party or parties, and often with good reason. During the Italian elections of 1948 the State Department announced quite plainly that it would stop all aid to Italy in the event of a Communist victory.[6] Whether as a result of this pressure, or in spite of it, the Communists lost at the polls.

[6] See *New York Times*, March 16, 1948, 6:4; also Secretary Marshall's statements, *Department of State Bulletin*, XVIII (March 28, 1948), p. 424.

External pressure on the internal politics of the beneficiary nation inevitably breeds resentment. The American people should understand this more than most. We have already observed that in the 1790's our French ally, seeking to get its money's worth out of a costly alliance, interfered outrageously in American domestic politics.

AMERICAN ARMS IN FOREIGN HANDS ARE UNCONTROLLABLE

After World War II, we supplied France, our NATO ally, with huge quantities of military hardware as a means of restraining or blunting a possible attack on Western Europe by Communist Russia. We were later shocked to learn that French troops, armed with our weapons, were shooting the Algerian rebels in North Africa. We could not completely forget that we also had fought for our independence many years earlier against a colonial overlord.

We likewise sent vast quantities of arms to India and Pakistan, next-door neighbors but bitter foes, in an effort to bolster them against a possible assault from Red China. Pakistan was our loyal ally in the Southeast Asia Treaty Organization (SEATO) and our quasi-ally under the Central Treaty Organization (CENTO), which was designed to hold the line against Red Russia. Each of the rivals —India and Pakistan—deeply resented the arming of the other by the United States.[7]

In 1962 the Red Chinese suddenly attacked India's northern borders, and we rushed additional arms to the victims. The Pakistani were alarmed and embittered. In 1965 they and the Indians clashed in a full-scale war over a long-disputed prize—scenic Kashmir. Our taxpayers were treated to the unlovely spectacle of American tanks and other weapons clashing head-on in furious battle. Washington promptly halted further shipments of arms, and when both sides began to run low on tanks, parts, and other material, the fighting ground to a halt.

The arms-giving nation can attach all the strings it desires, but in a crisis they will be cut and the weapons will be used as the recipient chooses.

[7] Particularly through 1965 relations between the United States and Pakistan were badly strained. President Ayub Khan declared that they would probably remain strained as long as we supplied arms to India. *New York Times,* January 4, 1965, 12:5.

NEVER THROW GOOD MONEY AFTER BAD

The American foreign aid program—the "multibillion dollar boondoggle"—has had its ups and downs. One of the worst failures occurred in Laos, where the tiny jungle land was virtually drowned in American dollars, with scandalous waste and graft. The greatest success was the Marshall Plan for the rehabilitation of postwar Europe.

"Marshall Plan" came to connote in a favorable sense what "Munich" has come to mean in an unfavorable sense. Some of the men in Washington and many in Latin America evidently arrived at the questionable conclusion that what had worked in Europe, with an industrially sophisticated people, would work elsewhere in the world. The Alliance for Progress of President Kennedy, launched for Latin America with much fanfare in 1961, flowed in part from this belief. Conceived in anxiety and born in haste, it worked much less well, largely because conditions in this hemisphere, industrial and otherwise, provided a less favorable seedbed. Not all of the world's ills can be cured by rubbing gold dust into them.

The Peace Corps, also launched by Kennedy in 1961, has enjoyed greater success. For the modest expenditure involved, it has perhaps returned richer dividends than any of our other foreign aid ventures since World War II. One basic reason is that it has brought a helping hand and a warm heart to the Cold War— individual assistance at the rice-paddy level rather than expensive machinery at the top level.

American foreign aid should attempt to combat the causes of discontent, rather than the results; to attack the roots, rather than the branches. To give lavish assistance to a people whose population is exploding beyond food supplies, and who are unwilling or unable to practice birth control, is a losing game. It is like pouring quarts of oil into a fuel tank while gallons are leaking out at the bottom. The only gain is that disaster may come somewhat more slowly.

The rich are indeed getting richer, but the poor are getting poorer, hungrier, more vocal, and more populous. Peoples—or better, ruling classes—who are unwilling to try to stand on their own feet, who refuse to make needed land reforms and tax reforms, who export their savings to Swiss banks, cannot easily be rescued by American dollars. They are unacceptable risks, whether from the standpoint of banking or diplomacy.

We should be willing to cut our losses and pull out of a given country, no matter how much has been poured down the rathole, when we discover that on balance the national interest is not being served. In some cases we have had no choice, as when our aid was summarily barred from Cambodia by Prince Sihanouk in 1963.

Critics have also urged, in Congress and out, that foreign aid be spread over a five-year period or some other long-term basis, rather than the present year-by-year basis. As President Kennedy told Congress in 1961, "Piecemeal projects, hastily designed to match the rhythm of the fiscal year, are no substitute for orderly long-term planning." [8] Clearly the "disadvantaged" nation could plan projects on a more beneficial basis if it could be guaranteed sustained support. But Congress (and the voters) wants to be sure that we receive our money's worth, and that the attached strings are not snipped. A five-year plan would obviously weaken the strings, while an annual hand-to-mouth accounting is more likely to keep the "client nation" under the thumb of Uncle Sam. In the folklore of American children there is an old saying, "Just before Christmas, I'm as good as I can be." And Christmas comes once a year, not once every five years.

FOOD IS A WEAPON

In many ways food is the most potent type of foreign aid, and it can be the most effective type of propaganda—"people-to-people diplomacy." At various times since 1917 the Moscow regime has exported grain for political purposes—"political wheat" or "food imperialism," even though many of its own people were hungry or actually starving.

The United States, with enormous surpluses of grain, embarked upon its Food for Peace Program in 1954, and over a period of twelve years shipped some $16 billion worth. The common practice was to sell the food to the ill-fed country, which paid for it in "soft" local currency, good only for expenditure locally. These lush "counterpart funds" have enabled junketing congressmen to live off the fat of the land.

[8] *Public Papers of the Presidents of the United States: John F. Kennedy, 1961* (1962), p. 204 (March 22, 1961).

If food is a weapon, it is a two-edged weapon. In the case of India, it has enabled millions of people—ill-fed, ill-clad, ill-housed, and illiterate—to survive famine and produce millions of new babies, thereby further contributing to the alarming overpopulation and disintegration. For many centuries famine has been one of the most important worldwide curbs on population growth.

Free food, which is only a crutch, causes still other problems for the give-away nation. The dumping of vast supplies of wheat may undermine local efforts to get a viable agricultural program rooted. When huge grain surpluses existed in America (as they did into the mid-1960's), the recipient often accused us of shipping them because they were too costly to store. At the same time we usurped the normal markets of other friendly nations, like Canada and Australia. In those cases where we declined to sell grain, notably to Red China, we incurred accusations of inhumanity, and when we ran out of surpluses, we incurred charges of selfishness or worse.

AVOID BEING PENNYWISE AND POUND FOOLISH

Foes of the foreign aid program in this country, pointing to its undoubted extravagances and failures, have complained loudly about the cost. The Republic, they insist, cannot afford such outlays forever. But successive Presidents since 1945 have argued that the nation, in the interests of its own defense against Communist aggression, simply cannot afford to withhold these global doles.

The sums disbursed have undoubtedly been fantastic, but they must be assessed in relation to the national income or the gross national product. By the mid-1960's the French, assisting primarily their former colonies on a mutual-interest basis, were actually disbursing more in foreign aid on this relative basis than was the United States.[9] We were appropriating less than one percent of our total. And while the figure for our gross national product was rising, the figure allocated for foreign aid was falling, on both a relative and absolute basis.

The Marshall Plan, over a period of several years, cost some $12 billion, of which about $2 billion was in loans. Pleading with Congress for an additional $600 million for foreign aid in 1963, President Kennedy noted that this sum, designed to help the de-

[9] "French Economic and Financial Aid to the Developing Countries," *French Affairs,* No. 197 (Sept., 1966), p. 2.

veloping nations of the world to become strong and free, was smaller than the nation's annual outlay for lipstick, face cream, or chewing gum. In his undelivered Dallas address, he was planning to say that "Dollar for dollar, in or out of government, there is no better form of investment in our national security than our much-abused foreign aid program." He had added, with the Alliance for Progress probably in mind, that the United States could surely do as much for its nineteen "needy neighbors" as the Communist bloc was doing in the island of Cuba alone.[10]

It is shortsighted to deny a few million dollars to keep small nations from becoming Communist, and then have to spend billions in shooting them after they have become Communist. In President Kennedy's day Congress was speedily appropriating about $50 billion a year for national defense, chiefly designed to contain the Communists, while begrudging less than one-tenth of that amount to strengthen the independence of the "expectant" nations and to "cure the social chaos," as Kennedy put it, "in which Communism always has thrived."

President Kennedy stressed much more than the military and defensive aspects of foreign aid. He insisted that the program was "right" because it served the cause of humanity. It also helped to strengthen our own nation by strengthening neighbor nations, who in turn could buy our products and in other ways invigorate our economy. All this added up to "enlightened self-interest" on a global scale.

[10] *Public Papers of the Presidents of the United States: John F. Kennedy, 1963* (1964), p. 893.

CHAPTER XVI

The Communist World

"It has become one of the 'self-evident truths' of the postwar era that, just as the President resides in Washington and the Pope in Rome, the Devil resides immutably in Moscow."

SENATOR J. W. FULBRIGHT, 1964

PROLOGUE

The Communists have parlayed Lenin's suitcase of 1917 into control of about one billion persons or approximately one-third of the human race. In achieving their goals they have been tough negotiators: intelligent, calculating, hard-headed, suspicious, and often unscrupulous, untruthful, shameless, arrogant, cynical, and even insulting. At the bargaining table, they believe in give-and-take, that is, "You give and we'll take." Put another way, "What's mine is mine; what's yours is negotiable."

The Communists have still other advantages. They are counting on the long haul, while we are more concerned about the short haul.[1] They are not greatly worried about public opinion at home, which they can delude, or about world opinion abroad, which they can deceive. They are not worried about the next election, for they can count on something like 99% of the vote. They confuse their adversaries with double-talk and upside-down language. They

[1] Adlai Stevenson remarked in 1952, "The contest with tyranny is not a hundred-yard dash—it is a test of endurance." Edward Hanna, et al., eds., The Wit and Wisdom of Adlai Stevenson (1965), p. 7.

have, for example, imposed "People's Democratic Republics," which are not democratic, not republics, and not of the people, at least not in the sense that the Western world understands these words. In brief, the Communist leaders have stopped at nothing, from prevarication to depopulation, in their ambitious attempt to Communize the world. Joseph Stalin allegedly remarked that "sincere diplomacy" was a contradiction in terms.

COMMUNISM IS NOT A MONOLITHIC MONSTER

Ever since the Bolshevik Revolution in Russia, countless worried peoples in the free world have assumed that Communism was one gigantic and granitic monolith, and that Communist parties all over the globe took their orders from Moscow like soldierly robots.

Communism, though presenting a fearsome front, has never been monolithic. Lenin and Trotsky were never in complete agreement as to the course their world revolution should take, and after Lenin died and Stalin came into power, Trotsky was exiled and later murdered. A tiny following of Trotskyites still lingers in the United States and elsewhere.

In 1948 the defection of Marshal Tito of Yugoslavia advertized to the whole world the rift within the Communist fold. In the years since then we have also witnessed the noisy rupture between Moscow and Peking. Elsewhere throughout the Communist world we have noted the stiffening resistance to dictation or even guidance from Moscow, and we have even observed the cut-throat rivalry between the Red Soviets and the Red Chinese for control of the emerging nations, especially in Africa.

On the one hand, the furious quarreling within the Communist camp is to the advantage of the free world, for it weakens the might of our most potent adversary. On the other hand, it promotes fanatical irresponsibility, as in the case of Red China. The age-old game of divide and conquer may be working to the advantage of the United States, provided that we play our cards right.

The more countries that go Communist, the less monolithic Communism becomes and the more infighting develops. The policymakers in Washington have evidently not given this profound truth the emphasis it deserves. If we had permitted Vietnam to go

Communist after the Geneva Agreements (disagreements) of 1954, a united Vietnam, if its previous history meant anything, might have resisted Chinese control. If so, the free world might have benefited from a species of Far Eastern Titoism.

In brief, the more Communism spreads, the more Titoism there is bound to be, and this, though risky, is a relatively inexpensive way of fighting Communist attempts to revolutionize the world.[2] If the Reds cannot agree among themselves how to dominate the globe, they are less likely to dominate it.

Even the presumably formidable Communist parties in countries like France and Italy are less alarming than their sheer numbers portend. Most of their members are evidently first of all nationalists, without any desire to submit to foreign dictation. More often than not they join the Communist party as a means of protesting against existing parties or of supporting local reforms.

IDEAS CANNOT BE BOMBED OUT OF EXISTENCE

Ideas are tough. They cannot be killed with bayonets or bombs. They skip across international boundaries or billowing oceans. They can be successfully combated only with better ideas, effectively communicated.

Revolutions are not carried in suitcases: as a rule, they can be neither imported nor exported. If internal conditions are not ripe for revolution, there can hardly be one, no matter how zealous or how gifted the agitators. On the other hand, nothing is seemingly more irresistible than a revolution, like the French Revolution, whose time has come.

The United States, in its efforts to fight Communism, has been only dimly aware of these fundamental truths. But to make sure, we have used both propaganda and napalm. In the short run, at least, the American bombs on North Vietnam in the mid-1960's strengthened the enemy's will to resist.[3]

---

[2] In August, 1966, the government of North Korea, in whose behalf the Chinese had suffered enormous casualties during the Korean War, declared its independence of control from both Peking and Moscow. *New York Times,* August 13, 1966, 1:6.

[3] In World War II, the anger and determination of both British and German civilian populations seem to have been increased by aerial bombing. For the Germans, see Sir Charles Webster and Noble Frankland, *The Strategic Air Offensive Against Germany, 1939–1945,* 4 vols. (1961), III, 288.

Force can be futile in another area. The Eisenhower Doctrine for the Defense of the Middle East, approved by Congress in 1957, authorized the President to employ the armed forces against aggression from countries controlled by Communism. A dramatic landing of American troops came in 1958 on the beaches of Lebanon, in response to the request of President Chamoun. This spectacular stroke proved that we had military muscle and could deploy it rapidly. But it also proved that the iron fist was ineffective against the insidious hand of subversion—the most worrisome threat in the Middle East.

In the late eighteenth and early nineteenth centuries, three-pronged American republicanism, constitutionalism, and liberalism were the world's most feared isms. If we are to win the battle for men's minds, we shall be well advised to recapture some of the dynamism that made democracy such a fearsome force in a monarchical world. We have become fat, sated, and lethargic. It is the Communists who have the crusading zeal, the stars in their eyes.

PEACEFUL COEXISTENCE IS BETTER THAN NO EXISTENCE

The supreme Leninist–Stalinist goal was Communist world revolution, to be achieved by propaganda, by subversion, and, if necessary, by force.

The "line" softened under Premier Khrushchev, who in 1956 denounced Joseph Stalin as a bloody and despotic cutthroat. The statues and portraits of Stalin came tumbling down, and his body was moved to a less conspicuous spot. The new "line" was "peaceful coexistence" with the West, except for local wars of "national liberation." These, however, cover much territory. After rebelling Hungary was crushed in 1956, Premier Khrushchev boasted of his determination to "bury" us. But he later explained, in a more sober moment, that he meant a burial under competitive coexistence in the economic world.

The Peking regime, dedicated to Leninist world revolution by whatever means or cost, broke with Moscow over this "soft" line. Significantly, the real kernel of the quarrel was over *how* to bury the West: by force of arms or by a peaceful takeover. The free world could take only scant comfort from the name-calling between the rival undertakers.

Many anti-Reds in America and elsewhere have deplored peaceful or competitive coexistence with Communism. Some of them have favored showering nuclear bombs on the Soviet Union and Red China, while we presumably still had a preponderance of such weapons. But as "the balance of terror" developed and the retaliatory power of the Soviet Union was plain for all to see, the alternatives were clear. Either we would uneasily coexist with the Soviet Union, or neither would exist, except perhaps among radioactive ruins.

A COMMUNIST CAN KEEP AGREEMENTS WHEN THEY PAY

The true-blue Communist is not hampered by bourgeois morality. "Promises," wrote Lenin, "are like piecrusts, made to be broken." In Communist thinking the end justifies the means, whether deception, bad faith, subversion, or plain murder.

It would be easy to compile a lengthy list of Soviet promises and agreements that have been broken, beginning with the pledges that the Russians made at the time we extended formal recognition in 1933. But all such lists must be inspected in the knowledge that there is a Soviet interpretation, often based on semantics, as well as an American. From a narrowly legalistic point of view the Communists are often right, especially when they argue that a slight infraction of an agreement by the United States releases them from all obligation to honor the remainder of the agreement. They are most likely to abide by treaties if the commitments on both sides are spelled out with the utmost precision.

But diversity of ideology does not necessarily mean diversity of interests. On many occasions the Soviets find that their own interests force them to keep an agreement with capitalistic nations, especially where commercial contracts and future business dealings are at stake. We have already noted the agreement for control of Antarctica (too cold for the Cold War) and the partial Nuclear Test-Ban Treaty.[4] In December, 1966, the Russian and American

---

[4] When the Nuclear Test-Ban Treaty of 1963 was under discussion, the American press claimed that the Soviets had broken 50 out of 52 or 53 agree-

representatives in the UN, together with those of all other nations, approved a draft treaty banning weapons of mass destruction in outer space.

In short, the Communists can cooperate with the Western world, and they have done so when such cooperation was clearly to their advantage.

TRADE CAN BECOME A PROPAGANDA WEAPON

For many years after the Communist takeover of China in 1948–1949, the Washington government imposed an embargo on trade with Red China. The reasoning was that if we withheld our goods, the regime would be weakened and would, we hoped, collapse.

This policy had some validity insofar as strategic goods were concerned, such as machine tools for manufacturing munitions that might one day be fired at American troops. But the rigid embargo policy evidently did not achieve its basic aim of undermining the Communists. The Red Chinese were further driven into the arms of Red Russia, and this tightened embrace did not accord with American overall policy. Moreover, barriers against trade proved to be barriers against good will and good understanding, both of which must be achieved if the nations of the world are to live together in peace.

Critics have often argued that an outflow of cheap American consumer goods, such as refrigerators and radios, would do more to convince the Communists of the advantages of capitalism than anything else. If we could distribute hundreds of thousands of copies of the Sears-Roebuck or Montgomery Ward mail-order catalogs in the Soviet Union and other Communist countries, the impact would be shattering. For this very reason they are not allowed to enter in quantity.

The few mail-order catalogs that have been permitted to come to the American embassy in Moscow have been a source of wonder-

ments. The State Department, in a memorandum (August 22, 1963) to the Senate Foreign Relations Committee, conceded that the Russians had violated a large number of international agreements, but listed seventeen that they had in general "satisfactorily observed." The memorandum concluded that self-interest was the governing principle. *Hearings on Executive M.*, Senate Foreign Relations Committee, 88th Cong., 1st sess., pp. 967–968.

ment to the Soviet underlings employed there. The pages have been well thumbed, and especially prized on those occasions when the Kremlin has allowed such employees to purchase a limited amount of goods through such channels.

COMMUNISTS CAN CHANGE THEIR STRIPES

Side by side with the myth of a mighty Communist monolith is that of Communist immutability.

The Communists can change, and have changed, both their grand strategy and their local tactics. As for tactics, they apparently are beyond embarrassment. They are quite capable of beating a complete retreat when they run up against a stone wall, as they did at the time of the Cuban missile crisis in 1962.

As for grand strategy, the Soviets have adopted significant changes. Between 1917 and 1921 the Bolshevik leaders installed Communism in Russia, and it failed. They then shifted to a form of state socialism or state capitalism which is called Communism but which is, in fact, something else. (The Russian leadership spoke of returning to Communism after the war-ravaged Soviet Union had achieved a more solid foundation.) We have also noted the shift from armed violence to peaceful or competitive coexistence in an effort gradually to achieve the grand goal of world revolution.

A complete abandonment of the revolutionary ideal by the Kremlin, or by other important centers of Communism, is not unthinkable. Such a shift would be hardly more of an about-face than some reversals already made. The trend is certainly toward a "softer" line in the Soviet Union, once the head and center of the so-called Communist monolith. As the Russian people become more fully aware of the outside world and create irresistible pressures for more consumer goods, the momentum is in the direction of more private enterprise—or "creeping capitalism." Once such sweets are tasted, the long-suffering Soviet peoples will not lightly give them up.

Not the most unthinkable of unthinkable thoughts is the prospect that one day the United States, softened by "creeping socialism," will clasp hands with the Soviet Union, softened by "creeping capitalism." Together they may stand foursquare against Communist China in defense of the new socialist–capitalist world.

We shall have to learn to live with the bumptiousness of nations on the make: they may eventually "arrive" and become less
noisy. We should know; we were that way ourselves in the nineteenth century. The Russians, having shaken off their inferiority
complex with their first Sputnik in 1957, are cooling down.[5] Perhaps
the Communist Chinese will one day complete the same cycle. In
this hope, American policy-makers may do well to pursue a course
of patience and persistence.

Above all, the planners on the Potomac should never fall into
the error that men and nations never change, and that a policy
that was viable for the Soviet Union of 1933 is still viable. Change
is the law of both life and history. We should deal with nations as
they are today, not as they used to be. The mere existence of Red
China belies the smug belief that neither ancient habits nor human
nature can be altered.

CONTAINMENT SHOULD BE SELECTIVE

George F. Kennan, a brilliant planner in the State Department
in the late 1940's, is credited with devising the doctrine of "containing" the power of Soviet Communism. This policy was imple-
mented most spectacularly in 1947 with the Truman Doctrine for
Greece and Turkey, and with the Marshall Plan for Western
Europe.

The architects of containment, in their initial planning, did
not envisage the use of large bodies of American troops to restrain
the rising tide of Soviet Communism. Arms would be provided to
the prospective victims, as well as vast amounts of economic aid.

Containment took on an ominous new dimension in 1950, when
President Truman sent troops into Korea to halt North Korean
aggression. The policy took still another turn in 1964 when American forces clashed on a large scale with those of North Vietnam in
an effort to prevent Communist domination of South Vietnam.

---

[5] Sputnik I demolished the stereotype, persisting since Tsarist days, that
the Russians were bovine, stupid Slavs, incapable of independent scientific
achievement. We were startled by their detonation of an atomic bomb in 1949,
but assumed that this unexpectedly early success was due primarily to German
scientists shanghaied from Hitler's collapsed Germany, and to the theft of
American atomic secrets by Soviet agents. These last two assumptions were
only partly valid.

Testifying before the Senate Foreign Relations Committee in 1966, Mr. Kennan declared that while his policy had not changed substantially, the world situation had. In 1947, there had been only one real center of Communist power; by 1966 there were several centers. Containment, he argued, meant concentrating on those areas that were most vital to the United States. In his view, his original policy had been expanded beyond what he regarded as reasonable or prudent.[6]

The truth is that the United States, powerful and rich though it is, does not have the military might or the economic resources to challenge every act of Communist aggression that may erupt anywhere in the world. By 1966 several hundred thousand American servicemen were involved in faraway Vietnam, aside from the more than two hundred thousand holding the line in Europe. Available manpower resources were buttered so thin over the globe that if a comparable crisis had developed in Korea or elsewhere, we would have faced critical shortages.

In brief, Uncle Sam cannot be an Uncle Don Quixote tilting at every Communist windmill, but should conserve his economic and military strength for the more crucial areas. Not all Communist countries, including Albania and Romania, are a direct menace to the United States.

COMMUNISM MAY CLOAK IMPERIALISM

One of the cleverest triumphs of Communist propaganda has been its success in "selling" the uncommitted world on the idea that Red Russia and Red China are not imperialistic powers but that the United States and its Western allies are. While we were divesting ourselves of the Philippines, while the British, Dutch, and French were liquidating their vast colonial empires, the Kremlin was extending its sway over tens of millions of "enslaved" peoples. Deeds are ordinarily stronger than words, but propaganda often speaks louder than actions.

One of the slickest tricks of Communist agents is to encourage anti-colonialism and nationalism in the underdeveloped countries of Asia and Africa, such as Indonesia and Ghana. Then, when

[6] See J. William Fulbright, *The Vietnam Hearings* (1966), pp. 130–131 (Feb. 10, 1966).

nationhood has been achieved, these same Communist agents have tried to subvert the new nationalism and bring the people under an internationalist sway exercised from Moscow or Peking.

In the nineteenth century, Tsarist Russia was one of the foremost imperialistic and expansionist powers of all time. A change of government does not ordinarily result in a change of basic national aspirations. The presumption is strong that even if Bolshevism had never come to the Soviet Union, an aggressive Russia would today pose a menace to those neighboring nations upon which it looks with more than fraternal interest. Precisely the same observation may be made about Red China, which in earlier centuries was the scourge of Asia. She has old scores to settle with the land-grabbing Russians, who took full advantage of her weakness in the nineteenth century to seize enormous areas long claimed or desired by the Chinese.

A HEALTHY DEMOCRACY IS AN ANTIDOTE
TO COMMUNISM

One of the best ways for America to fight Communism abroad is to foster democracy at home. Perhaps the most damning indictment of McCarthyism in the 1950's was that in concentrating on the handful of alleged Communists under the bed, we lost sight of the millions overseas. The "thought control" spawned by this witchhunt bore ugly resemblances to that under Hitler and other dictators. American democracy received a black eye abroad from which it has never fully recovered.

The internal Negro Revolution of the 1960's was another source of acute embarrassment to the United States in its battle to stem Communism in the emerging nations of Africa and Asia. The violent repressive measures that we directed against Americans— black and white—further sullied our national image.

The workaday American, preoccupied with the prospective occupant of the house next door, is tragically shortsighted. He does not seem to realize that every time he is guilty of an act of intolerance or injustice against members of a different race, he is playing into the hands of Communist propagandists. He is in truth striking a blow against the successful implementation of his nation's foreign policy.

CHAPTER XVII

The Non-Communist World

"Never have the nations of the world had so much to lose or so much to gain. Together we shall save our planet or together we shall perish in its flames."

PRESIDENT KENNEDY, to UN General Assembly, 1961

PROLOGUE

The globe since 1945 has divided itself roughly into thirds, like a gigantic but irregularly cut pie: the Communist world, the democratic world, and the noncommitted world—"the third world"— which could gravitate into either camp. The Communist nations and the so-called free nations are locked in a desperate and costly struggle for the allegiance of the in-between nations, which are in the favored position of being suitored by both sides. A large segment of American policy since 1945, particularly the costly foreign aid program, has been affected by this colossal tug-of-war. The United States has rung up gains, and it has suffered losses. Some of the most serious losses have come in nations—Cuba, for example—which we kicked around in a day when no one dreamed that we would need their sympathy, if not their active support, in a contest for survival. Past sins have a nasty habit of returning to plague us.

NATIONAL TRAITS CAN BE MISLEADING

A dangerous pitfall is to make easy assumptions about the national character of the people with whom we are thrown into contact.

Before the Pearl Harbor debacle, we had learned that the Japanese were fanatically militaristic, that they were wholly lacking in inventive genius, that they could not construct airplanes, and that, since they all wore thick glasses, they could not see well enough to fly them. One rumor had German aviators flying aircraft for them.

Pearl Harbor ripped away the veil of illusion, and the postwar years jarred our thinking about inborn Japanese militarism. One of the major tasks confronting American policy-makers in the 1960's was to persuade the Japanese to raise even a token army and to share some of the cost of their own defense.

Similar miscalculations have often betrayed us. We have formed misleading stereotypes about the imperialistic Briton, the unscientific Slav, and the excitable Frenchman. We assumed that the French, with their passion for change, could construct only collapsible governments. This, of course, was before the heyday of President Charles de Gaulle.

Two world wars with Germany taught us some harsh lessons that were hard to unlearn. We concluded that the Germans were cruel, arrogant, militaristic, and docile enough to goose-step behind any kind of Hitler who would promise world domination.[1] After World War II, we discovered that the so-called militaristic Germans, shattered by air raids and invaders, simply did not want to raise a new army. They finally consented to do so, in what were conceived as our interests as well as their own, after much arm-twisting on our part and feet-dragging on theirs. By this time we had learned that there are good Germans as well as bad ones.

All these experiences should warn us against hasty judgments

---

[1] Jakob Cats (1577–1660), the Dutch poet, wrote:
> "When the Hun [German] is poor and down
> He's the humblest man in town;
> But once he climbs and holds the rod
> He smites his fellow-man—and God."

Winston Churchill, speaking to the United States Congress (May 19, 1943) recalled the old saying, "The Hun is always either at your throat or at your feet."

about national traits. Insofar as they do exist, they can change with changing circumstances. The American people and their policy-makers should keep this vital truth in mind, and not deal with nations in the twentieth century on a nineteenth century basis.

Rudyard Kipling warned in 1889, "Oh, East is East, and West is West, and never the twain shall meet. . . ." The West has not only met but collided with the East. The United States itself has been involved in fighting in the Philippines (1899–1902), China (1900), Burma (1942–1945), Korea (1950–1953), and Vietnam. Kipling also warned us that only a fool would try "to hustle the East." Yet we have witnessed, in recent generations, the amazing trans-formation of feudal Japan and the even more astonishing "leaps forward" of China in the years since 1949. Old stereotypes require new looks.

BEWARE OF SELF-DECEPTION ABOUT FOREIGNERS

A glaring example of the folly of self-deception is provided by the Chinese. It points up the necessity of avoiding sentimentalizing and of securing reliable information.

Early American missionaries and diplomats in China created the false impression that the heathen Chinese despised all foreign-ers, except those from the United States. The truth is that the Chinese, with their ancient civilization, regarded all other nations as "barbarians," including the American upstarts. The nationalistic Chinese Boxers of 1900 butchered American missionaries as blood-ily as those from other lands.

We assumed in the 1940's and 1950's that Chiang Kai-shek loved the Americans. His recollections have appeared in book form, but the expurgated edition has been most widely circulated in the United States. His original comments on the Americans were so unflattering that they might well have hurt his chances of secur-ing continued financial aid on Taiwan.

We believed that the Chinese were loyal and self-sacrificing allies during World War II. Yet Chiang fought with one eye on the Japanese and the other on the Communists, against whom he diverted many of the few arms we were able to send him. Here we find a partial explanation of the sourness that developed between him and the American General Joseph ("Vinegar Joe") Stilwell.

During World War II we fondly imagined that China was a great power, one of the Big Four, including the United States, the U.S.S.R., and Britain. Partly to bolster sagging Chinese morale, President Roosevelt promoted this fiction and managed to secure a permanent seat on the Security Council of the UN for China. Yet Winston Churchill wrote in 1944, "That China is one of the world's four Great Powers is an absolute farce." [2] Red China finally did emerge as a major power in the 1950's, when she fought a coalition of Western nations to a standstill in Korea.

In the 1940's we also deceived ourselves in thinking that the backward and docile Chinese Communists were simply "agrarian reformers," and that their ancient family system effectively barred Communism. Many red-blooded Americans believed that Chiang Kai-shek lost out because we did not send him enough help in arms and money, and because we sent him no American troops at all. The truth is that Chiang had forfeited the confidence of his own people, and in these circumstances few regimes can survive. Outside armed intervention, as was evidently true of the invasion of Bolshevist Russia after 1917, may even defeat its ends by arousing patriotic opposition.

BAD NEIGHBORISM IS HARD TO ERASE

For many decades we have been the overshadowingly dominant power in this hemisphere, and on numerous occasions we have taken advantage of the weakness of our Latin neighbors to seize their territory or land troops. Such interventions have occurred most frequently in the Caribbean area in defense of the Monroe Doctrine and our Isthmian viscera.

Small nations have long memories, and they nurse these slights and bruises long after we have forgotten our misdeeds. In 1914, when Franklin D. Roosevelt was Assistant Secretary of the Navy and Josephus Daniels was Secretary of the Navy, President Wilson ordered the bombardment of Vera Cruz. More than 200 Mexicans died. Yet in 1933 President Franklin D. Roosevelt, who evidently

[2] Winston S. Churchill, *Triumph and Tragedy* (1953), p. 701. Franklin Delano Roosevelt was fond of recalling the two fortunes which his Delano grandfather made in the China trade, and this recollection seems to have left him with an emotional attachment to China itself. Frank Freidel, *Franklin Roosevelt: The Apprenticeship* (1952), p. 13.

had forgotten this brutal business, appointed Josephus Daniels as our Ambassador to Mexico. The Mexicans, who had not forgotten, received Ambassador Daniels with grave misgivings. But his friendliness and sympathy dispelled their doubts, and he turned out to be an unusually popular envoy.

The Bad Neighborism, as evidenced by repeated landings of the marines was publicly disavowed by President Franklin Roosevelt in 1933. From then until 1965, when President Lyndon Johnson ordered troops to Santo Domingo, the record remained unblemished. But an hour of interventionism can wipe out three decades of noninterventionism, and countless Latin Americans reacted with anger and horror at this return to the old "gunboat diplomacy."

As a rule, the smaller the country, the greater the sensitivity; the weaker the nation, the thinner the skin. Weak neighbors are suspicious neighbors, and for many of them suspicion is the first line of defense—in fact, the only line.[3] The American public and their representatives, whether officials or newsmen, would do well to lean over backward to respect the sovereignty of these less privileged nations.[4]

REVOLUTIONS DO NOT STOP TO PLEASE AMERICAN INVESTORS

The investment of American dollars in underdeveloped countries normally involves more risk (and hence a higher interest return) than investment at home.

When revolutions have erupted, say in Nicaragua, the investors have naturally clamored for American marines to defend their dollars. The marines are supported by all the taxpayers, but the profits from these investments (with the risk thereby reduced by the presence of the marines) flowed into the pockets of a self-selected few.

[3] A Haitian came to the United States in the 1920's thinking that the Yankees were bent on devouring his country. His fear turned to resentment when he discovered that most Americans did not even know where Haiti was.

[4] In 1959 a U.S. embassy official in Bolivia was quoted in the Latin American edition of *Time* (March 2, 1959) as having remarked that Bolivia's economic ills could be cured by dividing the country among its neighbors. Mobs stoned the embassy. An official investigation by Washington resulted in a soothing denial that any such statement had been made by the staff.

The problem became most acute with the Mexican upheaval of 1911, which developed into a genuine revolution designed to restore Mexico to the Mexicans. The new regimes expropriated the oil concessions and other holdings of foreigners, including the "gringos" from the North. President Wilson was under enormous pressure from American investors to intervene, but Mexico, unlike Nicaragua, is an immense and populous country, capable of waging a protracted guerrilla war. The right of revolution was permitted to take precedence over the rights of foreign investors, who came out on the short end.

The Cuban revolution under Castro resulted in the expropriation of hundreds of millions of dollars worth of American holdings. Again Washington was under enormous pressure to intervene, but it compromised by resorting to embargoes and boycotts. Its hope was that Castro would ultimately collapse, and that the sugar refineries and other American properties would be restored to their rightful owners.

There is a tendency among conservative investors in foreign lands to regard social reform, including badly needed redistribution of land in Latin America, as a Communist plot. Official Washington should be cautious in listening to those financiers who cry Communism in their attempts to secure armed intervention to protect their holdings.

MULTILATERAL INTERVENTION IS PREFERABLE TO UNILATERAL

The United States not only forswore intervention in Latin America in 1933 but in 1947 signed the Rio Pact. Under it, the twenty-one so-called Republics of the New World pledged themselves to stand together against aggression from the outside or against an armed attack from a sister nation in the Americas.

At the time of the Cuban missile crisis in 1962, the United States was fully prepared to invade Cuba and destroy the threat to its vitals. The other voting members of the Organization of American States, realizing that missiles that could shoot north from Cuba could also shoot south, unanimously backed Washington in this crisis.

A different situation developed in the Dominican Republic in

1965. There was seemingly no time for a meeting of the Organization of American States, with prolonged debate, with a probable
lack of unanimity, and with a possibly adverse vote. President
Johnson promptly sent in troops, and in subsequent days several
other Latin American states added small contingents. The occupation force then took on something of a Pan-American coloration,
but certainly not a strong coloration.[5] In any case, the northern
Colossus was thus able to make its intervention look somewhat less
brutal.

DISTANCE WEAKENS DIPLOMACY

The United States has been more successful in twisting arms
in the Americas than in either Europe or the Far East. This
partially explains why, during the nineteenth century notably, we
pursued a policy of nonintervention in Europe, intervention in
Latin America, and cooperation with the powers in the Far East.
We recall vividly that in 1962 the Soviets undertook to challenge
us frontally in our Cuban front yard. One basic reason why they
backed down no doubt was a realization that the cards were
stacked in our favor, for Cuba was some 6,000 miles from the
U.S.S.R. and only 90 miles from the U.S.A.

In more recent years, we have increasingly become go-it-alone-
ists in the Far East. Nominally the Korean War was a sixteen-nation
operation (aside from the South Koreans) but we bore virtually
the entire burden. We came out of this conflict poorer and sadder
but somewhat wiser, and with the precept ringing in our ears, "Never
again an open-ended war in Asia in which we are up against the inexhaustible manpower of China." [6]

In the 1960's this lesson was ignored in Vietnam, possibly because the Pentagon planners were convinced that bombers alone,
using "conventional" weapons, could turn the trick. We became

[5] Participating members were the United States, Brazil, Costa Rica,
Honduras, Nicaragua, and Paraguay. The last four provided only token forces.
A Brazilian general was placed in command, even though the United States had
the preponderant contribution. See John B. Martin, *Overtaken by Events* (1966),
p. 699.

[6] General Douglas MacArthur was quoted as saying, "Anybody who com-
mits the land power of the United States on the continent of Asia ought to have
his head examined."

bogged down in Vietnamese jungles, in virtually a solo operation, except for the war-weary South Vietnamese. And again—the "lessons" of history brushed aside—we were in an area adjacent to the "inexhaustible manpower of China" and under pressures from American extremists to carry the war into Red China itself. We seemed to forget that China then had over 700 million people; we had fewer than 200 million, about 7,000 miles away, at the end of an attenuated supply line. For the foreseeable future there will always be hundreds of millions more Asiatics than Americans, and fighting a foot-soldiers' war on their ground is an uphill game.

Down through the ages foreign hordes have swept into China, but there she stands, with the longest continuous national government in existence. The invaders have come, have been outbred and inbred, and then have disappeared. Speaking to a joint session of Congress in 1952, Prime Minister Churchill quoted a Chinese proverb: "China is a sea that salts all the waters that flow into it." [7]

The Japanese were the last large-scale invaders. They came in 1931 and again in 1932 and again in 1937. They threw several million soldiers into China; they overran vast areas of the country, including the most populous coastal and urban areas; and they finally failed. If the Japanese, as near neighbors with a powerful army, could not overcome a divided and devitalized China, the prospects of a successful conquest by the United States do not seem promising.

Distance weakens power. Great distance weakens power greatly.

SOUND PRINCIPLES KNOW NO HEMISPHERE

We have already observed that the United States, notably in the so-called isolationist nineteenth century, pursued different policies in different hemispheres. This was especially true in the Western Hemisphere, where we could best make our muscle felt.

The picture has changed. We now live in one world. It is like a giant drum, and if we thump it anywhere, it vibrates almost everywhere.

Back in the nineteenth century, and even later, we looked upon Europe as the main show. There dwelt the "great powers."

[7] *Cong. Record,* 82nd Cong., 2nd sess., p. 277.

What happened in Europe was of the first importance; what happened elsewhere was secondary or a minor-league operation.

In 1931 the Japanese militarists staged their epochal *coup* in Manchuria. President Hoover, the lifelong Quaker, was unwilling to join with the other powers—assuming such willingness on their part—to bell the Japanese cat. The American public agreed with him, for we felt that China's Manchuria was really no business of ours. We also believed that the faraway Far East was the back door of the world, and nothing that could happen at the back door could possibly affect the front door.

No nation is an island, and the halting of Japan's naked aggression, assuming it could have been stopped by joint action, was a concern of all nations, including the United States. By one way of reckoning, Tokyo's defiance of the League of Nations in Manchuria led inexorably to World War II. The League betrayed its fatal weakness to the fast-ascending Mussolini and Hitler, both of whom launched upon a mad course that ultimately wrapped the globe in flames.

SOVEREIGNTY IS THE PRICE OF
INTERNATIONAL ORGANIZATION

The United Nations has proved to be a grave disappointment, as was true of the League of Nations before it, largely because we have expected the impossible. It was "oversold" at the outset. It was supposed to preserve international order and prevent war without being clothed with the authority or organized to achieve these ends.

None of the great powers has been willing to yield effective control over its affairs to the United Nations, certainly not to a supranational police force under that body's jurisdiction. Each of the superpowers in the Security Council has retained the right of veto, without which the organization would not have come into being. A legally dubious attempt to clothe the General Assembly with power to act, when the Security Council was deadlocked by the veto, was made in the Uniting for Peace Resolutions of 1950.[8] But since then the Assembly has been hamstrung by the pocketbook veto—that is, the refusal of Russia, France, and other nations

[8] Adopted November 3, 1950. *United Nations General Assembly, Fifth Session*, Agenda Item, 68, pp. 1–8 (Nov. 4, 1950). (Uniting for Peace, Resolutions. A/1481.)

to pay financial assessments to support armed operations in the Congo and other areas.

The UN has undoubtedly served a useful purpose in varied walks of life, but its usefulness is severely limited. The Charter badly needs overhauling, but the prospect that the major powers will yield more sovereignty becomes fainter by the year.

The principle of one-nation-one-vote in the General Assembly has yielded a disturbing harvest. The balance of power is now held by the Afro-Asian bloc (the "Asafs"), consisting largely of poor and weak nations recently freed from colonialism. At times they show incredible irresponsibility. This was shockingly true in 1964, when African spokesmen passionately opposed the sending of aircraft into the Congo by the Americans and Belgians to rescue white civilians, including missionaries, who were being butchered by the natives. From time to time spokesmen for the great powers have argued for weighted voting—that is, adjusting the weight of a vote to the population and strength of the member. But the likelihood that the weaker nations will consent to this kind of downgrading becomes even dimmer as more of them enter the UN. More than half of the current membership had not yet attained nationhood when the organization was founded in 1945.

Increasingly we shall have to face up to the painful prospect of being outvoted in the General Assembly by these newcomers, some of whom are patently feeling their oats. From the early days of the UN the Soviet Union has routinely used the veto in the Security Council—more than one hundred times—to safeguard its interests against an unfriendly capitalistic majority. The United States may have to resort to the same weapon to protect itself against a growing bloc of anti-colonial and anti-capitalistic neophyte nations.

A WORLD ORGANIZATION REQUIRES WORLD MEMBERSHIP

The UN continues to limp along without superpopulous Red China, which, with nuclear weapons, is becoming more of a menace to its numerous weak neighbors.

The problem of admitting Communist China is not a simple one. The Charter of the UN stipulates that the organization is open to "all other peace-loving states" (Article 4). In 1951 the UN Assembly formally branded Communist China an aggressor, after it had attacked the multination UN force in Korea. Technically, this war is still on; only an armistice was agreed upon in 1953, and it is a precarious armistice. In 1959 the "peace-loving" Chinese, invoking old claims, overran and absorbed Tibet, and in 1962 invaded India's frontier.

If the UN consisted only of good boys, we should have all the more reason to keep China outside the gates. But in truth the UN is not a collection of Eagle Scouts. The Soviet Union, with the blood of the Hungarians of 1956 on its hands, to say nothing of other sins, remains among its members. Many others, including America with its Vietnam involvement, are not lily-white.

The United States, which in the days of Secretary Hay enunciated the Open Door for China, is now supporting a Closed Door at the UN. We do not approve of the Red regime and feel that we shall dishearten the peace-loving nations of Asia and the rest of the world if we permit Chinese Communists to rub elbows around the same table with them. On the other hand, now that Red China has achieved the nuclear breakthrough, the worldwide feeling grows that she can be controlled more effectively within the UN than without. A sense of urgency causes many former critics to overlook certain blemishes on Peking's character.

The question of nonseating is now largely academic, because Peking has proclaimed that it will not accept membership in the UN, except on its own terms. These involve an unseating of the rump Taiwan regime and other modifications of the Charter which are clearly unacceptable to many of the other charter-member nations.

One lesson is obvious. If we do not invite prospective members into the club when they want to join, we may find them spurning our advances when their interest has cooled.

PART V

War and Diplomacy

CHAPTER XVIII

The Politics of Power

"The Pope? How many divisions has he got?"

REMARK ATTRIBUTED TO MARSHAL STALIN, 1935

PROLOGUE

A nation's power, whether military or economic, is not in itself evil, any more than a powerful police department in a large city is evil. If armed forces are used for self-defense, for discouraging aggression, and for upholding legitimate policies, they usually escape moral condemnation. But power as an end in itself, rather than a means to an end, is generally regarded as wicked, as evidenced by the unpleasant overtones attached to the term "power politics." Adolf Hitler, a foremost practitioner of this art, brought incalculable misery upon countless millions of innocent people. Lord Acton observed that power corrupts; he might have added that it can also intoxicate and madden.

POLICY WITHOUT POWER IS IMPOTENT

President Theodore Roosevelt, a former Colonel of the Rough Riders, declared in 1905 that he never took a position in foreign affairs unless "assured that I shall be able eventually to carry out my will by force." He realized that military might is the teeth of diplomacy, and that policy is seldom more effective than the capacity to implement it. He might well have had in mind the observation attributed to Oliver Cromwell: "A man-of-war is the best ambassador." [1] Robert McClintock, Ambassador in Lebanon when we landed some 14,000 troops in 1958, writes: "There can be no effective diplomacy without the existence of some form of power, whether military, economic or psychological." [2]

Might tends to make right, and preponderant power usually calls the tune, as was true when big-navy Britain made her views on impressment prevail over weak-navy America prior to the War of 1812. Generally speaking, the seas were free in the nineteenth century only so far as the Mistress of the Seas would permit them to be free. In later years, especially during World War II, the United States was indisputably the dominant naval power. We were in a position to make our interpretation of neutral rights stick, and usually did.

Another favorite axiom of President Theodore Roosevelt was "Speak softly and carry a big stick, [and] you will go far." He did not always speak softly, but he did wield a Big Stick to beat nations, especially the small ones, into line. The Rooseveltian proverb is but another way of saying that courtesy, plus a show of strength —the iron hand in the velvet glove—is one of the more civilized ways of producing results.

The strong can afford to be polite; the weak have to bluster. The United States, as the weaker naval power in the controversy with Britain over Oregon in 1846, resorted to bluster, after which President Polk was luckily able to secure a fair compromise. The British came to the negotiating table for reasons that had little to do with America's impressive show of verbal strength.

A Big Stick is an asset, but a statesman should not make an undue display of it: to a diplomat of the old school, armies and navies were unmentionables. Premier Khrushchev, of the new Bolshevist school, used to brag in the 1950's of the nuclear bombs and rockets that the Soviet Union was prepared to rain on the United

---

[1] In 1908 Admiral Robley D. Evans, speaking in San Francisco, declared, "If you want to preserve the peace of the world, give us more battleships and fewer statesmen." Quoted in Robert A. Hart, *The Great White Fleet* (1965), p. 167.

[2] *The Meaning of Limited War* (1967), p. 123.

States. All of the great powers, and many of the small ones, have efficient spy systems. Diplomats should remember that their adversary is probably almost as well-informed as they are about their own military strength—in some cases better informed. Loud talk may even spur the intended victim to renewed efforts to increase his defensive arsenal. As the German proverb has it, "The best enemies are those who make threats."

ABUSE OF POWER BREEDS RESENTMENT

A strapping young Uncle Sam, during his more bumptious years at the turn of the nineteenth century, threw his weight around in an obnoxious fashion. His rule seemed to be: forbearance with the strong, impatience with the weak. President Theodore Roosevelt was deferential to a strong Japan during the San Francisco schoolboy crisis of 1906, but highhanded toward a weak Colombia, from which he wrenched the Canal Zone in 1903.

Bullying has no place today in conventional diplomacy, for to bully diplomatically is to blunder diplomatically. Smaller nations, bruised and resentful, may one day be able to get their knife into their tormentors, and in some noteworthy cases have done so. "Brave little Finland," despoiled of her territory by a brutal Stalin in 1940, stabbed the Russians in the flank when they were reeling under Hitler's ferocious surprise attack in 1941. By a narrow margin the Finns lost again, but their intervention worsened the already desperate plight of the Soviets.

One form of power-abuse is crushing butterflies with a sledgehammer. The punishment should fit the crime, and a nation should tailor its response to the magnitude of the grievance. It should react but not overreact. In 1891 two American sailors from the U.S.S. *Baltimore* were killed and nearly a score injured following a brawl in a Chilean saloon. President Harrison forced the Chileans to crawl, and they have never forgotten this humiliation.[3]

---

[3] Samuel Guy Inman, a distinguished United States authority on Latin America, recalls that at the end of a lecture to a student group in Chile, he threw the meeting open for questions. "How do you explain the *Baltimore* incident?" was the first question. To his acute embarrassment, Inman could not remember ever having heard of it. Carleton Beals, *et al.*, *What the South Americans Think of Us* (1945), p. 349.

It is well to have a giant's strength but not to use it like a giant in browbeating small nations. The greater the power the greater the responsibility to use it responsibly.

TURN ON THE HEAT BY DEGREES

In the Cuban missile crisis of 1962, President Kennedy exemplified gradualism in a masterly way. He first of all proclaimed a defensive "quarantine" of offensive weapons being shipped into Cuba. This was actually a war blockade, but he used the softer term "quarantine" to keep the temperature down. If the "quarantine" had not worked, Kennedy could have widened the blockade to all weapons (offensive and defensive), then to all incoming shipments (whether weapons or not), and then to all shipments of any kind (incoming or outgoing). He could then have landed troops, followed, if needed, by "surgical bombing" with conventional bombs, and then saturation bombing, with either conventional bombs or nuclear weapons.

Applying the heat gradually has the added advantage of enabling one's adversary to back down with a minimum of humiliation and without the risk of a "spasm reaction." Stepping up the pressure by degrees is much less dangerous than having to back down from an initial overuse of power. More options are preserved, and the preservation of optimum options is one of the major goals of diplomacy.

Never draw the sword when a rattle of the scabbard will suffice. A saturation bombing is irreversible.

POWER CAN PRESERVE THE PEACE

Military power in itself, as we have noted, is not necessarily evil, but its misuse and abuse are bad.

The longest period of general peace known to Western civilization came during the centuries when the Roman Peace (*Pax Romana*) prevailed. Some writers have referred to America's four-year nuclear monopoly after World War II as establishing a kind of Pax Americana, as far as a European conflict was concerned. Winston Churchill was but one of many observers to conclude, whether correctly or not, that America's atomic bombs were all that kept the Soviets from surging across Western Europe to the North Sea.[4]

[4] See Kay Halle, ed., *Irrepressible Churchill* (1966), p. 9 (March 31, 1949).

In 1949 the Russians detonated their first atomic bomb and a balance of bomb-power, or Pax Atomica—not a Pax Americana—has since prevailed. The U.S. and the U.S.S.R. could in theory impose their will on all other powers except each other.

POWER IS RELATIVE

In assessing power we must ask ourselves against whom it is potentially to be used—and where. The Soviets are stronger than we are in Eastern Europe, but we are stronger than they are in the Eastern Caribbean.

In 1812 Napoleon invaded Russia with some 500,000 men; simultaneously the United States, his quasi-ally, invaded Canada with some 5,000 men. Napoleon was stronger than we were in Europe, but we were stronger than he was in North America because he had no way of getting his army here. (His British arch-enemy controlled the seas.) In 1812 the United States, as regards the size of its army and navy, was a relatively weak power, that is, outside of its North American domain. But we were in no danger whatever of destruction, and in little danger of conquest.

Today we have immense power, nuclear and otherwise. We can theoretically destroy many times over—"overkill"—every inhabitant of the globe. Yet paradoxically we are in danger ourselves of nuclear annihilation, and the outlook grows more ominous as new and more irresponsible nations attain nuclear capability. The more powerful we become, the more vulnerable we are. In time of so-called peace, we are in more danger of destruction than we ever were in the worst of our wars.

Sheer force cannot solve all political problems. In the mid-1960's the United States, with a population of about 200 million and with overwhelming air and naval power, could not impose its will on a nation of some 17 million war-weary and poverty-stricken Asiatics in Vietnam. Ingenious new techniques of guerrilla warfare have strengthened the position of irregular troops—"raggety little bastards in black pajamas"—fighting in jungles. The eagle in the sky, combined with the whale in the ocean, cannot overcome the elephant in the jungle—so the Asiatic saying goes.

The United States could have unleashed its fearsome nuclear weapons and left the Vietnamese jungles uninhabited and uninhabitable in a matter of minutes. But such a diabolical course would have been no real solution of the problem and would further have branded us as monstrous in the eyes of hundreds of millions of people, including Americans. There is little satisfaction in creating a desert and calling it peace.

Our power has never been greater, but the greatest part of it is of little use in anything short of a nuclear incineration. We have the power to destroy the world but not to rule it. We are potent but not omnipotent.

POWER BREEDS APPREHENSION

Even in the best of circumstances, overweening power creates uneasiness in others. It can generate outright fear if a nation uses that power to aggrandize itself at the expense of its neighbors.

The United States came to be the much-hated Colossus of the North, in the eyes of Latin Americans, especially after it seized about one-half of Mexico in 1848 and continued intermittently with a policy of aggressive imperialism south of the Rio Grande. The high point—or low point—came during the first three decades of the present century, what with a protectorate over Cuba, the Americanization of Puerto Rico, the "rape" of Panama, and numerous landings of marines on the palm-fronded shores of the Caribbean.

Machiavelli observed in *The Prince* that, while a people would like to be both loved and feared by foreign nations, the two emotions are mutually incompatible, and that if a statesman has to choose between them, "it is far safer to be feared than loved." There is actually a more desirable middle course, and that is to seek to win respect.

MAKE ALLOWANCES FOR THE STRENGTH OF WEAKNESS

Someone has well said that only the very strong and the very weak can operate with reasonable safety in the jungle of diplomacy. The strong can take care of themselves; the weak can often count on forces outside themselves, including the balance of power or the balance of terror. A weak and helpless China was probably saved from partition at the end of the nineteenth century because none of the great powers could trust the others to grab only their fair share.

The weak can also count on humanitarianism, justice—"the might of right"—and the force of world opinion to restrain an avenging hand. A gentleman does not slap a woman (or did not in the old days), and a powerful nation does not ordinarily slap a weak one. Frenzied Egyptian and Indonesian mobs have sacked and burned United States Information Libraries in their capitals. American nuclear forces could retaliate with obliteration. But the misbehaving nations know that we will not, and they continue such indignities because they enjoy the strength of weakness—a cheap strength but often an effective one.

THE WILL TO USE POWER CAN BE AS IMPORTANT AS POWER ITSELF

"Human waves" of Chinese Communists swept into Korea late in 1950 and hurled back General MacArthur's advancing armies. The United States possessed the nuclear weapons to wipe out not only the Chinese bases but all the principal Chinese cities as well. We refrained from doing so, partly out of regard for world opinion, and partly out of a fear that the Soviets, allies of China under the treaty of 1950, would be drawn into the inferno and World War III would convulse mankind.[5]

Thus the United States, theoretically capable of winning a crushing victory in Korea, finally settled for a frustrating stalemate. For understandable and perfectly rational reasons, we lacked the nerve to play the game of "nuclear chicken."

During the Cuban missile crunch of 1962, we had both the power and the *will* to force the Soviets to withdraw their offensive weapons from Cuba. The situation was strikingly different from that in Korea, where the national interest was less critically involved, and where we had the dragging anchor of more than a dozen nervous allies. We were determined, if necessary, to go the whole way, and Moscow got the message.

POWER IMPOSES RESPONSIBILITIES

From those to whom much has been given, much is expected. When a nation becomes powerful and wealthy, it is supposed to

[5] For the text of the pact see Henry Wei, *China and Soviet Russia* (1956), pp. 343–347.

help less favored neighbors and use its power for the betterment of all peoples. This obligation accounts in part for our fantastic outpouring of foreign aid after World War II, although considerations of security and prosperity were also involved.

Great nations must act greatly in response to recurring crises or they abandon greatness. Just as nobility imposes obligations (*noblesse oblige*), power imposes obligations (*puissance oblige*), as do riches (*richesse oblige*). We should prefer to return to the relatively carefree days of the nineteenth century, when Britain was the dominant world leader, but the iron hand of destiny has tapped us as leader of the free world. If we fall, presumably the other democratic nations will fall, like a group of mountain climbers roped together behind a giant. To flee from these obligations would not only be the coward's course but would probably create chaos that would ultimately engulf us. In our own interest, if for no better reason, we are compelled to face up to these burdensome new responsibilities.

During World War I, we were forced into the position of leader of the nations, but in isolationist panic we fled to the wings. Today we are locked on the world stage. There is no place to hide. We either acquit ourselves like adults or like adolescents.

POWER ABHORS VACUUMS

In 1945 American officials, responding to an outcry from anxious sweethearts and relatives to bring the boys home, hastily dismantled the most potent striking force ever assembled. We had made the error in 1919 of bringing the fire department home before the fire in Europe was completely extinguished, and we repeated the same blunder in 1945.[6]

The withdrawal of the all-conquering Americans created a power vacuum into which the Soviets instinctively moved. They avoided unleashing their armies upon the nations of Western Europe, presumably out of fear of our atomic bomb monopoly. But they sought the same end by trying to take over the governments, notably those of Italy and France, through their powerful Com-

[6] Wholesale demonstrations by soldiers to spur demobilization may be regarded as technical mutinies. See R. Alton Lee, "The Army 'Mutiny' of 1946," *Journal of American History*, LIII (1966), pp. 555–571.

munist parties. The United States belatedly plugged the gap with the Marshall Plan, followed by NATO. This filling of the power vacuum was followed by a new, costly, and frantic arms race, which resulted in an uneasy balance of power.

Those dictators who seek to conquer their neighbors are usually peace-loving, provided that they can get what they want without fighting for it. Hitler, declared one contemporary punster, was piece-loving: all he wanted was a large piece of Czechoslovakia and then of Central Europe, as *hors d'oeuvres*. If a dictator covets power and wealth, he defeats his own ends when he destroys the cities, factories, and mines of his victims. Bank robbers seldom burn down banks.

Power is the only language that bullies respect, including certain postwar Communists. If the aggressors think that their victim is weak enough to crush, and they want to crush him, they will move in; otherwise they will hold back. A postwar Soviet spokesman remarked that when your knife hits bone, withdraw; when it hits mush, push.

TO THE AGGRESSOR BELONGS THE INITIATIVE

American foreign policy after World War II was widely criticized for its negativism. It consisted primarily of a number of holding actions or reactions to the actions of the Soviets, as was conspicuously exemplified by the Truman Doctrine, the Marshall Plan, the Berlin airlift, and the North Atlantic Treaty Organization.

This negativism was inevitable, because the United States had no designs on its neighbors, whereas the Soviet Union did. The aggressor knows who his potential victim is; and since in the years after World War II we did not know who was next on the Communist grab list, our actions generally had to be governed by the defensive philosophy of containment.

The Washington government has never taken the position that the Soviets are not entitled to Communism or socialism or any other "ism" they want. But they are not to force it on all other nations, including the United States. "Live and let live" is a philosophy that can work only on a two-way street, and the Soviets were operating on a one-way street, with the weaker neighbors being crushed beneath their juggernaut.

NEVER OVERESTIMATE THE STRENGTH
OF DICTATORSHIP

A favorite theme of Secretary of State Dulles in the 1950's was that dictatorships are less powerful and democracies less weak than they seem.

Hitler brutally challenged the democratic world in 1939, and at first his mechanized might seemed invincible. Britain was beaten in 1940 but did not know enough to know it. Behind the on-the-surface weaknesses of the British, as is true of most genuine democracies, lay unsuspected reservoirs of strength. Behind the glittering and awesome martial array of Hitler lay the rottenness of a bloody and corrupt regime of gangsters. In World War I and World War II the democratic nations, after initial disasters, finally triumphed over their foes. The will of free men seeking to preserve their freedoms is not to be taken lightly.

Countless dictators have strutted briefly across the stage of history. Hitler's self-proclaimed Thousand Year Empire lasted only twelve years. And where are the Mussolinis, the Stalins, and the Tojos of yesteryear?

MORAL DISAPPROBATION BREAKS NO BONES

In 1931 the American people thoroughly disapproved of Japan's military *coup* in China's Manchuria. We deplored aggression, and our sympathies traditionally went out to the underdog, even though a large-sized one. But the Hoover administration, unwilling to use force or unable to command sufficient force, had to content itself with the Hoover–Stimson Doctrine of nonrecognition (1932). Secretary Stimson proclaimed that the United States would not recognize any "situation, treaty, or agreement" brought about contrary to the Kellogg–Briand Pact of 1928, which had outlawed war (except in self-defense) as an instrument of national policy. Japan had signed the Kellogg–Briand Pact.

The Stimson nonrecognition policy was a cheap and apparently safe way of satisfying the American conscience. It did not bother the Japanese perceptibly or stop them in their ambitious career of conquest, for it was not even a slap on the wrist. Winston Churchill observed in 1937, "Moral force is, unhappily, no substitute for armed force, but it is a very great reinforcement." [7]

There is seldom such a thing as a cheap defense, but there are cheap catastrophes. The nagging, moralistic course that we pursued in the Far East, as a veritable "paper tiger," led us to proclaim a pro-Chinese, anti-Japanese policy that ultimately blew up in our faces at Pearl Harbor.

The moral disapprobation of the outside world does not halt tanks, as the Soviet "Butchers of Budapest" demonstrated in 1956. Nor did it halt the "peace-loving" Prime Minister Nehru of India in 1961 when he suddenly seized the centuries-old Portuguese enclave of Goa. If a real showdown comes, harsh words are a poor substitute for defiant deeds.

[7] See Kay Halle, ed., *Irrepressible Churchill* (1966), p. 136.

CHAPTER XIX

The Mission of the Military

"We dare not tempt them [our adversaries] with weakness. For only when our arms are sufficient beyond doubt can we be certain beyond doubt that they will never be employed."

JOHN F. KENNEDY, INAUGURAL ADDRESS, 1961

PROLOGUE

War has now become, or can again become, total war. Military men in America are increasingly involved in civilian life, and civilians are increasingly involved in military life. The interlocking of these interests has produced some disturbing problems, notably the preservation of civilian control over the military. Under our Constitution the President is made Commander-in-Chief of all the armed forces, yet in recent years, except for President-General Eisenhower, he has had no military experience whatever, or only limited experience at the lower levels. Headstrong generals naturally resent taking orders from a rank amateur, especially if an exalted reputation is at stake, as was General MacArthur's in his titanic but uneven tug-of-war with Commander-in-Chief Truman. But for more than a hundred years this "general problem" has existed, and it is one of the many prices we have to pay for our time-honored tradition of free speech.

PROFITABLE WARS ARE SELF-STARTING WARS

Aggressors usually do not pick a fight unless they are confident they can win. By the same token they do not ordinarily start a war unless there is something in it for them, or they think there is.

In 1812, for example, the United States declared war on the British. We had burning grievances, chiefly growing out of Britain's high-handed maritime practices during her war with France. But we almost certainly could have endured these grievances somewhat longer had not Canada been there, an alluring object of conquest, apparently defenseless and seemingly capable of being overrun with ridiculous ease.

In the 1930's, the tables were turned and a fabulously rich and fatuously unprepared America invited the cupidity of the aggressors. We were lucky to come out of that crisis with a relatively whole skin.

IMBALANCES OF POWER PROVOKE WAR

After Europe burst into flames in 1914, the assumption was hardly challenged in America that the baleful balance of power had ignited the conflagration. President Wilson was determined to have no more war-breeding alliances: he would have all the nations of the world joined in one grand alliance for peace known as the League of Nations.[1]

It is true that war engulfed Europe in 1914 in part because of rivalries between two delicately poised balances of power. But war came again in 1939 because of an obvious imbalance of power. The backdown of Britain and France at Munich in 1938 had nakedly advertised their weakness, and Hitler plunged into Poland the next year because he was confident he could win, as he came perilously close to doing.

Soviet Russia emerged as the colossus of Europe after World War II, and the United States strove desperately to redress the consequent imbalance of power. A major result was the North Atlantic Treaty Organization, which doubtless put something of a damper on Soviet designs.

[1] See Edward H. Buehrig, *Woodrow Wilson and the Balance of Power* (1955).

Balances of power have long been traditional first lines of defense. And while they do not guarantee peace, they are certainly more effective guarantors than gross imbalances of power. "One sword keeps another in its scabbard," runs a German proverb.

UNPREPAREDNESS INCITES ATTACK

Homer Lea, the American author-soldier who foresaw ultimate conflict with Japan, wrote feelingly of *The Valor of Ignorance* (1909). For generations Americans believed that they could win wars without preparing for them, and they found support for this delusion in their superpatriotic history textbooks. These manuals misleadingly taught that we had won all of our wars, including the miserable little War of 1812, without adequate preparedness.

After World War I erupted, President Wilson opposed prudent defense measures. Not only was he steeped in the American tradition of isolationism and neutralism but he feared that if we had an army, we might succumb to the temptation to use it overseas. He reluctantly reversed his position in 1915, but tragically late. By 1917, when the Germans in desperation undertook to sink all ships in the war zone (including American), Wilson had no Big Stick with which to back up his position. If he had possessed a formidable army, with adequate transatlantic transportation, the Germans might well have had second thoughts about forcing us into the fray.

We relearned the forgotten lessons of 1812 and 1917 again after Pearl Harbor in 1941 and in Korea in 1950. It is more comforting to have arms and not need them than to need them and not have them.

A PUBLICIZED NO-STRIKE-FIRST POLICY INVITES DISASTER

In the years after World War II the Washington authorities repeatedly proclaimed their determination never to strike first with atomic weapons. This was a high-sounding moral position, consonant with American traditions, but it was so unrealistic as to be branded by Winston Churchill as a "silly thing." It meant in effect that while you carry a costly pistol for your defense, you must never shoot until you are shot dead or nearly dead. You must lose a hundred million or more of your people in your enemy's first salvo and count on having enough nuclear weapons left to annihilate him. If he believes that he can wipe you out completely with his first strike, without danger of retaliation, he will be tempted to strike first.

Crises will conceivably develop in which the Washington officials will have unmistakable evidence that our adversary is just about to cut loose with a surprise nuclear salvo. In these circumstances, ruthless realism would call for shooting first and without warning. If the United States on moral grounds must cling to a policy of no-strike-first, then at the very least we should keep our adversary guessing (and on his good behavior) by not advertising such a policy. Artemus Ward has observed:

> "Twice is he armed that hath his quarrel just;
> And three times he who gets his fist in fust."

REPEATED BLUFFING BLUNTS
DIPLOMATIC EFFECTIVENESS

A policy of bluff-and-back-down introduces an element of uncertainty into diplomacy and produces the possibility of war by miscalculation. President Theodore Roosevelt's frontier maxim was, "Never draw unless you mean to shoot."

After World War II, Russian spokesmen repeatedly threatened the Western powers with war if they created a German army. A German army was created—and nothing happened. The Russians repeatedly threatened to turn Berlin over to the East Germans if the Western Allies did not move out. Several deadlines passed without comment, without explanation, and without war. The notorious capacity of Moscow for bluffing no doubt helped stiffen the backbone of President Kennedy when he stared the Russians down during the Cuban missile crisis of 1962.

But we must never assume that a bluffer is always bluffing, and we must especially be on our guard when a nonbluffer is said to be bluffing. Experts declared that tiny Japan was bluffing when she stood up to gigantic foes like China in 1894, Russia in 1904, and the United States in 1941. In each instance she took the initiative in a surprise attack.

The famed Supreme Court Justice, Oliver Wendell Holmes, Jr., once remarked that on a certain point "a page of history" was "worth a volume of logic." In view of Japan's record of unannounced assaults, one is all the more amazed that the American forces were caught with their planes down at Pearl Harbor. We were humiliated largely because the strategists in Washington did not feel that the Japanese were strong enough or stupid enough to gamble on a devastating first strike.

We must never assume that our opponent is always prudent, or that he would never do in a given situation what we would not do. Different peoples have different values, and they reason from different premises.

DIPLOMATIC AND MILITARY AFFAIRS
ARE SIAMESE TWINS

The generals and the diplomats should cooperate in both peace and war. Each should know what the other is doing, so that military means can be adjusted to diplomatic ends, and so that the warriors can know what policy they are supposed to uphold in what part of the world and with what. The opening in 1946 of the National War College in Washington, where diplomats and military men are trained together, was a significant step in the right direction. "The soldier is the stateman's junior partner," declared General Matthew B. Ridgway in 1954.

An absence of adequate communication between the diplomats in Washington and the commanders at Pearl Harbor helped set the stage for the disaster of December 7, 1941. Washington can see the global picture, while the theater commanders naturally think in terms of their immediate responsibility. The commanders in the field should be kept as fully informed as security precautions will permit.

MASSIVE RETALIATION CHOKES OFF ALTERNATIVES

During the Dulles–Eisenhower years the emphasis was on "massive retaliation," that is, responding to aggression with devastating nuclear power. This strategy of "peace through deterrence" appealed to many Americans because it was cheaper than maintaining large standing armies—"more bang for the buck," as the saying went.

Cut-rate defense is often costly defense, and this type had one terrifying drawback. It made no adequate provision for controlling localized "brush-fire wars" which might be stamped out with conventional forces before they spread into global forest fires. In the event of a crisis, one side had to back down or there would be nuclear incineration. Fortunately for sanity, during the Cuban missile crisis of 1962 the Soviets backed down.

In short, the alternatives under massive retaliation could well be humiliation or holocaust, surrender or suicide. With conventional ground forces, which were built up under Presidents Kennedy and Johnson, there were other choices, including the portentous commitment of troops to South Vietnam. The greater the variety of weapons, the greater the variety of options—and also involvements. If one does not have conventional forces to commit, one is less likely to commit them.

Massive retaliation, rather than a "flexible response" or "graduated deterrence," has another drawback. Frequent and loose talk about it may produce a callousness which in turn may help bring it on. Mankind learns to live with horror. We were shocked when German Zeppelins during World War I dropped a relatively few bombs on London. In subsequent wars "civilized" man moved forward to the point where he had not the house-buster, or the block-buster, but the city-buster. The atomic flash that flattened Hiroshima seemed to be the ultimate weapon, and although humanity recoiled in horror, our "shock-proof generation" gradually got used to the idea. Then came the vastly more destructive hydrogen bomb, and mankind also got used to the thought of wiping out a hundred million or more persons in a nuclear salvo. "Crisis," observed former President Eisenhower, has now become "normalcy"—and man must learn to live with it.

NEVER BACK YOUR ADVERSARY OR YOURSELF INTO A CORNER

A nation should never back its opponent into a corner, unless perchance it wants war. Even a rat will fight when cornered, and burglars seldom become murderers if they are given a chance to

flee. In short, we must never compel our opponent to choose between national existence and war or national honor and war. In
1812 we tried to force Britain to give up the impressment of seamen, which she deemed necessary for her national preservation
against the deadly threat of Napoleon. The result was an armed
clash.

The United States, in dealing with the menace of Napoleon III
in Mexico after the Civil War, operated more skillfully. Rather
than driving him into a corner, Secretary Seward pushed him
gently toward the open exit.

Conversely, a diplomat should not back himself into a corner
from which there is no retreat, honorable or dishonorable. Ideally,
there should always be various alternatives or fall-back positions,
despite the danger that when such exits exist, one is tempted to
fall back too soon. In 1954 Secretary Dulles was pressing the
French to integrate the proposed German army into a six-nation
force—the so-called European Defense Community (EDC). Despite
Washington's insistence, Paris finally rejected the whole idea, leaving a red-faced Secretary Dulles without any real alternatives to
propose. Western diplomats, notably those of Britain, helped come
to the rescue with a compromise scheme.

One way to steer clear of corners and retain flexibility of
maneuver is to avoid ultimata, especially those with a specific time
limit. A nation should not ordinarily go out on the end of such a
limb, unless it is fully prepared to start a war if its adversary does
not consent to its terms. On September 3, 1939, two days after Hitler's fateful invasion of Poland, Great Britain, an ally of the Poles,
presented a note to Berlin stating that unless word arrived by 11
A.M. that the Germans had withdrawn their troops, Britain and
Germany would be at war. No such word was forthcoming, and the
clash came. But by this time diplomatic relations with the war-mad
Hitler had so far deteriorated that there was no hope of withdrawal.

BEWARE OF THE SOLDIERLY ITCH FOR ACTION

The so-called "military mind" has often been unfairly condemned. Brass hats do not necessarily mean brass heads. There are
rigid and obtuse minds in all walks of life, military and civilian,
and there are exceptionally keen minds among the soldiers. But

some direct-actionists, bored with civilian routine or seeking release from tension, crave action,[2] and alarmingly a few are to be found in the Pentagon and sometimes among top advisers on the Joint Chiefs of Staff.

After the Cuban missile crisis was surmounted in 1962, some American military men regretted the peaceful settlement, even though the invasion of Cuba would have cost an estimated 40,000 to 50,000 American casualties, assuming that the Soviets remained on the sidelines. President Kennedy later estimated that the odds in favor of a nuclear Armageddon were "somewhere between one out of three and even." [3]

This is not to say that statesmen should not stand up for their rights even when the odds are highly unfavorable. In 1938 the Czechs, with a fine army and air force and a strong defensive position, bent the knee to Hitler when left in the lurch by the Western powers at Munich. We now know that the German army in 1938 was not really ready to march. In 1940, after the flight from France, the British carried on against seemingly hopeless odds, and finally (with the help of allies) fought through to victory. Elmer Davis, the able American writer and commentator, wrote in 1954, "The first and great commandment is, Don't let them scare you."

PROFESSIONAL SOLDIERS ARE SELDOM PROFESSIONAL DIPLOMATS

It is true that military affairs are increasingly becoming intertwined with diplomatic affairs. It is also true that General Eisenhower, as Supreme Commander in Europe, was involved in quasi-diplomatic negotiations with Winston Churchill and other European statesmen. He was, in fact, chosen for the position largely

[2] Young Colonel George Washington, after his first brush with the French in 1754, wrote that he heard the whine of bullets and there was something "charming" about the sound. They ultimately lost their charm. Winston Churchill, the young war correspondent, reported in 1906, "Nothing in life is so exhilarating as to be shot at without results." Bullets continued to have their exhilaration for him. Kay Halle, ed., *Irrepressible Churchill* (1966), p. 56.

[3] T. C. Sorensen, *Kennedy* (1965), p. 705. Shortly after the crisis passed, Kennedy remarked that an invasion would have been a "mistake." "But the military are mad. They wanted to do this. It's lucky for us that we have [Defense Secretary] McNamara over there." A. M. Schlesinger, Jr., *A Thousand Days* (1965), p. 831.

because of his well-recognized talents as a conciliator and an accommodator—a chairman of the board—rather than a Napoleonic genius. But political decisions were forced upon him that no general in the field should be required to make, including the fateful decision whether or not to occupy Berlin with American troops before the advancing Russians reached the city.[4]

During and after World War II, a considerable number of high-ranking military men were drafted for diplomatic or quasi-diplomatic tasks. Conspicuous among them were General Douglas MacArthur in Japan, Admiral William H. Standley in Russia, General Lucius Clay in Germany, General Walter B. Smith in Russia, and General George C. Marshall as Secretary of State. But the postwar problems were largely military problems, and the war had left the foreign service short of high-quality personnel.

Even so, professional military men should be brought into the diplomatic service only in unusual circumstances. We surely would not put a career diplomat in command of the Seventh Fleet, yet many persons would see nothing improper about putting the Commander of the Seventh Fleet in charge of an important diplomatic post.

President Eisenhower learned a good deal during his on-the-job training, and he was disturbed by the fact that over half the national budget of about $80 billion was going to the military. In his farewell radio and television address to the American people on January 17, 1961, he warned against permitting a powerful military-industrial complex to endanger our hard-won liberties. This timely warning, proclaimed as it was by a distinguished general, carried considerable weight. It further proved that a professional military man can become civilianized.

[4] Dwight D. Eisenhower, *Crusade in Europe* (1948), pp. 396 *ff.*

CHAPTER XX

The Iron Dice of War

"War is nothing but a continuation of political intercourse with an admixture of other means."

KARL VON CLAUSEWITZ, *c.* 1832 [1]

PROLOGUE

A declaration of war is a public confession that conventional diplomacy has failed. The diplomats then ordinarily go home. But this does not mean that in wartime the diplomatic front cannot be as important as the military front. The belligerents maintain diplomatic contact indirectly through third parties; during World War II, for example, Germany and the United States communicated with each other through the intermediary of neutral Switzerland.

Diplomatic intercourse is maintained directly with the neutrals, which can be of extreme importance if they are powerful. The United States of America defeated the Confederate States of America during the Civil War largely because the Washington government won the crucial diplomatic battles in neutral Britain and France. The Confederates were hopefully counting on the intervention of either or both of these two potent nations. Minister Charles

[1] Less well known is the observation of Mao Tse-tung in 1938: "In a word, war cannot for a single moment be separated from politics. Any tendency . . . to belittle politics, to isolate war from politics, and to become advocates of 'war is everything,' is erroneous and must be corrected." *Selected Works* (1954), II, 202.

Francis Adams, battling for the Union and nonintervention in London, played a role no less important than that of many of the leading Northern generals.

A PREVENTIVE WAR IS THE COUNSEL OF DESPAIR

To attack a powerful adversary because he is "inevitably" going to attack you at some rather distant date suggests cutting your throat for fear of dying a natural death.[2]

There was much talk in America of a preventive war against the Russians from 1945 to 1949, when we had the atomic bomb and they did not. (All this did nothing to ease tensions with the Kremlin.) The assumption was that the Soviet Union was hell-bent on our destruction. But with the passage of time the Soviets acquired terrifying nuclear weapons of their own, and not only calmed down but undertook to "coexist" with the United States. Red China may ultimately travel the same road.

To fight because war is "inevitable" flies in the face of history. The record reveals many instances of so-called "inevitable" clashes that never came off. Conspicuous examples are the "inevitable" war between Russia and Britain in the latter part of the nineteenth century and the "inevitable" war between Britain and the United States after the frustrating conflict ending in 1815.

Making war to preserve peace is a contradiction in terms. In 1956 the Israeli, responding to extreme provocation, attacked Egypt and drove toward the Suez Canal. Britain and France then pounced upon Egypt, declaring that they were forced to move to separate the belligerents and avert a world war. The real reasons were evidently a desire to regain control of the vital Suez lifeline and topple the supposedly embryonic Hitler of the Nile—President Nasser. The British and French, forced to back down by various pressures, came closer to starting a world war than preventing one.[3]

[2] The lack of immediacy distinguishes this situation from the strike first policy discussed on pp. 242–243.

[3] Although both the British Foreign Secretary and Prime Minister denied any prior collusion with the Israeli, ten years later the then French foreign minister, Pineau, revealed that a definite commitment had been signed by representatives of Britain, France, and Israel at a secret meeting near Paris. *Time,* August 5, 1966, p. 32. This is confirmed by Terence Robertson, *Crisis: The Inside Story of the Suez Conspiracy* (1965), p. 163. The author had interviewed Pineau.

WARS TAKE UNPREDICTABLE COURSES

Wars are much easier to start than to stop. One nation can begin hostilities, as Japan did when she attacked Pearl Harbor. But it takes two nations, or sometimes two nations and their allies, to bring the fighting to an end.

Washington was eager to halt the conflict in Vietnam in the mid-1960's on its terms, but the enemy was determined to continue resisting until we were willing to accept his terms and get out. In these circumstances we either had to acknowledge defeat or continue to fight. The obvious moral is that one should not start something unless one is prepared to finish it.

Localized wars, as critics of the Vietnam fighting repeatedly pointed out, run the grave risk of becoming global wars. In 1914 Austria–Hungary was determined to punish little Serbia by chastising her in a war confined to the Balkans. Before the shooting stopped in 1918, some fifteen nations had become involved, and over 10 million people had died. Hitler likewise planned a localized invasion of Poland in 1939, and was vastly annoyed when France and Britain declared war on him. He was further annoyed when they refused to undeclare it after his conquest of Poland.

Brush fires can easily become forest fires, and limited wars can have limitless consequences. When the guns begin to boom, one of the few certainties is that one side cannot win.

TOTAL VICTORY USUALLY SPELLS UNLIMITED WAR

Theodore Roosevelt had another favorite aphorism, "Never hit if you can honorably avoid doing so, but never hit soft." This is another way of saying, as Sir John Fisher put it, "The essence of war is violence, moderation in war is imbecility."

We departed from this basic rule during the Korean conflict, when we fought with self-limited means for self-limited objectives.[4]

---

[4] Limited wars are by no means new in human experience, certainly not in that of the United States. We had in view limited objectives when we fought Britain in 1776 and in 1812, Mexico in 1846, Spain in 1898, Germany in 1917, North Korea and China in 1950, and North Vietnam in 1964. None of our foreign foes accepted unconditional surrender (except Italy in 1943 and Germany in 1945), and all of our foreign wars (except Italy and Germany) ended in a negotiated settlement.

The Korea-type war did not lend itself well to nuclear bombing, and to attack neighboring China was risky business. We were understandably worried about our major adversary, the Soviet Union.

Certainly we did not "hit soft" when we dropped our two atomic bombs on Hiroshima and Nagasaki in 1945—an unappreciated "mercy killing" which may have saved hundreds of thousands of lives, both Japanese and American. This hypothesis, of course, rests on the assumption that Japan could not have been induced to surrender between August and November, when the amphibious assault was scheduled to begin.

The Japanese warlords, when they attacked Pearl Harbor in 1941, forgot that when an assassin strikes a king he must strike to kill. Their strategy was merely to wound the American giant by immobilizing his Pacific fleet while they pursued their master plan of conquest in the Far East. They succeeded in their immediate objective, but the crippled king finally arose from the mud of Pearl Harbor to crush them.

NONAGGRESSION PACTS DO NOT GUARANTEE NONAGGRESSION

Honest men do not need to sign agreements to be honest; peacefully disposed nations do not need to sign agreements binding them not to attack their neighbors. If the aggressor nation feels that its interests demand an attack, it will seldom be restrained by parchment fetters.[5] Hitler negotiated a series of nonaggression pacts with his neighbors, presumably to lull them into a false sense of security before he attacked. Stalin did likewise. The Hitler–Stalin nonaggression pact of 1939, which triggered World War II and which was to have lasted ten years, actually lasted less than two. Stalin's five-year neutrality pact of 1941 with Japan (renewable for five more years) lasted only four, and was violated by the Soviets.

To the extent that nonaggression pacts calm fears *on both*

[5] Germany had guaranteed the "perpetual neutrality" of Belgium in the treaty of 1839, yet attacked in 1914 after a twelve-hour ultimatum. Britain, a guarantor of the same treaty, declared war on Germany, and the German Chancellor blunderingly remarked, ". . . Just for a word 'neutrality,' a word which in war time had so often been disregarded—just for a scrap of paper, Great Britain was going to make war. . . ." Sidney B. Fay, *The Origins of the World War* (1928), II, 545. The "scrap of paper" phrase became a damaging weapon in the subsequent propaganda clash.

sides, especially among nations of relatively equal strength, they may help to create an atmosphere conducive to continued peace. But in crises where the preponderance of power is on the side of the potential aggressor, the nonaggression pact is a feeble shield indeed.

Nations seeking hostilities will always find some excuse. Hitler declared war on Poland in 1939, after a stage-managed attack by Poles, who were actually Germans disguised as Poles. He invaded Norway, Denmark, the Netherlands, Luxembourg, and Belgium in the spring of 1940, despite neutrality laws and nonaggression obligations. He struck without warning and without prior declarations of war, using the pretext, notably in Norway, that his enemies threatened to use these areas against him. A flimsy pretext is often worse than no excuse at all.

In short, diplomacy breaks down when there is no will to preserve the peace. One nation may deliberately force a war upon another, as Hitler did when he attacked Stalin, his accomplice in the ill-starred nonaggression pact of 1939. Hitler, in fact, regarded diplomacy as a means of preparing for war.

In launching his invasion of Russia, Hitler violated one of his own precepts growing out of Germany's defeat in 1914–1918: Never wage a two-front war, if avoidable. The folly of fighting more than one conflict at a time is so obvious that scholars still wonder why President Polk, though deep in a one-front conflict with Mexico in 1846, almost provoked Great Britain into an armed clash before the two English-speaking nations settled their boundary dispute over Oregon.

BRING MILITARY OBJECTIVES INTO BALANCE
WITH YOUR POWER

In the Vietnamese war of the mid-1960's we sought by military means to impose our will on the Communist regime in North Vietnam. We had the *power* to do so but not the *will* to use our nuclear bombs: humanity and world opinion would have been outraged. We may have had the manpower to win, assuming the abstention of Red China, but public opinion at home was unwilling to sacrifice that many lives. In this plight the only rational course was to retreat from the objective of defeating North Vietnam so decisively that we could dictate terms to her. The desirable had to be brought into line with the feasible, and a negotiated peace seemed the only possible alternative. In brief, we had to increase our power or decrease our objectives; we had to face reality rather than save face.

There is such a thing as knowing when one is thwarted or licked and redefining one's objectives. He who fights and then gives way, lives to fight another day—though perhaps with less prestige and more embarrassment. The French were run out of both Southeast Asia (1954) and Algeria (1962), as we have seen, yet emerged more prosperous and powerful than ever. Even Americans, spectacular though their achievements may be, cannot do the impossible; they cannot serve as both policeman and fireman for the entire world.

The much-ballyhooed Kellogg–Briand Pact of 1928, ultimately signed by all the leading powers, outlawed war as an instrument of national policy, except in self-defense.[6] (Aggressors almost invariably claim they are fighting in self-defense.) The result was not to outlaw war but to outlaw declarations of war in many cases. In 1931, 1932, and 1937–1945, Japan fought China without a formal declaration of war. This procedure helped to set a pattern for the dictators of the 1930's. Even the United States fought major actions in Korea and Vietnam without official declarations. A war that is not declared does not have to be undeclared; it can be ended without a treaty that must pass the senatorial hatchet. Besides, an official war may drag in other nations through the obligations of defensive alliances.

MISCALCULATION IS OFTEN THE MOTHER OF WAR

In 1812 the British pushed the United States into the abyss, partly through a misunderstanding. They mistakenly assumed that the anti-war and pro-British Federalist element in America represented majority opinion, and that a nation so divided would not or could not resort to arms.

More recent examples also come to mind. The Germans resorted to war in 1914, and again in 1939, partly because they mistakenly assumed or hoped that the British would stay on the

---

[6] Sixty-two nations ultimately signed. Nonsigners were Argentina, Bolivia, El Salvador, Uruguay, and Yemen.

sidelines. The North Koreans invaded South Korea in 1950, presumably because they interpreted Secretary Acheson's misleading pronouncement to mean that the United States would not intervene.[7]

Two obvious lessons are clear. First, we should appraise realistically the probable reactions of our adversary. Second, we should, as a general rule, make it unmistakably clear, as we did not in Korea, that we are willing to stand and fight if our potential foe steps over a given line. He then will be in a better position to anticipate our probable response.

WAR IS NOT A MONOPOLY OF THE MILITARY

Georges Clemenceau, the French Premier in World War I, has often been quoted as saying, "War is much too serious a business to be entrusted to the generals."

The civilian authorities in Washington should define the political objectives of a war—for example, the overthrowing of the dictators in 1941–1945. The military men should have a large voice in determining when, where, and with what to strike, in order to achieve these objectives. The civilian leaders should then keep elbow-jogging at a minimum.

In World War II the highest civilian and military authorities in Washington wisely decided to make Germany rather than Japan the first major target, and to launch a second-front invasion of Hitler's Fortress Europa. They persisted in this decision despite a loud public outcry of "Get Hirohito First."[8] The military men, with their highly technical training, were the only ones competent to decide precisely where and with what specific forces the invasion was to be launched on D-Day.

OVERALL MILITARY POLICY SHOULD BE SHAPED
BY CIVILIANS

The President should determine basic military policy. But he should act in close consultation with his military and civilian ad-

[7] See above, p. 20.

[8] One public opinion poll shortly after Pearl Harbor found 62.4% of the respondents in favor of making Japan the number one priority. *Fortune*, XXV (Feb., 1942), p. 97.

visers, and with the requirements of all defense theaters fully in mind. The commander in the field, like General MacArthur in Korea, has to carry out the President's orders, just as the lieutenants under MacArthur had to carry out orders from above, whether agreeable or not. If a general disapproves of his orders, he may remonstrate through proper channels or resign his command. But he should never attempt to delay, divert, or subvert the policy decided on by the highest authorities.

General MacArthur, with an exalted reputation as an all-conquering hero, naturally disapproved of waging a limited war in Korea for limited objectives. Like any successful commander, he wanted to fight through to military victory without shackles. But unlike a good soldier, he attempted to undermine the policy he was supposed to be carrying out in good faith. He had, as we have seen, a bad case of "localitis": that is, he was so deeply involved with the Korean problem that he did not give proper attention to the Soviet menace on the other side of the world. He may have been right, but we can normally have only one fundamental policy in one place at a time, whether good or bad.[9]

President Truman, his patience exhausted, finally dismissed MacArthur with unseemly brutality. In so doing, the Chief Executive reasserted the principles of civilian supremacy and subordination by subordinates. In our democracy, the military men should always be on tap, but never on top.

SOME WARS SOLVE PROBLEMS

The cliché that war never settles anything is palpably false. The American conquest of Mexico in 1846–1848 determined the fate of approximately one-half of Mexico. The Civil War settled the question of Negro slavery in the United States, but not the question of Negro–white relationships.

New vexations almost inevitably arise from the ashes of conflict, and sometimes they are more costly than the original war itself. The spoils of the Mexican conflict led directly to the Civil War, which cost some 600,000 lives and billions of dollars. World War II

[9] Truman's version appears in *Memoirs of Harry S. Truman* (1956), II, Ch. 27; Douglas MacArthur's in *Reminiscences* (1964), Pt. 9.

crushed Adolf Hitler, but it led to the ascendancy of Stalinist Russia, which in some respects was a worse menace. Modern wars can easily create more problems than they solve. New terrors seem to replace the old.

IT IS DIFFICULT FOR BIG NATIONS
TO HAVE SMALL WARS

President Eisenhower promised South Vietnam economic aid and military assistance, which subsequently involved about seven hundred American military "advisers" before his administration ended.[10] In December, 1961, President Kennedy sharply increased the number of "advisers," many of whom ultimately became active combatants. President Johnson, confronted with defeat or escalation of the war, bombed North Vietnam and committed several hundred thousand American troops. The more men we threw in, the more men North Vietnam threw in.

One obvious conclusion is that when a nation as big as the United States becomes involved in a small war the reverberations are worldwide. The escalation of the conflict in Vietnam in 1964 had a profound effect on the foreign policy of the two Red giants— China and Russia. It alarmed pro-Communist and anti-Communist neighbors in Southeast Asia. It aroused widespread criticism among America's fourteen NATO allies, most of whom were unwilling to see the bastion of Western freedom pour its blood and treasure down this Far Eastern rathole. In sum, not only the Communist world but the neutralist and allied world shook from seismic waves resulting from the small war waged by a superpower.

Uncle Sam is like a giant crowded into a small room with pygmies. Even his most casual movements, which seem normal to him, not only excite apprehension but create the danger of physical harm.

[10] For President Eisenhower's letter (Oct. 1, 1954) promising general assistance and his latter-day comment on it, see the *New York Times,* August 18, 1965, 1:6, 3:1. Whether or not he intended to provide military assistance in October, 1954, the fact is that he soon did provide it.

PART IV

Problems of Peace

CHAPTER XXI

The Perils of Peacemaking

"The conquered nation often sees it [peace] as only a passing evil,
to be repaired in after times by political combinations."

KARL VON CLAUSEWITZ, *c.* 1832

PROLOGUE

"Blessed are the peacemakers," declares the Sermon on the Mount, "for they shall be called the children of God." Perhaps they will be in Heaven, but they are often called less pleasant names here on earth. Not one of the Big Four who met in Paris in 1919—Woodrow Wilson, Lloyd George, Georges Clemenceau, and Vittorio Orlando—escaped either scathing criticism or ultimate political repudiation.

Peacemaking is a delicate art. It calls for more talent, or at least a different kind of talent, than warmaking. One of the reasons why the peacemakers at Paris in 1919 failed to do better is that the same men who had succeeded as war leaders—who had whipped up the passions that brought victory—changed hats and sat down at the conference table as peacemakers. Passion seldom produces a satisfactory peace.

UNCONDITIONAL SURRENDER ENCOURAGES
UNCONDITIONAL RESISTANCE

Franklin Roosevelt, in the spotlight of the Casablanca Conference in 1943, proclaimed a policy of unconditional surrender for the Axis enemy—Germany, Italy, and Japan.[1] One unfortunate implication was that the World War then being waged was a struggle between total virtue and total wickedness, and that because a nation's government was evil, all its people were evil.

"Unconditional surrender" may have prolonged enemy resistance. It disheartened those German liberals, scanty in number, who might otherwise have found the courage to kill Hitler and negotiate peace terms. It was a godsend to the German propaganda machine, which now proclaimed that there was nothing to do but to fight to the last burned-out bunker.

On the other hand, "unconditional surrender" probably encouraged the Soviets to resist any temptation—assuming they felt any—to make a separate peace with Hitler. The phrase reassured Stalin that the Allies were not about to conspire behind his back with the Nazis. It inspirited conquered peoples like the Poles, who were then under the boots of the German conquerors. It averted disruptive arguments among the Allies as to surrender terms, as well as a noisy quarrel, like that with Germany after 1918, over armistice terms.

Statesmen who advocate unconditional surrender must decide whether, on balance, they have more to gain than lose by such a harsh policy. They must determine whether the war probably will be shortened, and whether the political objectives of a complete overthrow are worth the risks involved.

Ironically, Japan's surrender was finally made *conditionally*, the condition being that she would be permitted to retain Emperor Hirohito. If this condition had been accepted sooner in Washington, the war in the Far East might well have ended sooner, and

[1] The phrase "unconditional surrender," rather than the concept, was surprising. Early in the war both President Roosevelt and the embattled United Nations had put themselves on record as fighting for "complete," "total," and "absolute" victory. This problem was discussed in a paper entitled, "The American Concept of Victory," read by Professor Raymond G. O'Connor of Temple University at the annual meeting of the American Historical Association, New York, 1966.

without the holocaust at Hiroshima which besmirched the moral position of the United States.[2]

TOTAL VICTORY IMPOSES TOTAL RESPONSIBILITY

Complete prostration of the enemy can create more problems than it solves, though the vexations of victory, onerous though they may be, are more agreeable than those of defeat. There is pith in the reported remark of the Duke of Wellington, the victor at Waterloo: "Madame, there is nothing so dreadful as a great victory—excepting a great defeat."

In 1945 the formula of unconditional surrender left a prostrated and fragmented Germany on the hands of the conquerors and at their mercy. There was no German government, as there had been in 1918. The upshot was that the victors divided Germany (and also Berlin) into four zones, which required an army of occupation and a host of civilians to lead the vanquished Nazis into the peaceful paths of democracy.

Unconditional surrender resulted in once-proud Germany's being divided into two parts, with little prospect of reunification, and with much prospect of continued friction. Berlin, deep in the heart of East Germany (and the Russian Zone), repeatedly brought Moscow and the West to the brink of catastrophe. In 1948 the Soviets closed off the land and water approaches to the city and forced the Allies to mount their amazing Berlin airlift until 1949. In the third decade after the war any prospect of a treaty of peace with a united Germany seemed remote.

The conqueror can seldom afford the luxury of smashing his enemy entirely. Destroying all prospect of a balance of power is like destroying the balance of nature that restrains the propagation of mice and rats.

MILITARY VICTORY IS NOT THE ONLY KIND OF VICTORY

In Korea, in 1951, General MacArthur understandably resented having to fight under wraps, and without the "will to victory." He

[2] See Robert J. C. Butow, *Japan's Decision to Surrender* (1954).

voiced the now-famous slogan, "In war there is no substitute for victory." [3]

Critics insisted that there is a substitute for military victory more satisfying and enduring than complete military subjugation, namely a sane and lasting political settlement reasonably acceptable to all parties concerned. The Truman administration, fearful of becoming bogged down in an Asiatic war which would weaken us in the face of our Soviet adversary, had to have the "courage to be timid" and settle for a stalemate. In deadlocks of this kind, stalemate is preferable to checkmate—at our expense.

General MacArthur also forgot that military victory does not keep. A cynical Russian proverb reads, "Eternal peace lasts only until next year." The American people assumed in 1918 that once the "bestial" German Kaiser was disposed of, peace would settle down on the world like a white dove. We won the war but brought the boys home prematurely, and then had to do the dirty job all over again a generation later. Some wag has said that history *does* repeat itself, and the price goes up each time.

In 1945 we assumed that once Hitler was disposed of, "permanent peace" would be our reward. Yet Stalin, Khrushchev, Mao Tse-tung, Nasser, Sukarno, and other assorted menaces popped up to take his place. The hands of the clock simply cannot be nailed down at a moment favorable to our side. The defeated and the disgruntled are always on the lookout to get their knife into the back of the relaxed victors.

OVEREAGERNESS TO TALK PEACE IS SELF-DEFEATING

Early in 1966, President Johnson launched a highly ballyhooed "peace offensive," ostensibly to bring the North Vietnamese to the conference table.[4] He could hardly have expected this gambit to succeed, because it was the one tactic best designed to drive the enemy away. Many critics therefore assumed that Johnson's primary purpose was to prove that both he and his nation wanted peace, and to put the blame for the forthcoming escalation of bombing on the other side.

[3] See his letter of March, 1951, in *Congressional Record*, 82nd Cong., 1st sess., p. 3380. For the contrary view of Mao Tse-tung, see above, p. 249 n.

[4] See *Department of State Bulletin*, LIV (Feb. 7, 1966), pp. 186 *ff*.

The North Vietnamese branded the peace drive a "trick," as indeed it was to some extent. Few proposals could have done more to convince them that either we were losing the war or were unwilling to pay the price of victory. In either case, the obvious response of the North Vietnamese regime was to continue fighting with the expectation of ejecting the intruder.

We should have learned our lesson from the negotiations that ended the Korean War. In 1951, when the Chinese and North Korean invaders were reeling backward under Allied counterattacks, they put out a peace feeler through Moscow which we grasped with overeagerness. Whether or not the continued Allied drive would have won a decisive victory is debatable: the farther we got from our base of supplies, the closer the enemy got to his.[5] In any event, the Communist negotiators, compounding denunciations with deviousness, dragged out negotiations in Korea to 575 meetings in over two years, while the fortunes of war seesawed at the front with mounting casualties. Allegedly the threat by the new Eisenhower administration to use the atomic bomb on China helped bring about the uneasy armistice of 1953.

When peace discussions continue while the fighting still rages, they reflect the changing fortunes on the battlefield. This was also true at Ghent in 1814, when the British and the American delegates came to the peace table. The demands of each side rose or fell barometrically with news from the fighting front. Late in 1814 Britain's fearsome invasion of northern New York failed, as did the assault on star-spangled Baltimore. With the military situation thus stalemated, both sides settled for a stalemated peace. Military men have long since observed that one can seldom win at the peace table what one has not won on the battlefield.[6]

[5] General Matthew B. Ridgway, who succeeded MacArthur, believed that he could have driven to the Chinese border, *if* our government had been willing to pay the price in casualties. He concluded that from a "purely military standpoint" the result would not have been worth the cost. His army, with lengthened lines and a broadened front, would still have been facing the Chinese "in great strength." *Soldier: The Memoirs of Matthew B. Ridgway* (1956), p. 219.

[6] The reverse sometimes occurs and a nation may lose at the peace table what it has won on the battlefield. At Ghent in 1814 the British gave up substantial portions of American territory, including about one half of Maine. See F. L. Engelman, *The Peace of Christmas Eve* (1962). In 1954 the North Vietnamese lost the expected fruits of their war at the Geneva Conference, and this partly explains their reluctance to negotiate again.

The United States reluctantly accepted a stalemate in Korea and at Ghent because we were unwilling to pay the price in blood and dollars for total victory.

MILITARY VICTORY IS THE ACHIEVEMENT OF WAR AIMS

A nation is generally judged the winner of a war if it imposes its will on the enemy and accomplishes what it set out to do. It is not necessarily victorious if it inflicts more casualties, seizes more territory, drops more bombs, or wins more pitched battles.

The Korean War of 1950–1953 was actually two wars. In the first one we proclaimed the objective of hurling back the North Korean invaders across the 38th parallel. We won this war, with minor help from our United Nations allies and with major help from the South Koreans. Then we adopted the UN's ambitious aim of conquering North Korea and of uniting and rebuilding the entire country. This war we did not win, for we finally settled on the compromise line of approximately the 38th parallel. To change war aims in the middle of a war can be both costly and confusing.

In the War of 1812 our primary purpose was to force Britain to respect our rights on the high seas. The immediate military objective was to conquer Canada so that we could compel the British to make the desired concessions. (As time passed, war aims became confused with military objectives, and some historians have mistakenly claimed that we fought primarily to seize Canada.) In any event, we did not conquer Canada and were lucky to beat off large-scale invasions launched from Canadian soil. The Treaty of Ghent, which ended the conflict, mentioned neither Canada nor American maritime rights, primarily because we had not won the war in a military sense.

At the time of the Korean "police action" many patriotic Americans argued that as a matter of national pride we had to fight through to complete victory. If we did not, this would be the first war that we had failed to win. The fact is that militarily we did not win or lose either the War of 1812 or the Korean War (phase two); neither side was able or willing to impose its will on its enemy.

A DICTATED PEACE IS A PERILOUS PEACE

A victor's peace often breeds a new war to undo it. The conqueror can have vengeance or he can have justice, but he cannot have both in the same treaty. If he chooses the path of vengeance, he may keep his hobnailed boot on the neck of the vanquished for a generation or so, but this may be the limit.

The classic case is the treaty that Germany imposed upon France in 1871 at the end of the Franco–Prussian War. The thirst of a humiliated France for revenge and for the recovery of Alsace–Lorraine was a prime combustible leading to the global conflagration of 1914–1918. The Germans forgot one of their own proverbs: "Revenge does not long remain unrevenged." A mild "peace of accommodation," which can enable the defeated to forgive and forget, may last, notably the peace treaty which we negotiated with Japan in 1951. (Ironically, Soviet opposition to such terms had resulted in a six-year delay, which in turn permitted passions to cool and a reasonable pact to emerge.)

These harrowing experiences demonstrated that it is better to have peace without victory than a victory without peace. Early in 1917 President Wilson, in a powerful address to the Senate, called upon the warring European powers for a "peace without victory." But both camps of belligerents, still hoping to win, spurned his earnest plea. The result was the Treaty of Versailles, which was more a victor's peace than a victory for peace.[7] It was more punitive than preventive, and from it flowed another and bloodier war. On hearing its terms, the deposed German Kaiser reportedly remarked, "The war to end wars has resulted in a peace to end peace."

If both sets of belligerents had only been willing to accept a stalemate peace in 1917—a "peace without booty"—the world would have been spared many calamities, including probably Adolf Hitler, Joseph Stalin, Benito Mussolini, and Communist world revolution.

[7] The vanquished should have a voice in the making of the treaty while it is being drafted, because they, being on the receiving end, can best point out unworkable features. The Germans were denied this privilege, but were handed a semi-final draft against which they lodged vehement but generally unavailing protests. See Alma Luckau, *The German Delegation at the Paris Peace Conference* (1941).

"Only a peace between equals can last," declared Wilson with prophetic vision in his famed "peace without victory" speech. A truce is ordinarily better than a victor's peace, which is often only the continuation of war by other means. Within limits, we can accept Benjamin Franklin's dictum, "There never was a good war or a bad peace," or the English proverb, "Better a lean peace than a fat victory."

HASTE MAKES WASTE IN PEACEMAKING

Immediately after the Armistice of 1918, there was considerable talk of patching together a preliminary peace with Germany. Then, after passions had cooled, a final treaty would be signed. But Red Bolshevism was licking into Central Europe, and speed seemed imperative. The result was a hasty and vindictive peace, which helped brew another global conflict.

After World War II, the victors took heed of a page from their previous mistakes. They not only created the United Nations separately from a treaty,[8] but undertook to negotiate first with the smaller nations, Hungary, Bulgaria, Romania, and Italy. The treaty with Japan was deferred for six years, as we have seen, and as a consequence the terms were "soft."

Another by-product of haste in 1919 was a flouting of the pre-Armistice contract. The Germans had laid down their arms after receiving solemn assurances that they would be granted a peace of justice based on Wilson's Fourteen Points.[9] In part because of war passions and the presumed need for a prompt settlement, this agreement was not honored by the Allies. The disarmed Germans cried betrayal, and this accusation was one of Hitler's strongest talking points during his meteoric rise to power.

President Roosevelt no doubt remembered this prolonged and

[8] The League of Nations, at Wilson's insistence, was made the first section of the Treaty of Versailles, and it was the League that sank the entire treaty in the United States. President Roosevelt was evidently aware of this fact when he supported an independent UN Charter.

[9] The Allies entered two reservations on the Fourteen Points: freedom of the seas and reparations. One weakness of the Fourteen Points was that some of them were embarrassingly specific, particularly with reference to Turkey. By contrast, the Churchill–Roosevelt Atlantic Charter of 1941 was much more vague, and hence less open to charges of broken promises. Even so, the Poles and others saw in the Charter assurances of self-determination that were never fully realized.

disruptive wrangle when he insisted on "unconditional surrender" for the Germans at the end of World War II. But we subsequently learned the harsh way that both unconditional and conditional surrender bring a procession of problems in their train. Pre-armistice contracts, if made, should be kept to the letter.

PEACE TREATIES ARE NOT SELF-EXECUTING

A good treaty can be ruined by the bad faith of those responsible for carrying out its terms. A bad treaty can sometimes work if entrusted to men of good will.

The Treaty of Versailles in 1919 was not hopeless, and it would have worked better if its terms had been executed in the manner intended. But the United States Senate refused to honor Wilson's signature by approving the document. Its implementation thereupon fell into the hands of war-ravaged and vindictive Europeans, who were determined to squeeze the last pfennig out of Germany. If the United States, as planned, had taken its rightful place on the Reparations Commission, we might well have kept the indemnity at a reasonable figure—say $8 or $10 billion—instead of the astronomical $32 billion finally assessed.

Under the Treaty of Versailles, reparations were designed not only as restitution but as revenge. The victors evidently forgot that such exactions impose further burdens on a nation already burdened by the exhaustion of fighting. They sow dragon's teeth that can sprout into new and costlier conflict, as was notably true of the indemnity that the Germans imposed on France at the end of the Franco–Prussian War in 1871. Germany collected a billion dollars, but the war of revenge that came in 1914 probably cost her more than $100 billion, to say nothing of millions of lives and abject defeat.

THE VICTOR REDEFINES JUSTICE

After World War II, many of the military and civilian leaders of both Germany and Japan were subjected to war-crimes trials. In Germany, ten were hanged; in Japan, seven "major" war criminals were executed (including ex-Premier Tojo). In the American Zone of Germany, thousands of lesser offenders were convicted and received sentences ranging from small fines to long imprisonment.

More than twenty years after Hitler's collapse, his mentally unhinged henchman, Rudolf Hess, was still in a German cell.

The United States was a leading prosecutor of these culprits, many of whom were clearly guilty of unspeakable offenses against humanity, including genocide.[10] But legalists the world over pointed out that the crimes of which the vanquished were accused had not previously been recognized as crimes under international law, and that to indict these men on such grounds was in effect to sanction *ex post facto* laws. Such are repugnant to our Constitution (Article I, Section 9).

The moral is that if one gets into a war, one should not lose it. The future winner now has ample precedent for serving as judge, jury, and hangman. The victors next time may be the vanquished, and American officials may be on the receiving end of the noose.

MIGHT MAKES THE RECORD RIGHT

The absent and the defeated are always wrong, we are told, and the victorious nation normally makes its version prevail as to the responsibility for starting the conflict.

Germany lost in 1918 and was forced, at bayonet point and under vehement protest, to sign a treaty containing the famous "war guilt clause" (Article 231). It declared that "Germany accepts the responsibility of Germany and her allies for causing all the loss and damage to which the Allied and Associated Governments and their nationals have been subjected as a consequence of the war imposed upon them by the aggression of Germany and her allies."

This is the view that generally prevailed in 1919, and to a large extent still prevails, despite two generations of revisionist scholarship. Many historians have concluded that while Germany was perhaps somewhat more guilty than any other nation in widening the Serbo–Austro–Hungarian quarrel, all the powers of Europe were in some measure responsible, whether positively or negatively, for the bloodbath that resulted.

To be right, be victorious. Generations of Southern children, many of them exposed to Yankee textbook versions of the Civil War, can testify on this sore point. The writing of history is often the continuation of war by other means.

---

[10] For the views of Robert H. Jackson, the chief United States counsel at the Nuremberg trials, see his *The Case Against the Nazi War Criminals* (1946).

CHAPTER XXII

Neutrality and Neutralism

"A wise neuter joins with neither, but uses both, as his honest interest leads him."

WILLIAM PENN (1644–1718)

PROLOGUE

Neutrality is ordinarily sound policy. Not getting involved in
others' quarrels unnecessarily is a desirable rule, whether in the
neighborhood of people or the neighborhood of nations. When a
country decides to depart from the true path of neutrality, it must
ask itself if the national interest is best served thereby, whether in
the short run or the long run. Switzerland decided to pursue a
strict neutrality in two world wars, and wisely so. So jealous is it of
its unique position, geographical and otherwise, that it is the only
qualified nation of any consequence which has steadfastly declined
to join the United Nations.

America, while nominally neutral during the earlier phases of
World War I and World War II, concluded that the national interest
would be best served by favoring one group of belligerents as
against the other. Both times we were finally sucked in beside the
Allies, whom we favored. Many people still argue that our best
interests in both instances would have been promoted by standing
rigidly aloof. Others maintain that by averting a collapse of the
Allies in both wars, we headed off far worse dangers than those that

we reluctantly embraced. But we shall never know what would have happened if we had taken the other path. Such are the mysteries of history.

NEUTRALITY IS IN THE AMERICAN TRADITION

The American people tried desperately to stay out of the wars that convulsed Europe following the outbreak of the French Revolution in 1789, but finally were drawn into the sideshow War of 1812 with Britain.

We took a holier-than-thou position when war engulfed Europe in 1914, stayed on the sidelines until 1917, and were finally involved. At the outset in 1914 we self-righteously declared that the conflict was none of our making, and that we would have nothing to do with it. We wound up in 1917 proclaiming that the war had been our war for democracy all along. Then, bitterly disillusioned, we ran out on the "wicked Europeans," leaving them exhausted and bleeding. Winston S. Churchill later wrote that it was not "open to the cool bystander, who afterwards becomes the loyal and ardent comrade and brave rescuer, to set himself up as an impartial judge of events which would never have occurred had he out-stretched a helping hand in time." [1]

When Hitler wrapped Europe in flames in 1939, we remained on the sidelines until late 1941, proclaiming that the war was not ours. Then, following the Pearl Harbor nightmare, we announced that the war was ours after all, and proceeded to help win it. As before, we wanted to retire to our own continent. But the specter of an engulfing Soviet Union forced us to reconsider at the eleventh hour, and we came to the rescue of Europe with the Marshall Plan and other forms of assistance.

Involvement in Europe as a permanent policy is of relatively recent vintage.

NEUTRALISM IS OFTEN THE REFUGE
OF THE WEAK

All the great powers were deeply enmeshed in the wars of the French Revolution and the Napoleonic Era. All were ultimately

[1] Colin Coote and Denzil Batchelor, *Winston S. Churchill's Maxims and Reflections* (1949), p. 169.

involved in World War I and World War II. But in both of the titanic conflicts of this century a half dozen or so of the tiny neutrals managed to remain bystanders. Spain, Switzerland, and Sweden all sat out the two great wars. They had strategic nuisance value; they were on the periphery of the swirling armies; they could sell crucial supplies to both sides; and they maintained armies that would have been tough nuts to crack.

Thus we have the paradox that these three comparatively weak nations—through foresight, wise statesmanship, geographical location, and good luck—were better able to control their destinies than were major powers like the United States. All three of them, while being courted by both sides and receiving favors from both sides, were able to enjoy some of the benefits of the Allies without being allied.

Ironically, the time-span of American neutrality has decreased with American power. Preceding the War of 1812 we remained neutral for about 107 months; preceding the 1917 involvement, 31 months; preceding the 1941 involvement, 27 months. If another world war should break out involving the major powers, we shall probably be in it from the very first day.

In the present nuclear-triggered world, power spells involvement.

NEUTRALITY IS OFTEN THE BEST POLICY

Neutrality is normally advisable for small or weak nations. They cannot usually control events in their own interests and must float along on the tide of events, trusting largely to prayer and luck. But neutrality ceases to be the best policy when events which a strong neutral has the power to control are developing in such an ominous fashion as to create a more disastrous situation than would result from armed intervention.

When Hitler invaded Poland on that fateful September morn of 1939, we reasoned that our interests would be best served by preserving neutrality. Presumably the British blockade would slowly strangle Germany, and German troops would bleed themselves white attacking impregnable French defenses. But when Hitler knocked France out of the war in 1940 and Britain was tottering under the aerial blitz, President Franklin Roosevelt abandoned all pretense of neutrality when he engineered the destroyers-for-bases deal with Britain and the Lend-Lease Act for those nations resisting aggression. On the one hand, we wanted to stay out. On the other, we felt that we could not afford to see the democracies sink and then have to stem the overwhelming might of the conquerors without allies. From unneutral neutrality before Pearl Harbor to open belligerency after Pearl Harbor was but a short step.

THE EQUAL TREATMENT OF ALL BELLIGERENTS CAN BE UNNEUTRAL

Anatole France once observed that "The law, in its majestic equality, forbids all men to sleep under bridges, to beg in the streets, and to steal bread—the rich as well as the poor." In the same vein a famous American jurist once remarked that there is no inequality so great as the equal treatment of unequals.

By 1939 Congress had prescribed neutrality legislation which forbade the export of arms to belligerents. Hitler's Germany, armed to the teeth, needed no American weapons; the unprepared democracies, France and Britain, desperately needed them. To apply the law with rigid impartiality to dictators and democracies alike was in fact to help the dictators and hurt the democracies. So Congress lifted the arms embargo in 1939, thus making weapons available to both sets of belligerents. But it realized full well that only the democracies, who controlled the seas, would be able to come and get them. We consequently abandoned an uneasy unneutrality favoring the dictators for an open unneutrality favoring the democracies. In situations of this kind a so-called neutral nation cannot possibly hold the scales precisely even.[2]

NEUTRALS MUST EXPECT BRICKBATS FROM BOTH SIDES

Walking the tight-rope of neutrality is a delicate task. Both sets of belligerents desire and often demand unneutral neutrality in

[2] A similar situation arose in 1914–1917, when arms flowed freely to the Allies, chiefly Britain and France. An embargo would have hurt the Allied cause, while continued noninterference hurt the cause of Germany and her allies.

their favor, if not open participation in the war on their side. All too often they feel that if the neutral country is not for them, it is against them. The United States has been on both the receiving and giving ends. During the wars of the French Revolution and the Napoleonic Era, we wanted only to sell produce to both sides, and as a result suffered the seizure of hundreds of ships by the British and the French. From 1914 to 1917 the British detained or seized scores of American ships (usually paying for the cargoes), while the Germans deliberately sank a few of them.

The neutral always has some weapons of his own, even though they may not be awesome. During the Napoleonic wars we withheld foodstuffs and other materials from both warring camps, under an embargo and nonintercourse policy. We hurt the clashing nations but we probably hurt ourselves even more. During World War II, the belligerents (including the United States) found it to their advantage not to force certain neutrals into the inferno of war. Both sides enjoyed access to Swedish ballbearings, Swiss precision instruments, Spanish wolfram, and Turkish chrome. By playing off one belligerent against the other, these neutrals not only remained aloof from the fighting but at the same time lined their pockets at the expense of the warring powers.

NEUTRALITY IN THOUGHT IS IMPOSSIBLE

When the guns of August began to boom in 1914, President Wilson urged the American people to remain "impartial in thought as well as in action." But this was the counsel of perfection. In a nation such as ours, the democratic processes would break down if the people were so ill-informed or so indifferent as to the causes and nature of a titanic war as not to have opinions and preferences.

President Franklin Roosevelt took a different tack. Perhaps remembering Wilson's admonition of 1914, he faced up to realities when Hitler ran amok in 1939. "This nation," he avowed in a Fireside Chat, "will remain a neutral nation, but I cannot ask that every American remain neutral in thought as well. Even a neutral has a right to take account of facts. Even a neutral cannot be asked to close his mind or his conscience." [3]

[3] *The Public Papers and Addresses of Franklin D. Roosevelt, 1939* (1941), p. 463 (Sept. 3, 1939).

A NEUTRALITY POLICY SHOULD BE KEPT FLEXIBLE

In the 1930's, the Congress of the United States, rightly fearing another world war, passed legislation tailored to keep us out of it. On the questionable assumption that the shipment of American arms to the belligerents and the traveling of American passengers on belligerent ships had dragged us into World War I, the legislators passed a series of laws designed to keep us out of a future World War II. Congress, with the active encouragement of Franklin Roosevelt, even embargoed arms to Spain, leaving the legal but leftist government of that war-cursed country to be systematically done to death by Franco, Hitler, and Mussolini.

The neutrality legislation worked well—in fact, too well, because it aided the aggressor rather than the victim. The American public finally concluded that, while it wanted to stay out of the war, it wanted even more to keep the democracies from collapsing and leaving us to face the wrath of the dictators alone. Under such pressures, Congress repealed or severely modified the neutrality restrictions. If these had remained on the books, and if they had been honestly enforced, we almost certainly would have avoided a conflict with Hitler, that is, until he overran Europe and we had to confront him alone.

One lasting lesson is that a nation, anticipating possible shifts of policy, should avoid erecting roadblocks in front of itself. President Franklin Roosevelt went along with the head-in-the-sands neutrality policy, and in some respects tightened it. Then when the dam broke with the collapse of France in 1940, he had to reeducate the citizenry to a reversal of policy. He found himself in difficulty because the masses had learned the lesson of neutrality so well that many of them were unable to unlearn it. On the very day of Pearl Harbor a strong majority of the voters, though reluctantly willing to aid the democracies at the risk of war, wished to remain aloof from the actual fighting.

NEUTRALISM CAN REDUCE INTERNATIONAL TENSIONS

The United States has often condemned those countries which refuse to line up with it against the Communists, and which insist on remaining a part of the uncommitted one-third of the world. Yet the more allies a nation has, the more complications it invites, as

American experience with the fifteen-nation NATO organization attests.

Vast countries like the Indian subcontinent, committed to neutralism under Prime Minister Nehru, reduced the area in which the free world and the unfree world could deploy their forces, whether diplomatic or warlike. For ten years after World War II, Austria was a bone of contention between the Soviets and the West. A treaty was finally concluded in 1955 which completely neutralized Austria, and all Soviet and Allied troops were withdrawn.

Various proposals for neutralizing Germany and other parts of Central Europe have been advanced from time to time, and if these were feasible, areas of tension would be reduced.[4] Neutrals with a pro-Western, anti-Communist slant—like Sweden and Switzerland—can be a definite asset to the free world, though not formally allied with it.

CIRCUMSTANCES ALTER NEUTRALIST VIEWPOINTS

In the last two world wars the British, naturally regarding their cause as righteous, were highly critical of the United States because it held back from casting its lot in with them. During the Cold War of the present era, Americans, involved in their quarrel with Godless and aggressive Communism, have been critical of the uncommitted nations that preferred to remain above the battle.

Secretary Dulles, in the early stages of his incumbency, publicly expressed the view that neutralism was "immoral." He was especially disturbed by India, which, under Prime Minister Nehru, was publicly condemning the United States for its aggressive militarism in holding the line against Communism. Nehru and his holier-than-thou followers seemed utterly oblivious to the fact that they were getting a free ride. They were unwilling to concede that the nuclear might of the United States, expensively maintained by the American taxpayers, was the shield behind which India could enjoy Communist-tolerating neutrality.

But India received an eye-opening jolt in 1962, when hordes of

---

[4] Various forms of "disengagement" have been proposed, notably the plan put forward by the Polish Foreign Minister Rapacki in 1957 and 1958. He envisaged a "de-nuclearized Zone" in Central Europe, including West Germany, East Germany, Poland, and Czechoslovakia, in which nuclear weapons would be forbidden and which would be guaranteed by the powers against outside nuclear attack.

Red Chinese troops came pouring down over its northern borders. Nehru, throwing consistency to the winds, cried out for hitherto-scorned American arms. Rather than indulging in we-told-you-so recriminations, we speedily airlifted in substantial quantities of military hardware to those people who had recently moralized against us.

The United States, given its own history of neutralism, should be able to appreciate, more than most powers, the desire of the uncommitted nations to fight shy of costly and dangerous entanglements. One man's neutrality is another man's enmity.

THE WAGES OF UNNEUTRALITY ARE OFTEN BELLIGERENCY

A nation cannot eat the cake of unneutrality and retain the blessings of neutrality, at least not ordinarily. A notable exception occurred during World War II, when the government of Franco's Spain pursued a course that was unneutrally favorable to the dictators, while avoiding open involvement. Many Americans, hating his illiberalism, favored shoving him over the edge. But Franco's hostility would have further imperiled the shipping lanes of the Mediterranean, and would have made virtually impossible the Allied invasion of North Africa. Referring to Franco's pro-Nazi neutrality in 1944, Prime Minister Churchill declared, "There is all the difference in the world between a man who knocks you down and a man who leaves you alone." [5]

But a great power like the United States has found that it cannot help the fighters on a large scale without getting into the fight. From 1914 to 1917, and again from 1939 to 1941, a "neutral" America so definitely tipped the scales of unneutrality in favor of the Allies as to become in effect a quasi-belligerent. In situations of this kind, active belligerency is the next natural step into the fearsome fray.

Neutrality is double-edged. On the one hand, it involves a respecting of neutral rights by the belligerents. On the other hand, it implies an obligation on the part of the neutral to act neutrally toward the belligerents. The way of the neutral is hard.

[5] Coote and Batchelor, *Churchill's Maxims,* p. 167.

CHAPTER XXIII

The Mirage of Disarmament

"The weapons of war must be abolished before they abolish us."

PRESIDENT JOHN F. KENNEDY, 1961

PROLOGUE

Historically, war can hardly be regarded as an abnormality. This does not mean that at any given time more men are fighting than are not fighting, but it does mean that wars have occurred so frequently as to be commonplace. In modern history there have been about three every five years, and since 1914 there has always been a time when at least one conflict of some consequence was being waged in some part of the globe.

When statesmen refer to disarmament, they usually mean arms limitation. None of the great powers, with one possible exception, has ever seriously proposed the outright abolition of all warmaking weapons. The exception is the Soviet Union, which on various occasions has urged complete disarmament. But the suspicion was strong that such gestures were made primarily for propaganda purposes, in an effort to put the other powers in the wrong, and in the confident belief that there would be no takers.

WEAPONS IN THEMSELVES ARE NOT IMMORAL

"There is no evil in the atom," declared Adlai Stevenson in 1952, "only in men's souls." [1] Nuclear power could be a boon rather than a bane, if mankind were to turn this awesome force solely to peacetime pursuits. Knives that are used to peel apples can be used to commit murder, if murder is in the heart. In short, weapons are neither immoral nor moral: they are amoral. The *purposes* to which they are put, whether aggressive or defensive, involve questions of morality or immorality.

Even if we could destroy all nuclear weapons, we could not destroy the scientists and technicians who have the skills to make replacements. If we eliminate all conventional weapons, such as howitzers and tanks, we yield a heavy advantage to the highly industrialized nations, which, if so minded, can turn tractors into tanks on short notice. If friction persists and peoples are determined to attack other peoples, they will find weapons, whether sticks, stones, or bones.

ARMAMENTS BETRAY INSECURITY

The aggressor, of course, may amass a potent force, as Hitler did, for the conquest of his neighbors, and not basically for defense. But the nonaggressive nation maintains costly armaments, at a heavy burden to its taxpayers, primarily because it fears attack.

The shell-shocked French emerged from World War I in 1918 determined to protect themselves against another periodic German invasion (which finally came under Hitler in 1940). Obsessed with a security psychosis, they maintained a large and expensive army, built up a network of alliances to the rear of Germany, and entrenched themselves behind the presumably impregnable Maginot Line (which the Germans in 1940 easily outflanked). If the French had felt secure against another German attack, they would not have piled up these armaments, which in turn spurred the Germans under Hitler to build up a terrifying striking force. Destroy suspicions and you destroy guns.

The French could not disarm as long as the Germans remained

[1] Edward Hanna, *et al.*, eds., *The Wit and Wisdom of Adlai Stevenson* (1965), p. 48.

bitter and vengeful. Germany had laid down her arms on the basis
of promises that were never fully redeemed; she had been dis-
membered; and she had been forced to sign a treaty in which she
acknowledged her "guilt" in bringing on World War I. A redress
of the vanquished's grievances must ordinarily take place before
an atmosphere is created favorable to arms limitation.

ARMAMENTS ARE BASICALLY THE SYMPTOMS OF A DISEASE

Suspicion and fear are great international diseases, both of
which spell insecurity. Treating the symptoms—that is, arms—is like
putting ice on the thermometer of a feverish patient. The disease
is still there, though the symptoms may be reduced for a time. If our
neighbor is a homicidal maniac, we fear him even if he has only a
paring knife in his kitchen. If he is normal, we sleep quietly at
night, even though he may own a veritable arsenal of revolvers and
hunting rifles. By the same token, political agreements among nations, easing suspicions and fears, should ordinarily precede viable
disarmament agreements, if any agreement is to be reached at all.

Yet the symptoms of a disease may in fact grow so serious as
to become a part of the disease or even a disease in themselves.
They can make war self-generating. A case in point is the frantic
naval race upon which Germany embarked with Britain, prior to
World War I. The Germans were shortsightedly determined to
wrest the trident from the Mistress of the Seas, who would suffo-
cate without a guaranteed access to the oceans. In this case the
arms race became a part of the disease known as insecurity.

The Atomic Age has brought new horrors, for, as Premier
Khrushchev warned the Chinese, in the event of a nuclear war the
survivors "would envy the dead." President Kennedy solemnly told
the UN General Assembly in 1961, "Men no longer debate whether
armaments are a symptom or a cause of tension. The mere existence
of modern weapons—ten million times more powerful than any that
the world has ever seen, and only minutes away from any target
on earth—is a source of horror and discord and distrust." [2]

[2] Maxwell Meyersohn, ed., *Memorable Quotations of John F. Kennedy*
(1965), p. 79 (Sept. 25, 1961).

DISTINCTIONS BETWEEN OFFENSIVE AND
DEFENSIVE ARMS ARE ILLUSORY

In 1932 President Hoover, the war-hating Quaker, urged the elimination of all offensive weapons. He apparently was unaware of the fact that the distinction between "offensive" and "defensive" depends on the use to which the arms are put.

An immobile coast defense gun is presumably defensive, but it could be placed on a railway car and used to attack a neighbor. Tanks are regarded as offensive weapons, but in 1950 the American troops in Korea discovered that when these monsters ran out of fuel or broke down, they could be used effectively as defensive pill boxes. An aerial bomber is normally an offensive weapon, but if it is used to destroy factories that are making bombers for destroying our cities, it becomes a defensive weapon.

Intercontinental ballistic missiles, armed with nuclear warheads, are obviously offensive. But if they are used to deter an attack from the Soviet Union with a threat of "massive retaliation," they become defensive weapons. The nuclear missiles that the Soviets attempted to sneak into Cuba in 1962 were offensive from our standpoint, but from Castro's standpoint they were defensive. American marines would not dare invade his island if, by pushing a few buttons, he could wipe out most of America's major cities. Much depends on purpose and on point of view—on which end of the gun you are looking at or into.

ARMS RACES RESULT IN AN UPWARD
SPIRALING VICIOUS CYCLE

In 1906 Britain launched the *Dreadnaught*, an all-big-gun battleship, which promptly outmoded all other battleships, including ironically her own. Germany, her chief naval rival, thereupon had to construct dreadnaughts. The more she built, the more Britain had to build, so as to maintain a margin of superiority. The frantic and costly race ended only with World War I, after which only the defeated disarmed, or were disarmed.

The United States acquired the atomic bomb in 1945, thereby tipping the balance of military power in its favor. The Soviets had to have the atomic bomb as a countermeasure, and they got theirs in 1949. We then undertook to make a vastly more lethal hydrogen bomb, on the valid assumption that if we did not, the Russians would, and then the advantage would be heavily on their side. The Soviets in the 1960's were making bigger bombs than the United States, though not so many of them. The Americans eased off in the competition only when they discovered that they had enough for "overkill"—that is, the capacity to kill all possible foes, many times over. At this point our nuclear armament existed mostly not to be used, except in the last extremity.

The race then partially shifted to countermeasures ("offensive" weapons inevitably spawn "defensive" weapons), and to the race into space, which has military implications. Thus, in a fateful cycle, fear begets new weapons and new weapons beget new fears. If a nation is ahead, it wants to stay ahead; if behind, it wants to catch up.

SUPERIORITY IN WEAPONRY DOES NOT GUARANTEE SECURITY

By the mid-1960's, if not earlier, we had enough nuclear weapons to incinerate the globe, although we were less secure than ever. China joined the exclusive Nuclear Club in 1964, though uninvited, and thus found herself in the same league with America, Russia, Britain, and France. Smaller nations, such as Israel and Egypt, will almost inevitably enter the magic circle in time, unless an effective multination agreement can be reached to limit such lethal arms.

A proliferation of nuclear weapons would cause the strength of the small nations to increase disproportionately. In the pre-atomic age, the United States could invade Cuba with relative ease, and in fact did so in 1898. But if Cuba should secure long-range nuclear weapons, she could take such a heavy toll of American urban centers as to make such an invasion prohibitively expensive.

The more atomic nations there are, the greater the danger of war through accident, miscalculation, or madness. If a small country, through design or mischance, should drop a bomb on the Soviet Union, the men in the Kremlin, suspecting an attack by the Pentagon, might well start activating missiles that would destroy our civilization. Such dangers are so overwhelming as to inspire some hope that genuine arms limitation is not a fantastic dream. To paraphrase Winston Churchill, when somebody can kill everybody, nobody will want to kill anybody.

DISARMAMENT WITHOUT ADEQUATE INSPECTION IS RISKY

Disarmament negotiations with Russia during the years after World War II all sank on the rock of inspection. The Soviets, dedicated to the goal of world revolution and completely unscrupulous as to their means, were plainly out to do us in. The Western world simply did not trust them to carry out disarmament commitments and not resort to cheating. They had cheated before, notably when they sneaked long-range missiles into Cuba in 1962, all the while lying and denying.

The Russians moreover retained the pathological suspicion they had shown under the Tsars, and wanted no foreign inspectors (spies?) poking around the ribs of Mother Russia and discovering weaknesses.[3] They believed that the hostile capitalist world was out to "bury" them. So with neither side trusting the other, agreement was impossible.

The partial Nuclear Test-Ban Treaty of 1962 was in no sense a disarmament agreement. It destroyed or restricted no weapons; it merely confined nuclear testing to underground sites. A basic reason why both sides accepted this handcuff was that violations of the ban could easily be detected by sensitive instruments without on-site inspection in either Russia or the United States.

UNILATERAL DISARMAMENT IS SELF-DELUSION

Uncle Sam was condemned as a "sucker" for having agreed at the so-called Washington Disarmament Conference of 1921–1922 to scrap fine new battleships, while the other nations, Japan and Britain, were scrapping fine new blueprints. The truth is that all three nations did scrap big battleships, but that the United States scrapped more ships and newer ships. This outcome led to the phrase "disarmament by example," as to some extent it was.

[3] Russia's traditional obsession with secrecy—"the peasant mentality"—may well have tipped the balance for peace during the Cuban crunch of 1962. We were about to seize Soviet ships headed toward Cuba with cargoes of missiles and other top-secret equipment, and the loss of such information could not have been lightly regarded by the Kremlin.

The term "Washington Disarmament Conference" is a mis-nomer.[4] No limits whatever were imposed on land armies, sub-marines, torpedo boats, destroyers, light cruisers, and heavy cruisers (except for maximum tonnage and armament). The only meaning-ful restrictions were imposed on capital ships (battleships and battle cruisers), and limited restrictions were placed on aircraft carriers. This meant that the naval race was virtually wide open in every other category, and if we fell alarmingly behind, as we did, we were not gulled by scheming foreigners. The tax-weary and wishful-thinking American people merely gulled themselves.[5]

DISARMAMENT NEGOTIATORS MUST DEAL
FROM STRENGTH

Unilateral disarmament has yet another disadvantage. It elimi-nates hope of mutual concessions or "the principle of balance."

The veteran American disarmament negotiator, Arthur H. Dean, after suffering through interminable negotiations with the Soviets, testified that "The essential foundation for negotiation on arms control and disarmament is respectable military strength on both sides."[6] If the Soviets were preponderantly powerful, they would have little reason to sit down at a conference table and divest themselves of the forces with which they could impose their will on the capitalistic world.

Doctrinaire pacifists argue that if we were to destroy all of our arms, we would create a more relaxed atmosphere that would contribute to the coming of world peace. Such zealots do not know the Soviets. Unilateral concessions in their eyes merely betray weakness, of which they hasten to take advantage. Arthur H. Dean concluded that "unilateral measures . . . which inequitably bear on only one side . . . will most likely lead not to acceptable dis-armament but to the political defeat of the weaker side and prob-ably also to greater dangers to peace." He further concludes that

[4] The official name from the outset was The International Conference on the Limitation of Armaments.
[5] The outcome evidently inspired Will Rogers' famous quip, "The United States never lost a war or won a conference." We certainly did not "win" the War of 1812 or the Korean War, and we have done exceptionally well in many conferences, particularly those involving the Latin American states, among whom we are the giant.
[6] Arthur H. Dean, *Test Ban and Disarmament* (1966), p. 65.

the emotional supporters of unilateral disarmament are "in reality the worst enemies of any realistic disarmament." [7]

One of the few real hopes for arms limitation is a mutual phasing out of weapons or "balanced disarmament." For example, if the United States, by agreement with Moscow, were publicly to destroy fifty bombers—"a bomber bonfire"—on the same day and at the same hour that the Soviets were supposed to destroy fifty bombers, some slight progress could be made toward disarmament. Perhaps the next fifty in a sequence could then be destroyed. But if the Soviets reneged and refused to carry out their part of the bargain in good faith, the relative loss to the United States would not be heavy, and all other attempts at mutual destruction of bombers, even obsolete ones, would end.

ARMAMENT AND DISARMAMENT BOTH ENTAIL RISKS

Arms races tend to incite war. Yet disarmament or inadequate armament invites attack from greedy or otherwise aggressive neighbors. Risks are involved in pursuing either course. But mankind may one day conclude that the risks of disarmament are less great than those of armament and act accordingly. Yet this blessed era is not likely to dawn until suspicions, fears, and tensions are substantially reduced. Disarmament of hearts must precede disarmament of arms. Security is basically a state of mind rather than a network of alliances or arsenals of weapons.

The stakes are now horrifyingly high, for the world may already have passed the point of no return in the proliferation of nuclear weapons. We can only hope that some day the nations will devote as much time, energy, patience, and brain power to a removal of the irritants that produce arms races as they do to arms themselves. We may then be closer to the solution of a problem that has thus far defied an answer.

The risks involved in limiting arms still seem great, but they should be compared with the enormous risks involved in an unlimited arms race in nuclear weapons. The members of the human race—the most dangerous of animals—must learn to live together as brothers or die together as fools.

[7] *Ibid.*

EPILOGUE

The future is darkened by the shadow of two bombs: the nuclear bomb and the population bomb. A prophet can hardly foretell whether we are in graver danger of blowing ourselves off the planet or elbowing ourselves off it.

Discontent is in the air. The underprivileged and overpopulated of the world, especially the two-thirds who are nonwhite, have in recent years shown increasing restlessness. They have glimpsed enough of the good things of this life to resent their squalor, hunger, disease, ignorance, and premature death. They want to join the human race. They are not always going to be content to plod along on bare feet while the rest of the world whizzes by in automobiles. The Revolution in Rising Expectations will not be easily checked, for tens of millions of "backward" peoples are shopping for a revolution.

The supreme paradox is that the United States must increasingly become entangled in world affairs to escape the full impact of world affairs. Except for a minority of isolationist die-hards, the ideal of an isolated Fortress America is becoming only a nostalgic dream: our democratic freedoms can hardly flourish, although they may exist precariously, in a sea of despotism. At heavy cost we have learned harsh lessons from two world wars, and we have become more sophisticated, more mature, and more responsible. Few peoples have had to grow old so fast.

If one were so presumptuous as to offer advice to the American people, one might say that they should learn to live with greatness, and to recognize that crisis may well continue to be a part of their daily diet. They should base their foreign policy more on what the world is and less on what they want it to be. They should try to change what needs to be changed in their own interests. Yet they should learn to accept what they cannot change, or can only change at too high a cost.

The American people need a clearer definition or redefinition of their national purpose, so that they can bring their policies more precisely into balance with their objectives. Democracy is again on the defensive, and tyranny is again on the march, as they were in the early years of the Republic, when in Abraham Lincoln's words, America was "the last, best hope of earth."

If the nation expects to survive, it would do well to recapture the faith in its democratic ideals that caused the United States in the nineteenth century to shine forth as a beacon light of liberty in a world of despotic darkness.

Bibliography and Notes

GENERAL

This book is designed as a supplement to, not a substitute for, the author's *A Diplomatic History of the American People*, 7th ed. (1964), which contains full bibliographical references and notes, with the emphasis on historical development. The reader is directed to them, if he wishes more investigation in depth, as well as to the older Samuel Flagg Bemis and Grace Gardner Griffin, eds., *Guide to the Diplomatic History of the United States, 1775–1921* (1935), and to Oscar Handlin, *et al.*, eds., *Harvard Guide to American History* (1954). The bibliographies of the present book emphasize the more recent literature, much of it devoted to current affairs rather than to deep-rooted historical problems.

Chapter I. THE ROLE OF THE PRESIDENT

Two older works are still basically useful: Edward S. Corwin, *The President's Control of Foreign Relations* (1917), and *The President, Office and Powers, 1787–1957*, 4th ed. (1957). They should be supplemented by Sidney Warren, *The President as World Leader* (1964), and Edgar E. Robinson, *et al.*, *Powers of the President in Foreign Affairs, 1945–1965* (1966). See also Elmer E. Cornwell, Jr., *Presidential Leadership of Public Opinion* (1965). Useful books of a general nature are Louis W. Koenig, *The Chief Executive* (1964); Clinton Rossiter, *The American Presidency*, 2nd ed. (1960); James M. Burns, *Presidential Government* (1966); Wilfred E. Binkley, *The Man in the White House* (1959); Richard E. Neustadt, *Presidential Power* (1960); Thomas A. Bailey, *Presidential Greatness* (1966); and T. C. Sorensen, *Decision Making in the White House* (1963). See also *Administration of National Security* (1965), a report of the Subcommittee on National Security Staffing and Operations, Senator Henry M. Jackson, Chairman.

Chapter II. THE DEPARTMENT OF STATE

The standard work on historical development is Graham H. Stuart, *The Department of State* (1949), now considerably outdated. An historical interpretation of merit is Alexander DeConde, *The American Secretary of State* (1962), with bibliographies. The classic multivolume is S. F. Bemis and R. H. Ferrell, eds., *The American Secretaries of State and Their Diplomacy,* 15 vols. (1927–1966), with volumes being added on the more recent incumbents. The twentieth-century Secretaries are assessed in much briefer compass in Norman A. Graebner, ed., *An Uncertain Tradition* (1961). Emphasis on administrative aspects appears in Norman L. Hill, *Mr. Secretary of State* (1963), with bibliographies; in Don K. Price, ed., *The Secretary of State* (1960); in R. E. Elder, *The Policy Machine: The Department of State and American Foreign Policy* (1960); in Senator Henry M. Jackson, ed., *The Secretary of State and the Ambassador* (1964); and in James L. McCamey, *Conduct of the New Diplomacy* (1964). More recent reflections by a veteran foreign service officer are in Smith Simpson, *Anatomy of the State Department* (1967). See also references for Chapter VII.

Chapter III. PICKING THE RIGHT AMBASSADOR

The standard work, though somewhat outdated, is Graham H. Stuart, *American Diplomatic and Consular Practice,* 2nd ed. (1952), which may be supplemented by Zara S. Steiner, *The State Department and the Foreign Service: The Wriston Report Four Years Later* (1958); W. F. Ilchman, *Professional Diplomacy in the United States, 1779–1939* (1961); William Barnes and J. H. Morgan, *The Foreign Service of the United States: Origins, Development and Functions* (1961); and *Administration of National Security* (1965), the report of Senator Henry M. Jackson's subcommittee. Especially revealing is E. Wilder Spaulding, *Ambassadors Ordinary and Extraordinary* (1961), an historical overview. The bibliographies in the Spaulding and Graham Stuart books are unusually helpful. See also J. J. Jusserand, *The School for Ambassadors and Other Essays* (1925), and Sir Ernest Satow, *A Guide to Diplomatic Practice,* 4th ed. (1957).

Chapter IV. UTILIZING THE AMBASSADOR

One of the best approaches to the problem is through the memoirs of former diplomats, and extensive lists of their contributions appear in the bibliographies of Graham H. Stuart, *American Diplomatic and Consular Practice*, 2nd ed. (1952), and E. Wilder Spaulding, *Ambassadors Ordinary and Extraordinary* (1961). Among the more useful memoirs of career officers to be published in recent years are J. Rives Childs, *American Foreign Service* (1948); William Phillips, *Ventures in Diplomacy* (1953); Perrin C. Galpin, ed., *Hugh Gibson* (1956); Charles W. Thayer, *Diplomat* (1959); Ellis O. Briggs, *Farewell to Foggy Bottom* (1964); Robert Murphy, *Diplomat Among Warriors* (1964); deLesseps S. Morrison, *Latin American Mission* (1965); and Henry S. Villard, *Affairs at State* (1965). See also J. P. Davies, Jr., *Foreign and Other Affairs* (1964).

Chapter V.　ADVICE FOR THE DIPLOMAT

An extraordinarily helpful book is Fred Charles Iklé, *How Nations Negotiate* (1964), which has a full bibliography, including the classic treatises in French and German. See also Harold Nicolson, *The Evolution of Diplomatic Method* (1954), and *Diplomacy* (1939; paperback revision, 1964). Emphasizing the United States is Elmer Plischke, *Conduct of American Diplomacy* (1950). See also Henry M. Wriston, *Diplomacy in a Democracy* (1956), and Lester B. Pearson, *Diplomacy in the Nuclear Age* (1959). A British slant appears in William S. Strang, *The Diplomatic Career* (1962), and Charles K. Webster, *The Art and Practice of Diplomacy* (1962).

Chapter VI.　THE SUPREMACY OF NATIONAL INTEREST

Useful introductions to the general subject are Hans J. Morgenthau, *In Defense of the National Interest* (1951), and R. E. Osgood, *Ideals and Self-Interest in American Foreign Relations* (1953); Donald Brandon, *American Foreign Policy: Beyond Utopianism and Realism* (1966); A. A. Ekirch, Jr., *Ideas, Ideals, and American Diplomacy* (1966); C. A. Beard, *The Idea of National Interest* (1934); T. I. Cook and Malcolm Moos, *Power through Purpose: The Realism of Idealism as a Basis for Foreign Policy* (1954). See also Dexter Perkins, *The American Approach to Foreign Policy*, rev. ed. (1962); Thomas A. Bailey, *The Man in the Street* (1948); G. F. Kennan, *Realities of American Foreign Policy* (1954); K. W. Thompson, *Political Realism and the Crisis of World Politics* (1960); L. J. Halle, *Dream and Reality: Aspects of American Foreign Policy* (1959); E. McN. Burns, *The American Idea of Mission* (1957); and Dorothy Jane Van Hoogstrate, *American Foreign Policy: Realists and Idealists* (1960).

Chapter VII.   THE SHAPING OF POLICY

Particularly useful are Fred Charles Iklé, *How Nations Negotiate* (1964), which has full bibliographies. See also Burton M. Sapin, *The Making of United States Foreign Policy* (1966), and Frank Tannenbaum, *The American Tradition in Foreign Policy* (1956). Helpful studies by participants in the government are Andrew H. T. Berding, *Foreign Affairs and You* (1962); Henry M. Jackson, ed., *The National Security Council: Jackson Subcommittee Papers on Policy Making at the Presidential Level* (1965); E. A. Johnson, ed., *The Dimensions of Diplomacy* (1964); W. W. Rostow, *View from the Seventh Floor* (1964), *The United States in the World Arena* (1960); Charles B. Marshall, *The Limits of Foreign Policy* (1954); Louis J. Halle, *Men and Nations* (1962). See also K. W. Thompson, *American Diplomacy and Emergent Patterns* (1962); W. Y. Elliott, *et al.*, *United States Foreign Policy: Its Organization and Control* (1952); Joseph Frankel, *The Making of Foreign Policy* (1963); Henry M. Wriston, *Policy Perspectives* (1964); Richard C. Snyder, ed., *Foreign Policy Decision Making* (1962); Robert R. Bowie, *Shaping the Future* (1964); and C. O. Olsen, Jr., *Foreign Policy of the American People* (1961).

Chapter VIII.   THE POWER OF ECONOMIC INTERESTS

Works of a more popular nature are Paul Douglas, *America in the Market Place* (1966), and Peter B. Kenen, *Giant Among the Nations: Problems in U.S. Foreign Economic Policy* (1960). More technical studies are Henry G. Aubrey, *The Dollar in World Affairs* (1964); Don D. Humphrey, *The United States and the Common Market* (1962); James N. Rosenau, *National Leadership and Foreign Policy* (1963); Lionel Robbins, *The Economic Causes of War* (1940); and David A. Baldwin, *Economic Development and American Foreign Policy, 1943–1962* (1967). Historically oriented are Benjamin H. Williams, *Economic Foreign Policy of the United States* (1929); J. W. Angell, *Financial Foreign Policy of the United States* (1965); and William A. Williams, *The Tragedy of American Diplomacy* (1949).

Chapter IX.   THE DOMESTIC FRONT

General accounts are Dexter Perkins, *The American Approach to Foreign Policy*, rev. ed. (1962); Thomas A. Bailey, *The Man in the Street* (1948); Andrew Berding, *Foreign Affairs and You* (1962). On politics see Bernard Cohen, *The Political Process and Foreign Policy* (1957); C. V.

Crabb, Jr., *Bipartisan Foreign Policy: Myth or Reality?* (1957); and Holt
B. Westerfield, *Foreign Policy and Party Politics: Pearl Harbor to Korea*
(1955). The relationship of Congress is treated in R. A. Dahl, *Congress
and Foreign Policy* (1950); James A. Robinson, *Congress and Foreign
Policy-Making* (1962); Malcolm E. Jewell, *Senatorial Politics and Foreign
Policy* (1962); David N. Farnsworth, *The Senate Committee on Foreign
Relations* (1961); H. N. Carroll, *The House of Representatives and For-
eign Affairs* (1958). On sectionalism consult G. L. Grassmuck, *Sectional
Biases in Congress on Foreign Policy* (1951), and C. O. Lerche, Jr., *The
Uncertain South: Its Changing Patterns of Politics in Foreign Policy*
(1964).

Chapter X. THE PRESSURE OF PUBLIC OPINION

See the general works by Perkins, Bailey, and Berding cited in
previous chapter; also Gabriel A. Almond, *The American People and
Foreign Policy* (1950); James N. Rosenau, *Public Opinion and Foreign
Policy* (1961); Francis E. Rourke, *Secrecy and Publicity: Dilemmas of
Democracy* (1961); and Marion D. Irish, ed., *World Pressures on American
Foreign Policy* (1964). Emphasis on public opinion polls appears in Stuart
Chase, *American Credos* (1962); William Buchanan and Hadley Cantril,
How Nations See Each Other (1953); Harold R. Isaacs, *Scratches on Our
Minds: American Images of China and India* (1958); and A. T. Steele,
The American People and China (1966). For the press see Bernard C.
Cohen, *The Press and Foreign Policy* (1963); William L. Rivers, *The
Opinionmakers* (1965); James Reston, *The Artillery of the Press* (1967).
On pressure groups consult Roscoe Baker, *The American Legion and For-
eign Policy* (1954); R. J. Monsen, Jr., and M. W. Cannon, *The Makers of
Public Policy* (1965); Louis L. Gerson, *The Hyphenate in Recent American
Politics and Diplomacy* (1964). The outside world is dealt with in W. P.
Davison, *International Political Communication* (1965); W. P. Dizard,
The Strategy of Truth: The Story of the U.S. Information Service (1961);
Oren Stephens, *Facts to a Candid World: America's Overseas Information
Program* (1955); and J. B. Whitton, ed., *Propaganda and the Cold War*
(1963).

Chapter XI. TOP-LEVEL DIPLOMACY

See references for the preceding chapters, especially III and V, and
particularly Fred Charles Iklé, *How Nations Negotiate* (1964). A somewhat
different approach is taken in Norman L. Hill, *The Public International*

Conference (1929); Sir Maurice Hankey, *Diplomacy by Conference: Studies in Public Affairs, 1920–1946* (1946); Elmer Plischke, *Summit Diplomacy: Personal Diplomacy of the President of the United States* (1958); Arthur Lall, *Modern International Negotiation* (1966); Keith Eubank, *The Summit Conferences, 1919–1960* (1966). See also Sir William Hayter, *The Diplomacy of the Great Powers* (1961); S. D. Kertesz and M. A. Fitzsimons, eds., *Diplomacy in a Changing World* (1959); and H. B. Westerfield, *The Instruments of American Foreign Policy* (1963). Frustrating experiences with Communist negotiators in Korea are described in Charles T. Joy, *How Communists Negotiate* (1955), and William H. Vatcher, Jr., *Panmunjom: The Story of the Korean Military Armistice Negotiations* (1958).

Chapter XII. ETHICS AND MORALITY

Useful general works are Ernest W. Lefever, *Ethics and United States Foreign Policy* (1957); Erwin D. Canham, *The Ethics of United States Foreign Relations* (1966); Richard W. Sterling, *Ethics in a World of Power* (1958); Herbert Butterfield, *Christianity, Diplomacy and War*, 2nd ed. (1953); Paul Ramsey, *War and the Christian Conscience* (1961); David L. Larson, ed., *The Puritan Ethic in United States Foreign Policy* (1966); John C. Bennett, *Foreign Policy in Christian Perspective* (1966). On the ethics of the nuclear bomb, see Robert C. Batchelder, *The Irreversible Decision, 1939–1950* (1962), and John C. Bennett, ed., *Nuclear Weapons and the Conflict of Conscience* (1962); William Clancey, ed., *The Moral Dilemma of Nuclear Weapons* (1961); and Herbert Feis, *The Atomic Bomb and the End of World War II*, rev. ed. (1966). For espionage operations see Allen W. Dulles, *The Craft of Intelligence* (1963); Paul W. Blackstock, *The Strategy of Subversion* (1964); Roger Hilsman, *Strategic Intelligence and National Decisions* (1956); Sherman Kent, *Strategic Intelligence* (1949); Harry H. Ransom, *Central Intelligence and National Security* (1958); David Wise and Thomas B. Ross, *The U-2 Affair* (1962); and *The Invisible Government* (1964) [CIA].

Chapter XIII. ALLIES AND ALLIANCES

For the making and breaking of America's first entangling alliance see S. F. Bemis, *The Diplomacy of the American Revolution* (1935), and Alexander DeConde, *Entangling Alliance* (1958) and *The Quasi-War* (1966). On problems of World War II consult Herbert Feis, *Churchill, Roosevelt, Stalin* (1957), and John R. Deane, *The Strange Alliance* [with Russia] (1947). Among the numerous creditable books on NATO one may single out Robert E. Osgood, *NATO: The Entangling Alliance* (1962); Drew Middleton, *The Atlantic Community: A Study in Unity and Disunity* (1965); Henry A. Kissinger, *The Troubled Partnership: A Re-appraisal of the Atlantic Alliance* (1965), and William T. R. Fox and Annette B. Fox, *NATO and the Range of American Choice* (1967). A fuller bibliography appears in Donald Brandon, *American Foreign Policy* (1966), Ch. 9.

Chapter XIV.   THE ROLE OF THE FOREIGNER

General approaches are Franz M. Joseph, ed., *As Others See Us: The United States through Foreign Eyes* (1959); Andre Visson, *As Others See Us* (1948); Daniel J. Boorstin, *America and the Image of Europe* (1960); Harlan Cleveland, *et al.*, *The Overseas American* (1960). For Latin America, consult Donald M. Dozer, *Are We Good Neighbors: Three Decades of Inter-American Relations, 1930–1960* (1959); Bryce Wood, *The Making of the Good Neighbor Policy* (1961); and D. H. Radler, *El Gringo: The Yankee Image in Latin America* (1962). For general attitudes of the American public, see Stuart Chase, *American Credos* (1962); Harold R. Isaacs, *Scratches on Our Mind: American Images of China and India* (1958); and A. T. Steele, *The American People and China* (1966).

Chapter XV.   FOREIGN AID PROGRAMS

Historical backgrounds are developed in Merle Curti, *American Philanthropy Abroad* (1963), and Merle Curti and Kendall Birr, *Prelude to Point Four* (1954). Among accounts pointed toward more recent problems are Eugene Staley, *The Future of Underdeveloped Countries*, 2nd ed. (1961); Herbert Feis, *Foreign Aid and Foreign Policy* (1964); Edward S. Mason, *Foreign Aid and Foreign Policy* (1964); Jacob A. Rubin, *Your Hundred Billion Dollars* (1964); Charles Frankel, *The Neglected Aspect of Foreign Affairs* [cultural] (1966); Harold A. Hovey, *United States Military Assistance* (1965); Robert Heilbroner, *The Great Ascent: The Struggle for Economic Development in Our Times* (1963); W .G. Friedmann, *et al.*, *International Financial Aid* (1966); John D. Montgomery, *Foreign Aid in International Politics* (1967); Michael K. O'Leary, *The Politics of American Foreign Aid* (1967). See also Harry B. Price, *The Marshall Plan and Its Meaning* (1955).

Chapter XVI.   THE COMMUNIST WORLD

General approaches are found in George F. Kennan, *On Dealing with the Communist World* (1964); Frederick C. Barghoorn, *The Soviet Image of the United States* (1950); Marshall D. Shulman, *Beyond the Cold War*

(1965); Bernard S. Morris, *International Communism and American Policy* (1966); John C. Campbell, *American Policy toward Communist Eastern Europe* (1965). On Asia, consult Robert Blum, *The United States and China in World Affairs* (1966); Robert P. Newman, *Recognition of Communist China?* (1961); Harold C. Hinton, *Communist China in World Politics* (1966); A. Doak Barnett, *Communist China and Asia* (1960). For propaganda, see Allan A. Michie, *Voices through the Iron Curtain: The Radio Free Europe Story* (1963).

Chapter XVII.   THE NON-COMMUNIST   WORLD

On the United Nations, consult Lincoln P. Bloomfield, *The United Nations and U.S. Foreign Policy* (1960); Clark M. Eichelberger, *UN: The First Twenty Years* (1965); Franz B. Gross, ed., *The United States and the United Nations* (1964); James J. Wadsworth, *The Glass House: The United Nations in Action* (1966); and Hayward R. Alker and Bruce M. Russett, *World Politics in the General Assembly* (1965). See also Dexter Perkins, *The United States and Latin America* (1961); Adolf A. Berle, *Latin America: Diplomacy and Reality* (1962); George Wythe, *The United States and Inter-American Relations* (1964).

Chapter XVIII.   THE POLITICS OF POWER

More general references are William D. Puleston, *The Influence of Force in Foreign Relations* (1955); Thomas C. Schelling, *Arms and Influence* (1966) and *The Strategy of Conflict* (1960); Edmund O. Stillman and William Pfaff, *Power and Impotence: The Failure of America's Foreign Policy* (1966); Hans Morgenthau, *Scientific Man vs. Power Politics* (1946); Max Lerner, *The Age of Overkill: A Preface to World Politics* (1962); Klaus Knorr, *On the Uses of Military Power in the Nuclear Age* (1966); and Inis L. Claude, *Power and International Relations* (1962). Useful books by officials or ex-officials are Dean G. Acheson, *Power and Diplomacy* (1958); Harlan Cleveland, *The Obligations of Power* (1966); Thomas K. Finletter, *Foreign Policy: The Next Phase: the 1960's*, 2nd ed. (1960) and *Power and Policy: U.S. Foreign Policy and Military Power in the Hydrogen Age* (1954). Some of the most advanced thinking appears in Bernard Brodie, *Escalation and the Nuclear Option* (1966); Herman Kahn, *On Thermonuclear War* (1960) and *Thinking about the Unthinkable* (1962); and Henry A. Kissinger, *The Necessity for Choice: Prospects of American Foreign Policy* (1961).

Chapter XIX.   THE MISSION OF THE MILITARY

General treatments are Walter Millis, Harvey C. Mansfield, and Harold Stein, *Arms and the State: Civil-Military Elements in National Policy* (1958); Burton M. Sapin and Richard C. Snyder, *The Role of the Military in American Foreign Policy* (1954); Alfred Vagts, *Defense and Diplomacy: The Soldier and the Conduct of Foreign Relations* (1956); A. A. Ekirch, Jr., *The Civilian and the Military* (1956); Walter Mills, *Arms and Men: A Study in American Military History* (1956); Samuel E. Finer, *The Man on Horseback: The Role of the Military in Politics* (1962); Samuel P. Huntington, *The Soldier and the State: The Theory and Politics of Civil-Military Relations* (1957) and *The Common Defense: Strategic Programs in National Politics* (1961). Among the numerous more recent books of a specialized nature are Robert N. Ginsburgh, *U.S. Military Strategy in the Sixties* (1965); Morton H. Halperin, *Limited War in the Nuclear Age* (1963); and Arthur Herzog, *The War-Peace Establishment* (1965).

Chapter XX.   THE IRON DICE OF WAR

Excellent background accounts are Theodore Ropp, *War in the Modern World* (1959), and Alfred Vagts, *A History of Militarism: Civilian and Military* (1959). See also Robert E. Osgood, *Limited War: The Challenge to American Strategy* (1957); Robert McClintock, *The Meaning of Limited War* (1967); Raymond Aron, *The Century of Total War* (1954) and *Peace and War: A Theory of International Relations* (1967); Otto Heilbrunn, *Conventional Warfare in the Nuclear Age* (1965); Thomas E. Murray, *Nuclear Policy for War and Peace* (1960); Robert W. Tucker, *The Just War: A Study in Contemporary American Doctrine* (1960); and Anne Armstrong, *Unconditional Surrender* (1961).

Chapter XXI.   THE PERILS OF PEACEMAKING

For general background see Merle E. Curti, *The American Peace Crusade* (1929) and *Peace and War: the American Struggle, 1636–1936* (1936); and Dexter Perkins, *America's Quest for Peace* (1962). See also Mortimer J. Adler, *How to Think about War and Peace* (1944); Chester Bowles, *The New Dimensions of Peace* (1955); Richard N. Gardner, *In Pursuit of World Order* (1964) and (editor) *Blueprint for Peace* (1966); Robert A. Goldwin, ed., *Beyond the Cold War* (1966); Robert O. Byrd,

Quaker Ways in Foreign Policy (1960); G. F. Nuttall, *Christian Pacifism in History* (1958); D. S. Cheever and H. F. Haviland, *Organizing for Peace* (1954).

Chapter XXII. NEUTRALITY AND NEUTRALISM

A more recent general study is Cecil V. Crabb, Jr., *The Elephants and the Grass: A Study of Nonalignment* (1965). George F. Kennan's controversial views on disengagement were set forth in *Russia, the Atom, and the West* (1958). An illuminating study is Annette Baker Fox, *The Power of Small States: Diplomacy in World War II* (1959). The departure from American neutrality in the 1930's is described in Robert A. Divine, *The Illusion of Neutrality* (1962), and in William L. Langer and S. E. Gleason, *The Challenge to Isolation, 1937–1940* (1952) and *The Undeclared War, 1940–1941* (1953). For the period of World War I, consult Ernest R. May, *The World War and American Isolation, 1914–1917* (1959), and Thomas A. Bailey, *The Policy of the United States toward the Neutrals, 1917–1918* (1942).

Chapter XXIII. THE MIRAGE OF DISARMAMENT

Useful historical backgrounds appear in Merze Tate, *The United States and Armaments* (1948). More recent works are B. G. Bechhoefer, *Postwar Negotiations for Arms Control* (1961); Donald G. Brennan, ed., *Arms Control, Disarmament, and National Security* (1961); Hedley Bull, *The Control of the Arms Race* (1961); Henry W. Forbes, *The Strategy of Disarmament* (1962); Arthur T. Hadley, *The Nation's Safety and Arms Control* (1961); Ralph E. Lapp, *Kill and Overkill* (1962); Robert A. Levine, *The Arms Debate* (1963); Walter Millis and James Real, *The Abolition of War* (1963); Walter Millis, *An End to Arms* (1965); Thomas C. Schelling and Morton Halperin, *Strategy and Arms Control* (1961); J. David Singer, *Deterrence, Arms Control, and Disarmament* (1962); Arnold Wolfers, *et al., The United States in a Disarmed World* (1966); James J. Wadsworth, *The Price of Peace* (1962). On the Test-Ban Treaty of 1963, see Arthur H. Dean, *Test Ban and Disarmament* (1966), and Harold K. Jacobson and Eric Stein, *Diplomats, Scientists, and Politicians* (1966).

Index

See also Chronological Overview, pp. ix–xii.

Acheson, Dean, 9, 26, 29; quoted, 21, 22

Adams, Charles F., 67, 72

Adams, John, 42. *See* Chronological Overview, Adams

Adet, Pierre A., 74

Afro–Asian Bloc, 224

Alaska, 13

Algeria, 181

Ames, Fisher, 176

Antarctica Treaty, 145n., 209

Arab nations, 12

Atomic bomb, 232–233

Bay of Pigs. *See* Chronological Overview, Kennedy

Bemis, Samuel F., 107

Berding, A. H., 22; quoted, 64

Bismarck, Otto von, 54n.

Blaine, James G., 28

Bohlen, Charles E., 44n., 64

Bonaparte, Napoleon, quoted, 44, 83n., 95, 148

Borah, Senator W. E., 11

Bowers, Claude G., 51

Bowles, Chester, 37, 68

Braden, Spruille, 74

Brazil, 105

Bricker Amendment, 5, 6

Briggs, Ellis O., 55; quoted, 56

Brinkmanship, 24–25, 26, 247 (Cuban missiles)

Brown, Neill S., 64

Bruce, David K. E., 57

Bryan, William J., 10, 23, 27; quoted, 40

Bullitt, William C., 10, 74

Burlingame, Anson, 40

Byrnes, James F., 24

Caffery, Jefferson, 51

Callières, François de, quoted, 36, 37, 41, 41n., 43, 45, 50, 59

Cambodia, 202

Cameron, Simon, 39

Cassini, Count, 75–76

Castro, Fidel, 105–106

Cavour, Count, quoted, 156

Central Intelligence Agency, 33–34

Chiang Kai-shek. *See* Chronological Overview

Chiang Kai-shek, Madame, 64

China policy, 13, 14, 16, 25, 217–218, 222, 224–225

Churchill, Winston S., quoted, 25, 73n., 81, 95n., 107n., 116, 158n.,

Index

Churchill, Winston S.,
  quoted (*Cont.*)
  164n., 166, 168n., 174–175, 239,
  247n., 272
Civil rights, 115–116, 214
Clausewitz, Karl von, quoted, 249,
  261
Clemenceau, Georges, 139; quoted,
  255
Colby, Bainbridge, 11
Congo, 87, 224
Coolidge, Calvin, quoted, 107n.
Creel Committee, 129
Cromwell, James H. R., 73
Cuba, 28

Daniels, Josephus, 67
Davies, Joseph E., 59n.
Davis, John W., 49
Dean, Arthur H., quoted, 43n., 285
De Gaulle, Charles, 86, 141, 186,
  188
Denby, Charles, 48n.
Dodd, William E., 43–44, 50, 50n.
Dulles, Allen W., 33
Dulles, John Foster, 24–25, 26, 27–
  28, 30, 31; quoted, 21, 22, 23,
  62, 126, 137, 157

Earle, George H., 40
Eisenhower, Dwight D., 248;
  quoted, 122, 138. *See* Chronological Overview

Farland, Joseph S., 54
Finland, 231
Fisher, Sir John, quoted, 251
Fiume, 17
Flynn, E. J., 39n.
Food for Peace, 202–203
France, 85–86, 280
Francis, David Rowland, 58–59;
  quoted, 70

Franklin, Benjamin, 42, 53; quoted,
  268
Frelinghuysen, F. T., 28
Fulbright, J. W., quoted, 205

Gaulle, Charles de, 86, 141, 186,
  188
Germany, 110
Ghent, Peace of, 265
Gibson, Hugh, quoted, 137
Gluck, Maxwell H., 48
Gordon, Lincoln, 56
Grant, U. S., 67. *See* Chronological
  Overview
Grew, Joseph, 63, 72n.
Guatemala, 28, 33

Hamilton, Alexander, quoted, 156
Harding, W. G. *See* Chronological
  Overview
Harriman, W. Averell, 57; quoted,
  65
Harris, Townsend, 37
Harvey, George, 73
Hawley–Smoot Tariff, 96
Hawthorne, Nathaniel, 48
Hay, John, 29
Hayes, Dr. C. J. H., 46–47, 126n.
Henderson, Loy, quoted, 36–37
Hitler, Adolf, 280. *See* Chronologi-
  cal Overview, Roosevelt, F. D.
Hoover, Herbert, 106. *See* Chrono-
  logical Overview
Hoover, J. Edgar, 77
Hopkins, Harry L., 57
House, Col. E. M., 12, 57
Hughes, Charles E., 9
Hull, Cordell, 10, 23, 29

Imbrie, R. M., 39
India, 196n.
Indonesia, 87, 111–112, 149, 181
Inman, Samuel G., 231n.

Ireland, 13, 118
Israel, 11
Italy, 32, 47, 199

Jackson Subcommittee, 31, 35, 53, 56, 58, 66
Jay's Treaty, 146, 154
Jefferson, Thomas. *See* Chronological Overview
Johnson, L. B. *See* Chronological Overview
Jusserand, Jules, 56

Keiley, Anthony M., 50
Kennan, George F., 41, 63; quoted, 54, 212–213
Kennedy, John F., quoted, 89, 102, 113, 117, 167, 204, 215, 240, 279, 281. *See* Chronological Overview
Kennedy, Joseph P., 39, 69
Khrushchev, Nikita S., 16
Knowland, William F., 13
Korean War. *See* Chronological Overview

Lane, Arthur B., 66
Lansing, Robert, 11, 23, 43
La Paz, Bolivia, 38
Latin American policy, 234
League of Nations, 108–110. *See* Chronological Overview, Wilson, Harding
Leahy, W. D., quoted, 32
Lebanon, 42
Lenin, Nikolai, 206
Lincoln, Abraham. *See* Chronological Overview
Lodge, Henry Cabot, quoted, 24
Louisiana Purchase, 58, 92
Lowell, James R., 48
Luce, Clare B., 37n., 51, 68; quoted, 47n., 126n.

MacArthur, Douglas, 71; quoted, 221, 264. *See* Chronological Overview, Truman
McCarthy, Joseph R., 6–7, 29, 65, 214
McClintock, Robert, quoted, 230
McCloy, John J., 57
Machiavelli, Niccolò, 156; quoted, 83n., 131n., 163n., 234
McKinley, William. *See* Chronological Overview
McLeod, R. W. S., 29
McNamara, Robert S., 128
Madison, James. *See* Chronological Overview
Manifest Destiny, 116
Mao Tse-tung, quoted, 249n.
Marshall, George C., 23, 49
Marshall Plan. *See* Chronological Overview, Truman
Martin, John B., quoted, 46n.
Meredith, James, 116
Mesta, Pearl, 44
Mexican War. *See* Chronological Overview
Monroe, James, 68, 69, 176, 191–192
Monroe Doctrine. *See* Monroe, James
More, Thomas, quoted, 173
Morgenthau, Henry, 10, 33
Morrow, Dwight W., 46
Motley, John L., 67
Murphy, Robert, 10, 55–56, 76n.; quoted, 38
Munich Conference, 98, 99n. *See* Chronological Overview, Roosevelt, F. D.

Nasser, Gamal A., 31
National War College, 244
NATO, 31, 109, 180

Nicolson, Sir Harold, quoted, 58, 137, 185
Nixon, Richard M., 3, 19
Nomura, Admiral K., 45
North Atlantic Treaty Organization, 31, 109, 180

O'Dwyer, William, 51

Page, Walter H., 12, 53, 66–67
Pakenham, Richard, 68
Perón, Eva, 59n.
Perón, Juan, 74
Phi Beta Kappa, 36
Pinkney, William, 40
Polk, James K. *See* Chronological Overview
Porter, Horace, 73

Radio Free Europe, 17
Randolph, John, 38, 40
Rapacki Plan, 277n.
Reed, Thomas B., quoted, 119
Ridgeway, Matthew B., 265n.; quoted, 244
Roosevelt, Franklin D., quoted, 10, 16. *See* Chronological Overview
Roosevelt, Theodore, quoted, 229, 230, 251. *See* Chronological Overview
Rusk, Dean, 25n.; quoted, 52, 140
Russia. *See* Chronological Overview

Sackville–West, Lionel, 75
St. Petersburg, 38
Santo Domingo, 14. *See* Chronological Overview, Lincoln and Johnson, L. B.
Schlesinger, A. M., Jr., quoted, 32
Sickles, Daniel F., 44n.
Soulé, Pierre, 39, 46

Sputnik, 212
Stalin, Joseph, 15, 16; quoted, 127n., 206, 229. *See* Chronological Overview, Roosevelt, F. D. and Truman
Stettinius, E. R., Jr., 23
Stevenson, Adlai, 24; quoted, 102, 124n., 153–154, 205, 280
Suez seizure, 31, 87, 144–151, 162–163
Sullivan, J. M., 27
Switzerland, 249

Taft, W. H., 111, 142, 153
Tariff Reciprocity Treaties (1940's), 10
Tripoli War, 111, 114
Trotsky, Leon, 206
Truman, Harry S , quoted, 3. *See* Chronological Overview
Turkish missiles, 145. *See* Chronological Overview, Kennedy

U-2 Affair. *See* Chronological Overview, Eisenhower
Union of South Africa, 28
United Nations, 4, 24, 41, 116, 120–121, 196, 223, 224–225
Uniting for Peace Resolutions, 223
U Thant, quoted, 194

Van Alen, James J., 47
Vandenberg, Arthur H., quoted, 24
Versailles, Treaty of. *See* Chronological Overview, Wilson
Vichy, 17, 69, 76
Vietnam, 14. *See* Chronological Overview, Eisenhower, Kennedy, and Johnson, L. B.

Wallace, George, 24

War debts, 110
War of 1812. *See* Chronological Overview
Washington, George, quoted, 247n. *See* Chronological Overview
Webster, Daniel, 22
Wellington, Duke of, quoted, 263
White, Andrew D., 67
White, Henry, 37, 60
Whitney, John H., 49

Wilson, Woodrow, quoted, 102, 125n., 275. *See* Chronological Overview
Winant, John G., 10
World War I. *See* Chronological Overview
World War II. *See* Chronological Overview

XYZ Affair, 8, 125